The Historical Series of the Reformed Church
in America
No. 4

PIETY
AND
PATRIOTISM:

Bicentennial Studies
of the
Reformed Church
in America, 1776-1976

Edited by
James W. Van Hoeven

WM. B. EERDMANS PUBLISHING CO.
GRAND RAPIDS, MICHIGAN

James W. Van Hoeven

For my mother and late father,
Jacob and Nella Van Hoeven,
and
for my mother and father-in-law,
the Reverend and Mrs. Gerrit J. Rozeboom

Contents

The Historical Series of the Reformed Church in America

This series has been inaugurated by the General Synod of the Reformed Church in America, acting through its Commission on History, for the purpose of encouraging historical research and providing a medium wherein this knowledge may be shared with the academic community and with the members of the denomination in order that a knowledge of the past may contribute to right action in the present.

General Editor
The Reverend Donald J. Bruggink, Ph.D.,
Western Theological Seminary

The Commission on History

The Reverend John W. Beardslee III, Ph.D., New Brunswick Theological
  Seminary
The Reverend Donald J. Bruggink, Ph.D., Western Theological Seminary
The Reverend Marion De Velder, D.D., General Secretary, General Synod,
  R.C.A.
The Reverend Herman Harmelink III, S.T.M., minister, The Reformed
  Church, Poughkeepsie, New York
The Reverend Norman Kansfield, S.T.M., Western Theological Seminary
The Reverend Sharon T. Scholten, minister, Reformed Church of Keyport,
  Keyport, New Jersey
The Reverend Leroy A. Suess, minister, Saugerties Reformed Church,
  Saugerties, New York
The Reverend James W. Van Hoeven, Ph.D., Central College, Pella, Iowa

The Writers

The Reverend John W. Beardslee III, Ph.D., New Brunswick Theological
  Seminary
The Reverend James W. Van Hoeven, Ph.D., Central College, Pella, Iowa
The Reverend Elton J. Bruins, Ph.D., Hope College, Holland, Michigan
The Reverend Herman Harmelink III, S.T.M., minister, The Reformed
  Church, Poughkeepsie, New York
The Reverend Eugene P. Heideman, Th.D., Central College, Pella, Iowa
Professor John A. De Jong, Ph.D., Central College, Pella, Iowa
The Reverend Norman Kansfield, S.T.M., Western Theological Seminary
Ms. Barbara Fassler, M.A., Central College, Pella, Iowa

Acknowledgments

I am indebted to a number of persons who were helpful to me in pursuing this work. I wish first to express gratitude to my colleagues who contributed essays for this volume, and to Professor Donald Bruggink of Western Theological Seminary for his helpful editorial suggestions. I also extend my sincere thanks to Miss Elsie Stryker at the New Brunswick Seminary library, to Miss Mildred Schuppert at the Western Theological Seminary library, and to the librarians at Hope College, Central College, and Northwestern College, for helping me and the other writers track down numerous pertinent documents. I am, moreover, profoundly grateful to Barbara Fassler, John A. De Jong, and Eugene Heideman of Central College for reading the manuscript and offering valuable suggestions along the way. I am also indebted to Shirley Van Zee and the clerical staff at Central College, and to Alice Ver Meer, for typing the manuscript. In addition, I wish to thank the Pella National Bank, Pella, Iowa, for generously allowing me the use of their duplicating machine. And I thank President Kenneth Weller and Dean Harold Kolenbrander of Central College for encouraging me in this work. Most of all, I thank my wife, Mary, and our three children, Beth, Nancy, and Sarah, for their unfailing belief—expressed in countless ways—that what I was doing the summer of 1975 was significant.

Introduction

I regard patriotism with an American citizen as next to his religion, if not part of it.[1]

So wrote the Reverend Rufus W. Clark in 1876 as the nation celebrated its centennial. Clark was a minister of the Reformed Church in America, commissioned by the General Synod to discourse on "Religion and Civil Liberty." Referring to the sacred proverb that "Righteousness exalteth a nation," Clark asserted that "the precepts and principles of God's Holy Word have constituted the basis of every free, just, and prosperous government." He praised the fact that the Republic's Fathers were "inspired . . . by this grand truth," thereby "rendering the nation emphatically a chosen race," but warned that "this last and fairest experiment of human nature" could be destroyed if the people forsook personal righteousness. In this sense, patriotism and piety were necessarily tied together for the American citizen: "keep Christianity in the hearts of the people and you need not fear for the government."[2]

Since the founding of this Republic the Churches in America have worked to "keep Christianity in the hearts of the people." And the witness of some observers of the American religious situation suggests that the Churches have been successful at this task. Such, for example, was the opinion of the Frenchman Alexis de Tocqueville, who visited America in the 1830's, and commented upon American life and manners. He claimed that "the religious atmosphere" was the first thing that strikes a traveler from abroad, concluding that "there is no country in the world where the Christian religion retains a greater influence over the souls of men than in America."[3]

A contemporary traveler in America can still observe the kind of religious symbols that impressed Tocqueville, although he might not reach the same conclusions as the Frenchman. Church and seminary spires continue to dot the landscape of towns and cities throughout this always religious nation. Public officials still garnish their speeches with religious terms and images. And, to add a dimension Tocqueville did not observe,

most radio and television programming includes a liberal amount
of religious song and services, and ends appropriately each day
with a prayer.

Clark's discourse, as well as the religious symbolism of our
contemporary situation, raises the important issue of the relationship between piety and patriotism for American religion,
an issue that extends as far back as the colonial era and requires
fresh examination today. What is the responsibility of the
Church in a democratic state? Is there a point at which a
Christian's loyalty to Christ must transcend his loyalty to his
nation; when, in fact, he must protest his nation's policies?
How can the Church be certain that its corporate ethics and
theology are within the Christian tradition rather than a capitu-
lation to cultural vaules? These are some of the questions that
have been included in the issue of piety and patriotism in
American religious history. This Bicentennial volume studies the
manner in which the Reformed Church in America has responded to this issue, from 1776 to 1976.

The Reformed Church in America is part of the world-wide
family of Presbyterian and Reformed Churches which traces its
theological roots to John Calvin (1509-1564), one of the great
sixteenth century Reformers. Calvin was converted to evangelical views around 1534, and became a significant voice in the
Reformation beginning in 1536 with the publication of the first
edition of his *Institutes of the Christian Religion*. In the same
year Calvin was persuaded to help establish the "new" faith in
Geneva, Switzerland. From that time on, except for three years
that he was at Strasbourg, Geneva was the scene of his labors;
and Calvin turned that city into one of the most remarkable
centers of religious influence that the world has ever seen.

Numerous leaders of the second Protestant generation were
trained in Calvin's Geneva, and subsequently carried the message of the "Reformed" faith throughout Europe and beyond.
John Knox (1513-1572) spent some time in that "most perfect
city" and returned to begin Scotland's transformation. English
Protestantism was influenced by the life and thought of Geneva
and became a part of the Calvinist Reformation. In 1549
Zurich, where Ulrich Zwingli (1484-1531) had begun the Swiss
Reformation, accepted Calvin's view of the Lord's supper,
which taught a real but spiritual presence. Shortly thereafter,
much of Switzerland became Reformed. The movement also

affected the Rhineland, where certain princes, especially the Elector Palatine Frederick III (1559-1576), adopted it in the second half of the sixteenth century. His famous university in Heidelberg became a center of influence and the Heidelberg Catechism, published in 1563, became one of the Reformation's most important creeds. There were also significant Reformed advances among other German cities and states; and, in the 1550's Calvinism replaced Lutheranism in Bohemia, Moravia, Poland, and Hungary. France, too, was penetrated by the Reformed Church. It threatened to capture the country but then was eclipsed after a long and bitter struggle whose heroic nature is surpassed only by its pathos.

After the 1550's, Calvinism also began its conquest of the Netherlands, a fact of great importance for understanding the history of the (Dutch) Reformed Church in America. The seeds of the Reformation in the Netherlands had been sown earlier by many Augustinian canons who perpetuated the devotional emphasis of Gerhard Groote (1340-1384) and Thomas à Kempis (1380-1471), by Lutheran writings and converts, and by considerable Anabaptist activity. Gradually, however, beginning in the Walloon or southernmost French-speaking provinces, and with much help from Calvin, Reformed ideas came to dominate the Protestant movement in the country's seventeen provinces. In 1571 the Dutch adopted the Belgic Confession prepared ten years earlier by the Geneva-educated Guy de Bres. The conversion of William of Orange in 1573 was a vital turning point for these provinces, and by 1609 the Reformed Dutch had thrown off Catholic Spanish domination and became an independent Republic.

The same year, 1609, marks the beginning of the amazing commercial and imperial expansion of the Netherlands. All around the world its merchants, bankers, and seamen gained fame. One of these seamen, Henry Hudson, an Englishman in the employ of the Dutch East India Company, set sail from Holland on April 6, 1609. Subsequently, he steered his eighty-ton *Halve Maen* along the East coast of North America, and then one hundred fifty miles up the river that is named for him, engaging in a small amount of trade with several Indian tribes during the voyage. On October 14, 1609, Hudson set out to sea again for the long journey home.

The information brought to Holland by crew members of the *Halve Maen* awakened some interest among Dutch entrepreneurs in the possibility of trade in the New World. And later trading and exploring voyages to North America confirmed the earlier report and heightened this interest. Subsequently, the Dutch laid claim to all the land between the Delaware and Connecticut rivers. By 1613 they had a few trading houses on Manhattan, while a fort erected about this time on Castle Island (Fort Nassau, later Orange) was transferred in 1617 to the present site of Albany. After 1621 colonial affairs in America became the monopoly of the new Dutch West India Company. Two years later the first party of permanent settlers arrived at New Amsterdam and Fort Nassau, and established still other settlements on Long Island (Brooklyn), on the Delaware (across from the future Philadelphia), and on the Connecticut (near the site of later Hartford). With the appointment of Peter Minuit as director in 1626, New Netherland became a full-fledged colonial enterprise.[4]

In contrast to the efficient manner of these early years, however, the subsequent history of New Netherland is a story of mismanagement, dissension, and very slow growth. Perhaps the major factor in its mismanagement was the autocratic authority of the governors, who in addition were not temperamentally equipped to hold such extensive power. An equally serious mistake was the adoption in 1629 of the so-called patroon system. By this scheme, a qualified entrepreneur, or patroon, was given a tract of land in exchange for the commitment to settle, within four years, fifty colonists over fifteen years of age. The settlers, on their part, were obligated to pay the patroon a fixed rent for the land they worked as well as a share of the profits. The patroon was also given certain rights over his settlers with respect to fishing, hunting, milling, and justice. This archaic plan, intended to attract colonists, actually discouraged prospective settlers, while at the same time creating another divisive element in the colony.

Large-scale immigration to New Netherland was also hindered by the West India Company's close restrictions on the fur trade, which was the chief source of wealth, by the inadequacy of the land and climate for producing the necessary agricultural staples, and by the success of rival European countries in attracting large numbers of Dutch immigrant farmers and tradesmen. In addition, New Netherland also had to face the problem of remigration; the return of a significant number of Walloons and others to Holland, either because they had fulfilled the term of their contract or because they were no longer of service to the Company. Periodic skirmishes with the Indians also discouraged some emigration from Holland, while at the same time causing others to return home.

By 1650 several Dutch communities and farms had grown up in New Netherland, but only one was anything like a real town. This was New Amsterdam, on the lower tip of Manhattan, which had a population of less than one thousand. Next in importance was Fort Orange, still a wilderness community of only a few hundred people. There were also small Dutch settlements scattered up and down the Hudson River as well as several on western Long Island. In addition, there were two settlements to the south on the Delaware River. In 1664, when New England's population had grown to over fifty thousand, New Netherland numbered approximately eight thousand, about two-thirds of whom were Hollanders.

England had never conceded the Dutch claims in North America, and after the Stuart restoration in 1660 she was determined to challenge her commercial rival. To this end a vast proprietary grant, including the same land claimed by the Dutch, was deeded to James, Duke of York, the brother of Charles II. The duke then undertook the naval operation which secured New Amsterdam's quick surrender in 1664. The success of the English in this conflict might have been predicted for more than one reason. The lack of settlers in New Netherland was certainly a fundamental weakness. In addition, New Netherland lay geographically between the English settlements of New England on the north and Virginia and Maryland on the south. Moreover, internally the Dutch colony was very weak. The civil rights of the Dutch were being constantly encroached upon by a profit-obsessed company and an aristocratic Director General, with small regard for much else than to carry out the will of the nearly bankrupt Company. Consequently, in the money-making atmosphere which prevailed, there was little patriotism or public spirit among the colonists to inspire defense of the territory.

In the peace that followed, the Dutch holdings were divided; the Duke of York gained control only of New York, which he governed through a series of appointed deputies. Compared to Dutch rule the new government was liberal and humane, since by this time the economic advantages of religious liberty were generally conceded by colonial entrepreneurs; moreover, the conversion of James to Roman Catholicism in 1672 led him to seek toleration for his coreligionists. Compared with other colonies, however, the New York government was restrictive and arbitrary. The "Duke's Laws," approved by the Dutch deputies in 1665, encouraged the continued growth of big estates; and a few favored families—De Lanceys, Livingstones, Morrises, Schuylers, and others—acquired ownership of enormous stretches of land in the Hudson Valley. Most of their land remained uncultivated, however, although they collected rents from enough tenant farmers to enable them to live in an aristocratic style. For a few months in 1673-1674 the Dutch reconquered and held the territory; and when the Duke of York regained control he appointed as governor Sir Edmund Andros, who reinstated the "Duke's Laws" and resisted appeals for representative local government.

New York hardly prospered under Stuart rule, however. In 1678 there were about three thousand people in Manhattan, and not over twenty thousand in the whole colony. The great estates remained practically empty, and the wealth continued in the hands of a few landed gentlemen, merchants, and fur traders. The Duke's officials worked in close cooperation with these affluent aristocrats, who were permitted to exploit the small farmers and the urban craftsmen. In addition, the heterogeneity of the population heightened the problems of government. The Dutch were not particularly good subjects of the English crown, and the Puritans on Long Island regarded the Catholic James and his deputies with grave suspicion. And the constantly shifting boundaries made provincial loyalty or a sense of community difficult to develop. Only a tenth of the population was permitted to vote; and although protests about taxation without representation brought about the first meeting of the legislature in 1683, what progress it might have made was upset by Leisler's Rebellion[5] and the Glorious Revolution in 1688.

The religious situation in seventeenth century New York was feeble and disordered, reflecting the colony's political and social turmoil. This is interesting because during the same period the Reformed Church in the Netherlands was as profound as any branch of Christianity the age produced. It had manifested unity and strict adherence to the Reformed tradition at the Synod of Emden in 1571. Its universities at Leyden, Utrecht, Groningen, and Harderwijk, became famous as citadels of Reformed theological scholarship and their influence was felt at home and abroad. The Synod of Dort, called in 1618 to counteract the Arminian "heresy,"[6] became a virtual ecumenical council of Reformed Churches, and was the chief event in Reformed confessional history between the writings of Calvin and the Westminster Assembly of 1643. Even the Dutch rulers embraced the Reformed cause.

The religious activity of the mother country, however, was not matched by the Dutch colonists in New Netherland. The sponsoring West India Company recruited for commercial, and not religious reasons; its first charter in 1621 did not even include a provision for spiritual needs. Consequently, very few immigrants came to the New World with a fervent commitment to the Reformed faith. Subsequently, through the urging of the Classis of Amsterdam, the Company did "establish" a Dutch Reformed Church in New Netherland, but it was anything but conscientious in carrying out its commitment. Not until 1636, when the Classis of Amsterdam assumed full responsibility for sending ministers to New Netherland and for supervising congregations in matters of faith and church discipline, a responsibility it held until shortly before the American Revolution, was there possibility for religious growth and order among the colonists.

The first men who were sent out to look after the religious needs of the Dutch colonists were lay workers, officially called "comforters of the sick." They were Bastian Jansz Krol, who arrived in March, 1624, and Jan Huygens, who settled with his brother-in-law, Peter Minuit, in May, 1626. In addition to visiting the sick, a lay worker read prayers on appropriate occasions as well as a few chapters from the Bible and sometimes a sermon from an approved book of sermons. He also frequently assisted in the catechetical instruction of the youth. Although not permitted to administer the sacrament of the Lord's Supper, he was allowed by special permission to baptize and to perform marriages. During the eighteenth century, the lay worker frequently served as a general "all purpose man," whose religious duties were combined with those of church sexton, bell ringer, grave digger, schoolmaster, and town clerk.[7]

The Reverend Jonas Michaelius was the first ordained minister to come to New Netherland. Michaelius was born in 1584, had studied at the University of Leyden, had held several pastorates in Holland, and had served Dutch outposts in Brazil and Africa. He arrived at New Amsterdam on April 7, 1628, finding the two hundred seventy souls then at Manhattan to be "free, somewhat rough, and loose." Nonetheless, he soon organized a church at New Amsterdam, with approximately fifty communicants, and remained its minister until his return to Holland around 1632. The (Dutch) Reformed Church in America dates its formal beginning from the founding of this church in 1628.[8]

Michaelius was succeeded by Dominie Everardus Bogardus, who arrived in New Amsterdam in 1633. The second minister presided over the colony's religious life during its best years. He saw the old mill loft meeting hall replaced, first by a wooden church and then, in 1642, by a stone building. During his ministry, moreover, the congregation grew to nearly two hundred members. Bogardus was quick tempered, and frequently quarreled with Governor Kiefft, however; and when Peter Stuyvesant arrived in 1647, both the Dominie and Kiefft sailed for home to appeal their cases. Their appeal was determined by a higher judge than they planned, however, for both men drowned at sea.

In 1642 a third minister, the Reverend Jan van Mekelenburg, better known as Megapolensis, arrived to serve the manor of Patroon Kilian van Rensselaer, thereby becoming the first Dutch minister on the upper Hudson. In addition to normal pastoral duties, Megapolensis found time to study and write about the customs and language of the Mohawk Indians and to carry on mission work among them. On at least two occasions he gained the release of Jesuit missionaries held captive by the Indians. In 1649 Megapolensis became pastor of the church at New Amsterdam, a position he held until his death in 1670.[9]

From 1628 until the English conquest in 1664, some fifteen Dutch Reformed ministers served thirteen congregations scattered throughout New Netherland. During this period, moreover, the Dutch Church held a privileged position over competing denominations in the province. A regulation of March 28, 1624, for example, declared that the colonists "shall within their territory hold no other services than those of the true Reformed Religion, in the manner in which they are at present conducted in this country."[10] Similarly, the first article of Governor Stuyvesant's commission specified that he was "not to permit any other than the Reformed doctrine."[11]

These decrees, however, were not always well observed, primarily because the Dutch West India Company feared that a strict compliance would discourage emigration to the colony. The Jesuit missionary, Isaac Jogues, noted this in 1646: "No religion is publicly exercised but the Calvinists, but this is not observed, for besides the Calvinists there are in the colony Catholics, English Puritans, Lutherans, Anabaptists, . . . etc."[12]

The English conquest in 1664 naturally affected the Reformed Church in New Netherland. Most important was its change in status. Before 1664 it had been the established church in the province, legally the only religious body permitted to hold worship services. With the coming of the British, however, the Reformed Church was placed in a subordinate role and, as time went on, it was forced to practice its faith in a culture which became increasingly alien. Moreover, on several occasions the British authorities nearly succeeded in establishing the Anglican Church as the official Church in the colony.

In addition, the colonial Reformed churches faced several serious internal problems in the period after the English conquest. For example, because almost all immigration from the Netherlands ceased in 1664, there was little prospect for significant church growth. Correspondingly, there was a shortage of pastors. At the end of the seventeenth century, there were only six Dutch Reformed ministers in New Netherland, with twenty-three churches requiring pastoral services. As a result, a minister frequently served two or more congregations. Those churches without the care of a Dominie used lay workers, with an occasional visit from an ordained pastor for the sacramental services.

Moreover, there was the related problem of paying the salaries of the ministers. During the New Netherland period, the Dutch pastors had received their pay from the sponsoring West India Company. When the English took over in 1664, however, this practice stopped, and new laws were passed obligating each parish to support its pastor. This procedure proved impracticable, however, primarily because the people were not accustomed to supporting their churches and paying the minister's salary. In addition, most of the churches were lethargic, and there was precious little benevolent action of any kind. Beyond these factors, moreover, when the conservative Dutch clergy almost unanimously opposed Leisler's Rebellion in 1688-1689, which was a grass-roots revolt against the monied aristocrats, their relation to the people became strained, and some congregations were glad not to pay their Dominie's salary. Consequently, the lament of Megapolensis became typical: "On Sundays we have many hearers. People crowd into the church, and apparently like the sermon; but most of the listeners are not inclined to contribute to the support and salary of the preacher. They seem to desire, that we should live upon air and not upon produce."[13]

Despite such problems as a shortage of ministers, some alienation between clergy and people, inadequate funds, and occasional trouble with royal governors, the Dutch Reformed Churches managed some growth after the fall of New Netherland. This was especially true during the first half of the eighteenth century, when the Church grew from thirty-four congregations in 1705 to sixty-five churches in 1740. Much of this growth resulted from the natural increase of the Dutch population in the colony, although a number of Huguenot refugees from France and Palatine immigrants from Germany also affiliated with the Dutch churches. More significantly, however, the Church gained substantial new members through the spiritual renewal sparked by Dominie Theodorus Jacobus Frelinghuysen in central New Jersey.

Frelinghuysen, who deserves to be known as an important herald, if not the father of the Great Awakening, came to North America in 1720, and began his work the same year among six Dutch congregations in the Raritan Valley. Devotedly evangelical, he taught the necessity of personal conversion and subsequent holiness of life, and enforced strict standards for admission to the Lord's Supper. In preaching he was direct and outspoken, and occasionally antagonized some in his audience, particularly those who wanted to "keep things in the Dutch way."[14]

Despite considerable criticism, Frelinghuysen was very successful as an evangelical preacher. By 1727 a great revival was sweeping the central sections of New Jersey, and many were converted, including the deacons and elders of his various congregations. In addition, many of his sermons were published in both Dutch and English, and some of these inspired revivals in other colonies. When the eminent George Whitfield preached in the Dutch regions of New Jersey in 1739 and 1740, he attributed his success there in part to Frelinghuysen, who, he said, was "the beginning of the great work . . . in these parts."[15]

Since its beginning in North America, the Reformed Church had been subordinate to the mother Church in the Netherlands.

Although the arrangement had been necessary, it had created a number of problems. All important matters had to be decided by the Classis of Amsterdam, situated three thousand miles across the ocean. Although permission was granted occasionally for a small group of ministers in America to deal with a particular problem, such instances were rare. The Classis delayed months and sometimes years before making decisions. In addition, the requirement of training and ordaining ministers in the Netherlands had resulted in a chronic shortage of pastors. During most of the colonial period, there were about three times as many churches as ministers. Moreover, choices made by the Amsterdam brethren were often unwise. Sometimes they selected persons of mediocre ability who were unable to obtain pastorates in Holland.

Periodically a New Netherland divine or church suggested than an organization be established which could decide disciplinary problems, solve internal disputes, and examine and ordain young men for the ministry—all without the Classis of Amsterdam's imprimatur. As early as 1662, for example, the Reverend Johannes Polhemus of Long Island proposed that an association of ministers and churches be formed in New Netherland because "we stand in need of communication with one another in the form of a Classis, after the manner of the Fatherland."[16] Similar requests were made in 1706 and 1732, the latter by the Consistory of the Church in Schoharie, New York.[17]

The Classis of Amsterdam, however, consistently rejected these and similar suggestions. In 1709 it replied to the request of 1706 as follows: "The formation of a Classis among you, to correspond to ours at home, is yet far in the future, and we hardly dare to think of it," adding, "such a Classis would be the ruin of the churches of New York. This is so obvious that it needs no proof."[18]

By 1737, however, the "future" was present for some in the New Netherland churches. In that year several Dutch Reformed ministers and elders met in New York City to discuss the formation of an ecclesiastical union. In April, 1738, these men met again and drafted a constitution for a Coetus of the American churches. The Coetus was empowered to "consider, determine, give sentence upon, and settle all matters and dissensions that occur, or which are brought before us for action; for being on the ground, we are in the best possible position to judge them, and to check and smother them in their very beginnings." The Classis of Amsterdam was assured that the Coetus would conform "to the Churches of the Fatherland" and would correspond with them regularly. Anyone who felt himself aggrieved by its decisions could appeal to the Classis.[19] Nine years later, in 1747, the Amsterdam body approved most of this proposal, reserving to itself the power of ordination, and the Coetus was officially formed. And in 1754 the Coetus reorganized itself with power to ordain.

Not every leader in the American church endorsed this re-organized body, however. One in particular, Dominie Johannes Ritzema of New York City, organized a minority faction which refused to accept the actions of the Coetus, preferring instead continued subordination to the Classis of Amsterdam. Ritzema and his followers feared that the role carved out by the Coetus might lead to substantial changes in doctrine, liturgy, mode of worship, church government, and perhaps even the name of the church. They were especially worried that the ordination of ministers in America might result in a less learned and less respected ministry. Consequently, these opponents of the reor-ganized Coetus created an ecclesiastical body of their own. It became known as the Conferentie, and held firmly to the idea of subordination to the Classis of Amsterdam.

The effect of this schism, which lasted for nearly two dec-ades, was devastating for the colonial churches. Numerous Dutch Reformed families became discouraged and joined other religious bodies, particularly in New York City. Harsh language was frequently exchanged between the opposing factions. Both clergy and congregation entered the conflict, and on several occasions there were eruptions within chruches. At Hackensack, New Jersey, for example, there were two ministers, two dif-ferent consistories, and two opposing congregations, which agreed only on the established time for their separate functions at the church building. At times, there was even violence, with ministers being attacked and some groups being physically pre-vented from using an edifice for worship services.[20]

The swing of time, however, favored the Coetus faction, and its ranks and power steadily increased. This became especially true after 1766, when it succeeded in obtaining a charter to establish Queen's College (later Rutgers University), in New Brunswick, New Jersey. After 1766, moreover, the Coetus cause was helped by an unexpected source. Liberty-seeking Americans were then protesting the British imposed Stamp Act, and the clamor for political independence began to be heard in every American colony. This kind of rhetoric influenced the arguments of some of the Dutch Reformed Church leaders. Consequently, the Coetus informed the Classis on one occasion that it would not argue on the basis of past history as to whether the colonial churches should be subordinate to the Classis of Amsterdam, but would argue instead from "inherent rights."[21] It also asserted that "as a free people" it was a matter of their choice whether or not the ministers wished to correspond with the Amsterdam body.[22] In addition, the Classis of Amsterdam showed a greater willingness to compromise with the Coetus faction.

As a result of these developments, and the diplomacy of the Reverend John H. Livingston, the schism finally ended. Livingston, a member of one of New York's most prestigious families, had discussed the issue with a number of church leaders in the Netherlands while a student at the University of Utrecht during the 1760's. Ingratiating himself to that august body, he had secured their approval to prepare a plan for the union of the American churches. Later, in October, 1771, he succeeded in bringing the contending parties together for discussion in New York City.

A plan was finally drafted based on the ideas Livingston formulated in Holland. Known as the Articles of Union, it included the following basic points: 1) the churches would adhere to the doctrine and policy of the Reformed Church in Holland; 2) the churches would be divided into five centers, in which ministers and elders would meet together three or four times a year in special bodies known as Particular Assemblies; 3) each of these in turn would send delegates once a year to a larger body, known as the General Assembly, representing the entire colonial church; 4) the General Assembly would have the right to examine and ordain young men for the ministry; 5) the college at New Brunswick would be placed under the control of the General Assembly and provided with a Professor of Theology; and 6) close correspondence, including a yearly report, would be maintained with the Classis of Amsterdam. In June, 1772, the colonial leaders assembled again, and formally approved the Articles of Union. Thus, the Dutch Reformed Church in America was once again united.

During most of the next decade, the members of the Dutch Church, together with all of Colonial America, were deeply involved in the Revolutionary War. As a result, much of the life and work of the Reformed Church stopped, including its correspondence with the Classis of Amsterdam. When the war finally ended in 1783 the American Church began drafting a new constitution and liturgy appropriate for an independent denomination. This was completed and adopted in 1792, and the first meeting of the General Synod of the newly organized Reformed Protestant Dutch Church in North America was held in 1794.

The eight essays in this volume examine the history of the Reformed Church from the Revolutionary War to the present, roughly 1776 to 1976. In each case the writers have integrated an aspect of the denomination's life with an important matrix in the American experience: the War of Independence, westward expansion, immigration, international affairs, social and intellectual thought, social problems, education, and the role of women. The intent was to keep the developing history of the Reformed Church at center stage, while also giving attention to the interaction of that history with the American culture.

The informed reader will recognize that several important topics in the life of the Reformed Church were either excluded from this study or else were given cursory attention. These include the work of the Reverend John Kempers and his successors in Chiapas, Mexico, the black and Latin American influence, the mid-nineteenth century schism that gave birth to the Christian Reformed Church, and the contribution to the American life of such contemporary Reformed Church notables as A. J. Muste, Graham Taylor, and Norman Vincent Peale. Several of these topics can be examined in other volumes,[23] and each of them deserves a full-scale study. Space prevented a serious treatment of these topics in this book.

Although the writers in this volume worked independently, the eight essays point to several common themes which tie the composite together and suggest important character traits of the Reformed Church in the American experience. One such theme is the dialectic of derivative and indigenous: the Church's attempt to maintain its Dutch Calvinist heritage while at the same time taking seriously its life in the American culture. Whether the issue was mission, theology, education, or social action, the essays show that the denomination has tried to hold in tension its Old World tradition and the cultural norms of the American society. Eugene Heideman's chapter on theology and Norman Kansfield's essay on education are particularly insightful on this issue, showing that in those areas the denomination has attempted to keep in balance the derivative and indigenous polarities. In addition, in a somewhat different way Barbara Fassler's study of the role of women in the Arcot mission also develops this theme. She shows that the denomination's mission program in India was caught in the tension between the sex role concepts of American culture, and the demands of the mission goals and circumstances in India.

A second theme, related to the first, is the dialectic of the particular and the diverse: the denomination's effort to assert its parochial identity while at the same time becoming pluralistic. This theme emerges in nearly all of the studies in this volume. For example, both my essay on "home" missions and Elton Bruins' study in immigration show the tension between ethnic particularism on the one hand and pluralism on the other in the developing mission program of the denomination. Herman Harmelink's essay shows the same theme operating with regard to the denomination's world mission program, especially in relation to the question of ecumenism. And Eugene Heideman's study on the developing theology in the Reformed Church also points to this theme: the task of affirming the "Standards of Unity" on the one hand and accepting theological diversity on the other. Interestingly, the one issue where the denomination did not tolerate diversity was in regard to patriotism. John Beardslee's essay on the American Revolution, for example, shows that the Reformed Church, like the nation itself, quickly mythologized its history in regard to that conflict, assimilated within the denomination those Dutch who fought for the British, and never allowed its Tories to be proud of the fact that they were "on the wrong side." Similarly, John De Jong's essay shows that the denomination generally blended its piety with its patriotism on social issues, and usually found ways to nudge its more radical social activists out of the Church.

A third theme is the dialectic of the social and the individual: the Church's attempt to take seriously its corporate responsibility while at the same time emphasizing personal salvation and piety. This theme points to the democratizing influence of the American culture on the covenantal tradition and Old World "Standards" of the Reformed Church. On one level this was evidenced in the historical tension between presbyterianism and congregationalism. In addition, both Eugene Heideman's essay on theology and my chapter on mission show the Church caught in the tension between working for a Christian America on the one hand and preaching a Gospel of individualism on the other. This theme also appears in John De Jong's essay on social issues, which shows the social-individual dialectic at work as the Reformed Church became caught up in American evangelicalism.

These three themes—the derivative-indigenous, particular-diverse, and social-individual—suggest that the Reformed Church has felt most comfortable on the middle-ground during the two centuries, from 1776 to 1976. Historically the denomination has preferred compromise to extremism, finding the center of most issues more acceptable to its character than the polar edges. Through this process the Reformed Church has been able to carve out its own identity in the American culture. It is a fascinating history; the story of the Americanization of a denomination.

The American Revolution

John W. Beardslee III

In the writing of American History, secular historians have joined with writers of our denomination in depicting the Dutchman of the American Revolution as an enlightened, liberty-loving American, backing national self-government with enthusiasm, remembering his nation's struggle for freedom, suffering willingly for a great cause, and standing at the forefront of the patriotic rising against the backwardness and oppression that all right-thinking men and women saw in the British cause.[1] Two of the best of them join in telling us that Dutch Tories were few and far between, a little group of rich magnates and officials guided by self-interest and quite out of touch with the spiritual dynamic of their community.[2]

The reasons for this stand are clear. From the beginning, the young nation needed a common ideal and a unifying sense of its past. The glorification of the Revolution served this purpose. Only in recent decades have we really dared take a critical look at our origins, but in doing so we have found that, in spite of the defects of our founding fathers and the virtues found among their opponents, the revised and more realistic view is not only closer to abstract truth, but better fulfills the needs of a more mature nation.

If we undertake a similar realistic appraisal of our denominational past, a similar deepening of the appreciation of our origins, and the emergence of a more mature understanding of ourselves, will also result. The patriotic myths with which we have surrounded our past have, as a matter of fact, separated us from part of our spiritual heritage. For example, not only do writers on Brooklyn and Queens do their best to avoid an exploration of the lives of worshipping congregations with pastors loyal to the British Crown, but even writers dealing directly with the affairs of Manhattan Island, where continuous ministry since 1628 is part of our denominational glory, have been led to regard the history of the Reformed Church under British rule during most of the Revolution as a sort of interregnum or period of suspension with nothing happening, when in fact it was an important element in "establishment" society.³ The theoelogy that has accompanied this turning away from an element in our past is, in spite of the conscious orthodoxy of those who held it, a part of the American "civil religion."⁴ Facing needs similar to those of the new nation, a divided church faced them as did the nation, by finding an ideal in the national life and remembering only that part of the past that supported the ideal.

A minister whose family tradition remembered the facts, for instance, revealed the real theology of the early nineteenth century when he described the life of Reformed people of Bergen County, New Jersey during the Revolution in these terms:

"Some few were traitorous—some indifferent; others entered not as warmly into the cause as might have been expected; others again, urged on the cause of their country, as the cause of God. A few, no doubt, were excessive in profession of patriotism, and used it to cloak their love of plunder, and their individual resentments. Then came the strong political controversies, under the early years of our constitution."⁵

The dominie recognized the fact of a church divided over civil issues, and, as his catechism taught him to expect, infected by the old Adam. He minimized the number of "traitors"—Tories—who were, as a modern researcher has shown, one-third or one-half of the Dutch Church members in the area under consideration,⁶ but above all, he declared the nature of the prevailing theology, and the stand point from which we have studied our past, with his hearty approval of those who proclaimed the cause of "their country" as the cause of God. Similar attitudes in later generations and in later wars have not been unknown, but the American Revolution is above all that war which, for purposes of membership in the American community, our churches have felt constrained to take as an example of the identity of "cause of country" and "cause of God". To deny that divine providence produced the American Revolution has been the most unthinkable kind of un-American behavior. As a result, we have been unable to accept the fellowship of those who were not able to see "rebel" governments as representing their country, and we have understood the unity of our church in a way that excludes many of its members.

It is true that these Tories saw the cause of the king as the cause of God (an un-American perversion) and rejected the Revolution at least as violently as the Revolution rejected them. We have heard much of their loss, as supporters of a bad cause. What we have not heard, in our denominational history, is the story of our loss through separation from these brethren and rejection of their ideals.

To remedy this loss, we must first of all face the fact of Toryism among our forefathers of the American Revolution, and try to understand its relationship to the denomination's spiritual history. Its significance for us can then be understood.

With regard to the facts of Dutch Toryism, Professor Scott of Hope College, writing in 1876, listed forty-one ministers of the Protestant Dutch Church in New York and New Jersey,[7] sixteen foreign born and twenty-five natives. Of these, only four declared themselves as Tories, three of whom were foreign born. German born Johannes C. Rubel of Brooklyn was deposed after the war, for wife-beating, drunkeness, and the use of un-Christian language, with a strong rebuke for his disloyalty. He became a pharmacist in New York. Dutch-born Hermanus L. Boelen of Queens, Long Island returned to Holland in 1780. German-born John M. Kern, after a sojourn in Nova Scotia, retired in Pennsylvania, and American-born Gerret Lydekker, from Bergen County, New Jersey, ministered in British- occupied New York, and became an exile in England, abandoning his substantial family inheritance and living on the Loyalists' compensation provided by the Crown. During the war he had from time to time been employed by the British military government in translating proclamations into Dutch, which was still a significant spoken language in New York. Activities of the others, aside from supporting the royal cause by sermon and prayer, are harder to discover, but they identified themselves beyond equivocation with the losing side.

In the case of a number of other ministers, however, there is ambivalence in their relationship to the Republic. German-born Abraham Rosenkrantz of Herkimer, N.Y., on the frontier war zone, was a brother-in-law of the patriot hero, General Herkimer, by whom he was regarded as a Tory. He continued, however, in his charge and is known as a good pastor and a good American.[8] Perhaps he had that ability for non-political preaching that distinguished the learned Dutch domine of Hackensack and Shraalenburg (Dumont), New Jersey, Wormaldus Kuypers, whose son was employed in New York by the British Navy, but whose own only remembered political utterance seems to have been "trouble I hate", and who, in an area where military activity was constant for years, maintained a kind of neutrality as head of congregations with known Tory sympathies, undisturbed by the American authorities, and also became a good American in due time.[9]

Another German-born pastor in a frontier war zone, Johannes Schuyler of Schoharie, is described by a distinguished successor, Sanford E. Cobb, as "a patriot animating his brethren in the Revolutionary struggles", but at the time of decision it was reported that "the Domine does not dare to pray for King George anymore, and for Congress he will not pray".[10]

Perhaps the most interesting of the "neutrals", or secret Tories, was the stalwart conservative Hollander, Johannes Ritzema, in 1775 senior Dutch minister on Manhattan Island. He is obviously a key figure in our denomination's colonial history, and often a representative of what the later church has called the wrong side. Like his New York colleagues, on the outbreak of the Revolution he left the city, his home since 1744, settling in Kinderhook, where he ministered until his death. His letters to Amsterdam, after the war, are the letters of a faithful pastor, accepting the government under which he now lives, hurt deeply by his rejection in New York City and his inability to return to his former charge. He makes no explicit reference to political theory, beyond good orthodox disclaimers of the sin of anarchy, but he was not permitted to rejoin the Whig exiles of his congregation and minister to his former people. To what extent his age and health entered the decision, to what extent it was the heritage of the bitter church struggle in New York City, where he had been a conservative leader while "liberals" secured the innovation of English preaching, and at the same time disturbed the old power structure that Ritzema headed, and to what extent political sentiments were involved is difficult to say. Earlier historians who wrote from a Tory standpoint accepted the Domine as one of that party.[11] His importance in the history of the denomination made the conclusion unacceptable.

These facts were known—Ritzema had left New York City and remained in Kinderhook, and had left no political memorial behind him. His son, once a member of an honor guard for New England delegates to Congress, had deserted the American army and become a British lieutenant-colonel. With limited materials, research was guided by desire. By the end of the century, David Cole, probably recognizing the problem, ignored both the unwanted evidence and the question it posed, and, keeping a discreet silence on the Domine's politics, described him simply as an ornament to the church, in terms then accepted by the church. "He well understood and appreciated the necessity for our Americanization. And I believe he always meant to promote it." The conduct of his eldest son is described as "an unfortunate blot" on the name of a family that should always be honored.[12] A generation later, William H. S. Demarest even more completely used the American dream as a compensation for the absence of data, with a moving description of the four New York ministers, apparently united by love of God and country, going together into "exile" as the British occupied their city.[13] Since then, one startling fact has come to light— Governor Tryon of New York Province, a soldier-administrator distinguished by hatred for rebels, recommended Domine Ritzema (a non-conformist preacher under English law) for the chaplaincy of a British North American regiment, in which many American Dutchmen were serving.[14]

This review of clerical sentiment will help clarify our thinking about the relationship of the Reformed Church to the American Revolution, and it suggests a pattern for theological interpretation to which we shall come. But it does not change the fact that there was little overt opposition, except for four ministers out of forty-one, to the revolution, and much enthusiastic support. Governor Livingston of New Jersey, writing to Washington, used an often-quoted phrase about the Dutch clergy being patriots "almost to a man," and he was doubtless aware of the activity of Domine Du Bois of Monmouth County, who shouldered his gun for militia service, of Domine Hardenburgh of Raritan, sleeping with a loaded musket beside him for fear of "Tory neighbors" (Dutch or Non-Dutch?), of Domine Romeyn of Hackensack and Schraalenburg, encouraging the patriots in a war-devastated parish, corresponding with Trenton on defense problems, and at least once narrowly escaping being shot from ambush by Tory partisans, of Domine Jackson in what is now Jersey City, steadfastly upholding Revolutionary principles almost within sight of British headquarters, perhaps of Domine Froeligh, praying that God would strike the king's ships and send his soldiers to the bottom of the sea. To these might be added, for example, Domine Schuneman of Catskill and Coxsackie, New York, well-known for patriotic leadership and hospitality to home-sick soldiers. Tory exiles in Canada were said to have promised the Indians a reward for kidnapping him, but he went to and fro fearlessly and unhurt, in a scattered and exposed parish.

These were native Americans, but many immigrant pastors, as well, were enthusiastic for independence—Westerlo of Albany, a Hollander, Gebhard of Claverack, a German, who also faced danger from Tory irregulars, and Weyberg of Philadelphia, jailed during the British occupation because, preaching to them in their language, he urged Hessian soldiers to desert. These stories and others have been told by Corwin and a multitude of local historians.

We know better than to equate the opinions of the church with the opinions of the clergy, and when we turn to lay opinion during the Revolution we find evidence of a larger minority of Tories than among the ministers. It is interesting to note that it was our clergy, not our church, that Governor Livingston praised for patriotic zeal.

It may also be noted in passing that the overwhelming majority of the laity, although using Dutch or German in the family and for public worship, were native born, while over a third of the clergy, of 1775, were of foreign birth.

The best studies of Dutch Reformed lay sentiment in the Revolution come from students who are not members of our denomination—Adrian Leiby and Alice Kenney. Both write for particular areas where special local circumstances may have been operative. But with their help we may detect a definite pattern.

Leiby, writing on the struggle in northern New Jersey, and near-by New York, had access to well-preserved congregational records, and was able to discover the part played in the Revolution by individual church members. The organized structure of particular congregations also enabled him to determine the place of these persons, and their families, in the great schism which had recently disturbed the Dutch churches, and had been healed, on paper, in 1771. Such data, for significant numbers of laity, is probably irrecoverable for most areas. The intensity of the church struggle in the Hackensack Valley had resulted in institutionalized schisms—congregations had divided, called separate pastors, and kept separate membership lists, along a clear-cut party line. Leiby's findings merit a look backward at this dispute, as well as a look ahead, to the generation after the Revolution.

The dispute that divided and nearly ruined the Dutch Church of New York and New Jersey in the generation before the Revolution is called the struggle of coetus against conferentie. In the aftermath of the revival known as the Great Awakening, the church was cut in two, as the Presbyterians also had been. Many writers assume that this was a struggle of the vital, experiential faith of the revival against the dead formalism and traditionalism of unregenerate citizens. It is more helpful to see two styles of faith in a tension that for long was uncreative. The coetus party was indeed the revivalist, and in most ways the party of the future. They did emphasize personal spiritual experience and conversion, urging the necessity of personal decision. They favored an independent American ecclesiastical organization, such as the Congregationalists and Presbyterians already enjoyed, with power to ordain ministers. They were the originators of the demand for a Dutch Reformed college in America. The conferentie party, on the other hand, rejoiced in the Dutch connection, which by treaty gave the New York churches status as part of the national church of the Netherlands, rather than as "dissenters," although the legal meaning of this was vague. They cherished European traditions of ministerial education, and were anxious to have clergy educated in the Netherlands. They distrusted the emotional revivalistic preaching with its call for decision, as an open door to Arminian free-will doctrine.[15] They held firmly to the church order of Dort as well as to its theology, insisting on formal worship, observance of the traditional holidays of the church year, and the authority of classis and synod. While the coetus people proposed to organize their American classis, the conferentie declared that only the Classis of Amsterdam, their established parent body, could authorize ecclesiastical acts.

The resulting disputes divided congregations, embroiled pastors against consistories and people, and in some instances led to the establishment of separate, hostile congregations, each claiming to be the true one. With the passage of time, the conferentie party lost ground and became increasingly "conservative". In 1771, under John Livingston's leadership, a compromise was reached. The Classis of Amsterdam granted, in principle, the requests of the coetus, thereby withdrawing its support and prestige from the conferentie extremists, and depriving them of legal grounds for separation. Some churches held aloof from the union, and some sore wounds remained, especially in New York City, where the consistory had been neutral, but where a separate dispute over English preaching had produced a similar party division, and in northern New Jersey, where strong, well-organized, hostile congregations remained face to face.[16]

Leiby's careful survey of congregational records shows that, almost without exception, conferentie ministers and laymen, in northern New Jersey, supported the British cause, often very actively, throughout the Revolution, and coetus ministers and laymen, again almost without exception, supported the cause of independence. He has also shown that in the 1820's, when the "True Dutch Reformed Church"[17] split off from our denomination, it was, in northern New Jersey, descendants of coetus-Whig people who wanted to get out of the denomination, and descendants of conferentie-Tory folk formed a solid bloc that remained.

This is not the place to discuss the complicated theological questions posed by the True Dutch Reformed Church and the Secession of 1822, but an outline of Leiby's work indicates that the divisions among church people over the American Revolution were integrated into a long development of religious controversy. This fact, and the extremely close correlation of coetus-Whig and conferentie-Tory, supply the rationale for Leiby's further conclusion that the political decision for or against the Revolution should be seen primarily as a moral decision—"I believe", he says, "that most Dutchmen took sides for reasons of prinicple".[18] The modification of some of our historic myths lies in the evidence of a substantial clash of principle. The moral decision of supporters of the Revolution is not simply that of the "good guys," nor is it the sole expression of Christian principle in our tradition.

Outside northern New Jersey, data of the kind that Leiby used have not been found. The coetus-conferentie dispute had been institutionalized in other forms, and did not leave the same kind of church records. But Miss Kenney's study of the Albany Dutch[19] gives insights into the situation in another area of denominational strength. Her data are taken largely from secular records in what was then Albany County—the present counties of Albany, Columbia, Rensselaer, Saratoga, and Schenectady, besides parts of Greene, Schohaire, Warren and Washington. In this extensive and diversified area were eighteen largely rural Reformed Congregations besides the flourishing church in Albany, whose congregation included the "elite" of the second city of the Province. Miss Kenney based her research on the militia rolls, and on the lists of persons arrested as Tories, identifying "Dutch" persons by "family" names, and it must be remembered that not all Dutchmen are of the Reformed Church, and that, in various areas, a few prominent Reformed people already were found whose names cannot be recognized as Dutch or German (Livingston, Jackson, Christie, Smith). These examples, however, are not taken from up-state New York, and in that area few Dutchmen had as yet joined other churches, or lost their "Dutchness." However many never made a confession of faith, the church remained an important institution in their lives. Data regarding the ethnic Dutch are therefore highly significant as indices of the state of the Dutch Church. The Schohaire Valley, where many Palatine Germans were associated with the Dutch Church, is not included in Miss Kenney's study.

Thirty-eight per cent of the militia of the area (that is, of males between fifteen and sixty) she regards as of Dutch extraction, and thirty-two per cent of the persons arrested as Tories. But in local areas, significant variations appear. In Kinderhook, seventy-eight per cent of the arrested "Tories" were "Dutch," while only thirty-six per cent of the militia were of that group. In other words, Kinderhook was a specific center of Dutch Toryism. The Tories of Kinderhook and vicinity were, in fact, quite troublesome to the Revolutionary authorities, and the high percentage of Dutchmen among them, in the light of Leiby's findings regarding New Jersey, suggests that the conferentie sympathies of Domine Freyenmoet, pastor for over twenty years, were widely acceptable and influential. Many people behaved, in any case, like the conferentie brethren of New Jersey. Both conferentie sentiments and Tory guerilla activity in near-by Claverack are also important, according to a careful local historian.[20] The records of Poughkeepsie and of Kingston, let it be added, do not conflict with this pattern of Dutch Reformed life.

Eleven of the twelve persons first elected to the (Revolutionary) Committee of Safety in Kinderhook were eventually arrested as Tories. Nine of these, all Dutch, were either banished or went into voluntary exile, as a new group, including other Dutch elements, came into power. Parenthetically, a similar shift in the power structure, involving rejection of old Dutch leadership, seems to have taken place in Poughkeepsie. In Schenectady, on the other hand, this was not so. There the population was more solidly Dutch than in Kinderhook or Claverack—seventy-two per cent of the militia were Dutch, and only twenty-five per cent of detected Tories. Here at last is an area where Dutch adherance to the Revolution was not only outstanding, but far outstripped that of the local population in general. This becomes all the more striking by comparison with the adjacent West District of Rensselaerswyck, where the Dutch majority was divided in the same proportion as the rest of the population—seventy-two per cent of the militia and seventy-three per cent of arrested Tories were Dutch. The coetus-conferentie alignments in Schenectady are hard to determine, but like Albany, where the leadership of the Dutch church was a hall of fame of Revolutionary leadership, Schenectady had a Dutch church that represented the dominent social pattern of the town. And the pastoral leadership in Schenectady, from the beginning, had been heavily weighted toward the coetus. In the Revolution-oriented church of Albany, also, the pastoral work of T.J. Frelinghuysen's son Theodore had, not without opposition, brought the congregation into the coetus wing, without schism, and had established a current which the immigrant Domine Westerlo could not have stopped, even if he wanted to. Moreover, Westerlo himself was deeply influenced by a "support-group" of pietistic-revivalistic laymen.[21]

Without the precise data on laymen developed by Leiby, we can perhaps appeal to the adage "like parson, like people". In any event, lay behavior, in Bergen County, New Jersey and in Albany County, New York, shows the same pattern—a strong Tory minority attached to the Dutch church, especially where conferentie influence was powerful. There are, of course, many secular forces that affect political allegiance, and Miss Kenney has analyzed these for Albany County, as many historians have for the nation. But in considering the history of the church, it is important to recognize that Christian allegiance was involved in these choices, and that conscience, as Leiby suggests, may have determined individual action.

Reference to Albany and Schenectady recalls one significant fact—there was much real enthusiasm for independence among the Dutch—laity and clergy alike. Except for the mayor of the city, the prominent members of the Albany church were instrumental in setting up the new civil government. In both New York and New Jersey, Dutchmen, and the Palatine Germans of New York, religiously allied to the Dutch, are among the remembered heroes—Generals Schuyler and Herkimer, Colonels Van Schaick, Van Cortlandt, Gansevoort, and Du Bois, all of New York, for instance. There was also a host of largely unremembered people who served and suffered for what they obviously believed was right—people like Peter Van Orden of Schraalenburgh, New Jersey, who served in the militia of both New York and New Jersey in campaign after campaign, being forced to support a widowed mother and for a time moving to Kakiat, New York because of the destruction of his home.[22] The devotion to independence of the majority of New Jersey Dutchmen, and their hardihood in the face of suffering, are clearly indicated by Leiby's work, if, this late in time, such demonstration is needed.

But the Tories, remembered and unremembered, also brought whole-hearted devotion to their cause, and suffered for their principles. Those of Dutch extraction were a cross section of their community, including the mayor of Albany, who acquired a distinguished British military record, at least two sons of pastors, who served the British government, and a distinguished lawyer from Kinderhook. There were brave and efficient soldiers in the British army, dedicated undercover agents, and both plain citizens and self-seekers. One of the most energetic Tory partisan fighters in New Jersey, a man who eventually became little more than a robber, came, in fact, from a coetus family,[23] and Leiby mentions other coetus-Tory individuals, some of them more significant for churchmanship.

These "Dutchmen" who fought against one another, by foul means as well as fair, were drawn from the membership of one church. The evidence before us suggests that church membership was not incidental, but that religious convictions and church alignment played an important role in political decision-making by individuals. Further, neither side can be equated with the Reformed Church; both are part of our heritage.

Dutchmen of the American Revolution were obviously not apolitical, but it is a striking fact that, unlike the Congregationalists, Presbyterians, and Anglicans, we have no deposit of significant sermons, addresses, and pamphlets on the burning political issues. This is partly due to the fact that Dutch ministers of the period did little publishing. The Germans had a press in Pennsylvania; the Dutch had virtually none in America. But the manuscript material that survives—like the sermons of Laidlie and Livingston, is remarkably apolitical in content. A burning patriotic sermon by a minister later associated with our church has survived, but he was of Presbyterian background and was a Presbyterian when he gave the message and for some time thereafter. There is probably a theological and ecclesiastical reason for this reticence, and it can probably be found in the state of the church and in some dynamics of its theology.

The church, when the war came, was in the process of trying to reunite after a destructive controversy. Its energies were turned inward. The one thing that people did not need from the pulpit was another argument. "The times" called for conciliatory preaching. The spirit of the "union of 1771," which sought to unite the factions, discouraged the introduction of new divisions.

In New York City, the conflicting forces involved in the coetus-conferentie dispute were most clearly precipitated in the quarrel over English preaching. The effort to have one minister to preach regularly in English had divided the congregation, caused a law-suit, and resulted in the withdrawal of members. The English preacher was of Scotch birth and was accused of "jesuitical" and "republican" principles—like other Presbyterians, he was seen as a threat to royal authority. But in the controversy-ridden congregation, he and his friends too may well have been constrained to work for peace and not to stir up new troubles. This was certainly the attitude of John Livingston.

What energy the Dutch churches had not expended in controversy, they had devoted to an aim common to both coetus and conferentie—the preservation of ethnic identity. There was no desire to restore Dutch political rule, but a determination to remain Dutch. Church and language were both sacred. Except in New York City, coetus clergy clung to Dutch preaching as firmly as did the conferentie brethren. Coetus leaders laid the foundations for a separate Dutch Reformed College, although, like other spokesmen of undeveloped nations, they expected overseas friends ("rich and bountiful Holland") to foot the bill. The Classis of Amsterdam, feeling neither rich nor bountiful, urged participation in one of the existing American colleges, but even the advocates of ecclesiastical independence were determined on Dutch particularism.

The emphasis on this upholding of ethnic identity kept the Dutch somewhat out of the mainstream of the new American life. Many of them spoke English well for business purposes, but the church services, in Dutch, were a reflection of the particularistic concerns of the ethnic-religious community, not those of English-speaking neighbors. The growing English majority had already destroyed the Dutch flavor of much of New York City life, where both Anglicans and Presbyterians had outnumbered the Dutch, while in Albany, where the Dutch represented the community and monopolized elective office, they were "provincials" in more ways than one—appointed officers were royal officials sent by the New York English and were reminders of what had happened to Manhattan. In New Jersey the Dutch, always a minority, had played a subordinate political role.

The broader concerns of nation and government, therefore, were probably subordinated, in Dutch preaching and pastoral counsel, to the interests of the ethnic community, and insofar as the Dutch church had learned how to protect these ethnic interests under a British Government, there was no call for ecclesiastical, or "prophetic," resistance to that government. And, after some serious friction in the seventeenth and early eighteenth centuries, most Dutch churches had become quite well adjusted, and royal charters were being found to be satisfactory guardians of the privileges enshrined in the old treaty.

To people living in this spiritual mood, an orthodox Calvinism, and even, in principle, a "revivalist religion," offered excellent theological reasons for supporting the status quo. The rights of the church were not being infringed; the magistrate was doing his duty, and the Christian person should do his. Such understanding of Romans 13, I Peter 2:13-17, and similar texts can be held quite apart from the Belgic Confession, as the teaching of John Wesley and many another shows, but the Confession points toward a definite line of interpretation. To recognize that such theology suited the interests of wealthy Dutch families on Manhattan, or the well established proprietors of the Hackensack Valley, or of Long Island, or of Kinderhook, is to beg the whole problem. In theological terms, the causes of Dutch participation in the revolt, not of Toryism, call for explanation. A supporter of the government may not be-

come anyone's hero, but his stance, in itself, is hardly a violation of the Christian conscience as cultivated in Reformed
churches and families.

Contrary to the situation of the Dutch churches, Congregationalists and Presbyterians, although British and so of the
dominent ethnic group, had formed their ecclesiastical tradition, not under the reluctant but largely benevolent protection
of the British Crown, but in direct opposition to it. Puritan and
Scotch experience which they remembered made resistance to
their sovereign not contrary, or at most peripheral, to their
spiritual existence, but integral to it. The Presbyterians had
been overturning the religious establishment in New York, to
which the older Dutch tradition had become allied, and in order
to disestablish Anglicanism they had to attack existing political
institutions, and did not shrink from so doing. The Revolutionary party in New York was often called "Presbyterian," and
Tories saw Scotch-born Domine Laidlie as one of it. Many of
the more "Anglicized" or "Americanized" Dutch had become
Presbyterians, and others were influenced by them; the ardent
Revolutionist, Domine Dirck Romeyn, for example, had studied
at Princeton. Anglican doctrine and practice influenced some
Dutch people, many of whom joined that church, but Presbyterianism, the natural theological ally of the Dutch, influenced
others, and often supplied the revolutionary push that carried
the day. Presbyterians, including some ministers—Jacob Green
and John Witherspoon—took the lead in writing up Revolutionary theory for the Middle Colonies. This was not the Dutch
contribution.

Tories were, it must be remembered, a minority in the Dutch
church, but a minority important not only for numbers but
because of their legitimate theological stance within orthodox
Calvinism. The British government, for them, was not merely
benevolent; it was the government God had established.

That these convictions were generally respected is suggested
by the fact that, in spite of an often-quoted resolution of 1780
declaring the war to be "just and necessary," General Synod
(legally, the "General Body") was, in most of its war-time
pronouncements, quite apolitical, more so, from 1775, than the
Presbyterian synod. It spoke in general terms of the evils of the
day, the breakdown of morality, the need for prayer and for
divine guidance. It debated a few specific questions, such as the
baptism of illegitimate children.

It is possible, in short, that "theological Toryism" was more common among the Dutch than in any other non-Anglican community. Among the considerable German element in our church, in New York State, Lutheran influence had been strong, with long periods of close Reformed-Lutheran interaction. One wonders whether German Lutheran state church teaching had had an effect. Leiby found no evidence of such "Erastianism"[24] among the Lutheran Tories he studied, and it must be remembered that Lutherans furnished a fair share of Revolutionary leadership, and our German constituency did also. But one would like to know what lies behind Governor Tryon's description of Domine Ritzema as a "Dutch Lutheran," or the reference of another well-informed observer to Domine Rubel's Lutheran principles, in specific contrast to the "Calvinism" of his Whig colleague.

But whatever outside influences were at work, the Dutch Tory minority had substantial theological grounding for its stand. As the war progressed, and eventually led to a Revolutionary victory, it became apparent that another government was to be established, which could also be accepted as ordained by God. A shift in allegiance, whatever it might do to people's opinion of one as a citizen, was no vitiation of the Christian conscience. "Secret Tories" and "lukewarm patriots" in insurgent territory more freely took part in public affairs. In 1782, the year after Yorktown, known Tories were elected to the New Jersey Legislature—from Bergen County.[25] At the same time, many who had been living under British protection in New York found means, not without protest, to return. New Brunswick is mentioned as one of the cities that welcomed such.[26] Finally, with the evacuation of New York, the new nation was confronted squarely with the problem of those who had not helped establish it, but who wished to live in it. Many Tories, as is well-known, emigrated for various reasons. But with the ending of hostilities began a quiet process of amnesty which has been inadequately studied, but which was of major significance in the life of both the state and the church. In 1784, came the first of a series of New York amnesty acts, permitting specified Tory individuals named therein to return. Peter Van Schaak of Kinderhook was one.[27] Other acts of this sort followed, and in 1786, only three years after the peace, an important general law restored the rights of voting and office holding to those who had held office under the crown, born arms for the King, or left the state to avoid its service. This act affected many in New York, Richmond, Kings, Queens, and Westchester Counties—areas where there were many Dutch.[28] Finally, in 1788, other anti-Tory laws, considered contrary to the treaty of peace, were repealed. In New Jersey, meantime, a similar lifting of anti-Tory legislation was taking place.[29] By the time the Federal Constitution became law, amnesty, in these two states, was an accomplished fact—the past had been legally "forgotten".

The effects of this action on civil life are not our concern here. It has been said that ex-Tories were some of our best citizens, and certainly men like Philip Schuyler and Alexander Hamilton, who sponsored amnesty legislation, wanted some of them as citizens. But the effect of this amnesty on the church, and certainly on the Reformed Church, was also profound. Separated families could be reunited. Congregations could be re-established, and the good faith of brethren who had differed could be respected. The dead hand of a past dispute no longer lay over the church. Except for the Episcopalians, no religious body gained more than the Dutch Reformed. It is difficult to see how our divided church could have survived on any other basis, but in fact, separated brethren were now brought together, and, with the passage of time, developed unity in meeting new challenges, such as the missionary movement.

This new unity was not universal, and it is probable that wounds too deep to heal eventually contributed to the schism of the True Dutch Reformed Church in New Jersey. Livingston and other Reformed people contributed to the slow but salutory growth of a movement which, through Christian obedience, bound our church together and united it to other Christians. It was a great achievement, and anything that restored unity after the Revolution was a contribution toward it.

But one other fact needs to be noted. The new unity of the Reformed Church was gained not only by "forgetting" the past, but by denying part of its reality. The sons of the Tories were given no opportunity to be proud of their ancestors, and the Church, long after the amnesties, was unwilling to accept the facts. The same people who were unified in evangelical service were unified in a civil religion that denied one element in the Church's tradition. Instead of welcoming the full contribution of those who received amnesty, the Church pretended that amnesty had never been needed. A cult of the Revolution became part of the faith.

At one Fourth of July service, early in the nineteenth century, the benediction, pronounced by a Reformed Church pastor of European birth, a former Roman Catholic priest, was "The God of Abraham, the God of Isaac, and the God of Washington bless you all".[30]

With the passage of time, history was remembered from the viewpoint of the winners, and the disciples of Abraham Messler[31] gave us their picture of a pietistic-revivalistic coetus leadership as the typical Dutch Reformed churchmen, and at the same time extrapolated from Motley's *Dutch Republic* the progressive, tyranny-resisting Dutchman, steadfastly suffering for righteousness, as their American ancestor. The real sufferings of our past were thus forgotten.

The American Frontier

James W. Van Hoeven

The Lord in the Course of his Providence is opening a large Field in the Western Territory for the Extension of his Church and the Spread of his Gospel. . . . The Period is not far distant when the Fullness of the Gentiles shall come to the Knowledge of divine Truths as they are revealed to us . . . to insure to Thousands and Millions all temporal, Spiritual, and heavenly Blessings.[1]

So reported the Reverent Peter Stryker in 1800 to the General Synod of the Reformed Dutch Church. Stryker's report summarized the results of his nine weeks missionary tour of "Gentile" and Dutch outposts on New York's northern and western frontier. Enveloped in millenial expectations, the report intended to urge the Church to supply funds and clergy to "new settlers . . . who open an unbounded Prospect for usefulness in the Gospel ministry" and expansion for the denomination.[2]

By 1800 streams of "new settlers" were pouring into America's expansive western frontier. Most of these were poor, uneducated, and unchurched laborers from the East, who were attracted to the West by the hope of economic success or the chance for adventure. But the better class also migrated to the frontier. Fewer in number, but no less acquisitive, a large percentage of these pioneers were educated Calvinists—Presbyterian, Congregational, and a few Dutch Reformed—who left modest farms in the East in search of bigger fields and greater wealth in the West.

Many pioneers from these two classes settled in western New York and New Jersey, or eastern Pennsylvania. Others braved the difficult mountain passages over the Alleghenies and sought out land in the old Northwest. And when President Jefferson negotiated the Louisiana Purchase in 1803, new waves of settlers extended the continental frontier as far west as the Mississippi River.

In the three decades between 1792 and 1822 nine new states were added to the Union as a result of this westward migration: Kentucky in 1792, Tennessee in 1796, Ohio in 1803, Louisiana in 1812, Indiana in 1816, Mississippi in 1817, Illinois in 1818, Alabama in 1819, and Missouri in 1821. By 1830 more than a third of the nation's population lived west of the Allegheny Mountains.

The Reformed Church, in common with other eastern-based churches, was well aware of the challenge of the developing frontier. In the early 1800's, however, the denomination was ill-prepared to meet this challenge effectively. Crippled by the Revolutionary War, sparsely scattered in an alien culture, disrupted by long-standing disputes and controversy, and only recently organized as an independent, self-governing body, the Church was primarily concerned with the "reconquest of the East," rather than the "conquest of the West." In addition, the Reformed Church was egregiously Dutch and Dutch-speaking, committed to an educated ministry, and determined that worship be done "decently and in order," characteristics which did not easily lend themselves to a successful program of church expansion among predominantly English-speaking, uneducated, and ebullient frontier settlements. Consequently, during the first great era of westward migration in America, roughly 1790 to the mid-1830's, the frontier mission enterprise of the Reformed Church was generally ineffectual.

During this period, however, the Reformed Church managed to establish some "preaching stations" in several widely scattered areas. One of these was started in 1790 at the headwaters of the Potomac River, in Hardy County, Virginia. Informed that this region "held a large [English speaking] population entirely destitute of ecclesiastical privileges and the ministry of the Gospel,"[3] the denomination ordained and commissioned Jacob Jinnings, a physician from the Dutch Church at Raritan, New Jsery, to begin work there. Jinnings left for Virginia in the summer of 1790, but in April, 1791, he recommended that the denomination quit its work in Hardy County for the following reasons: first, most of the people were Arminians and "do not relish the Calvinistic Doctrines, which are repugnant to them"; second, the distance separating Virginia from the center of the Reformed Church in New York and New Jersey "renders [the program] impracticable"; third, mission work on the frontier seemed to be more successful under denominations with an "English Constitution" and an English-speaking heritage; and finally, his support from the Dutch Church was "very incompetent . . . so that I have been much shortened in my worldly circumstances."⁴ Because of these factors, Jinnings requested a letter of dismissal to the Presbyterian Church so that he could carry out a ministry "to a pious people . . . on the west side of the Aligany [sic] Mountains." The Reformed Church complied with Jinnings' request and, consequently, abandoned its work in Virginia in the spring of 1791, only eight months after the mission began.

The denomination began a second work in 1796 among Dutch settlers on the upper Salt River, near the present town of Harrodsburg in Mercer County, Kentucky. These pioneers had been part of a large Calvinist settlement in Conewago, Pennsylvania, but beginning in 1781 had migrated to Kentucky in search of better land. Once settled they remained strongly attached to the heritage of their forebears. Not only did they continue to converse in the Dutch language, but in 1795 they petitioned the Reformed Church for a minister who could preach in both Dutch and English. One year later, in 1796, the Classis of Hackensack, New Jersey, commissioned the Reverend Peter Labagh to the Salt River settlement, granting him thirty pounds for travel. Labagh quickly organized a congregation there, "consisting of about one hundred families,"⁶ but he left the field in 1797, noting that "on account of the distance of the congregation from the body of the Dutch Church, their unsettled state, and the improbability of extending the church to that quarter,"⁷ the work was impracticable for the denomination. Several years later, in 1804, the Reverend Thomas Kyle became pastor of the church and remained until 1816. When he left, the Salt River Church struggled on its own until 1817, when it merged with a Presbyterian congregation in the area.⁸

The Reformed Church began another frontier mission program in 1798, this time in Upper Canada (Ontario). In that year the Classis of Albany commissioned the Reverend Robert McDowell to English, German, and Dutch speaking settlements in the Bay of Quinte area. Informed that these settlers were "very desirous of having the Gospel preached to them," the denomination gave McDowell full authority to organize "new societies" for the Reformed Church among them.⁹ By 1799 McDowell had established six churches in the Ontario region totalling more than four hundred families, and had become the pastor of three of these churches—"Ernest Town, Fredericksburgh and Adolphus-town, on the northwest side of Lake Ontario."¹⁰ Subsequently, he organized eight additional churches, one at

Toronto, and another among German speaking settlers to the north of that city. This "parish" of fourteen churches encompassed an area of nearly three hundred miles. The indefatigable McDowell served all of these congregations alone until 1806, when he challenged the Church to send him aid, and advised that "if no assistance can be obtained from the Reformed Church . . . [he would] make application to the Presbyterian Church" for support.[11]

The Reformed Church was unable to provide McDowell with the help he requested, although for the next decade the denomination continued to show an interest in the work by occasionally sending itinerant missionaries to Canada on preaching tours. No Reformed Church clergyman was willing to set up permanent residence in that region, however. Moreover, the denomination was consistently without funds to support candidates interested in this work. Consequently, in 1819 McDowell joined the Presbyterian Church, taking with him to that sister denomination the eleven remaining congregations he had established.[12] Several of these churches still remain within the Presbyterian Church of Canada, and in June, 1975, that body honored McDowell's work by presenting an official plaque of the Province of Ontario Archives to the descendent congregations.

The final frontier mission program started by the Reformed Church during this period of westward migration was to predominantly Dutch settlements in New York, New Jersey, and Pennsylvania. This work became especially urgent in the 1780's, when a significant number of Dutch Reformed families, including some veterans returning from the Revolutionary War, began migrating westward within those states in search of economic betterment. In 1786 the denomination appointed its first committee on church extension to develop plans for reaching these settlers with the Gospel, so that they "may not remain scattered like sheep which have no shepherd."[13]

Situated in Albany, the committee's task was three-fold: to encourage each classis to search out and establish new congregations among Dutch settlements in their region; to find pastors to serve these new churches; and to solicit funds to support these programs of church expansion. It proved to be a painfully slow and disappointing business, and the committee's appeals for funds and clergy were consistently unheeded or undersubscribed. Despite these set-backs, however, nearly thirty frontier

congregations were established in the three eastern states between 1792 and 1821, although none of these churches was
supplied with a resident pastor. A half-century later, in 1871, all
but five of these frontier congregations had either been abandoned, or else had merged with Presbyterian churches in their
area.[14]

Few leaders in the Reformed Church were satisfied with the
denomination's frontier mission program during the early
1800's. And, indeed, there was little cause for satisfaction. Of
the four frontier programs initiated by the Church between
1790 and 1820—Virginia, Kentucky, Canada, and the three
eastern states—only the latter survived, and that program was
hard-pressed for support. Mission committee reports for those
years reflected this disappointment, and consistently mixed
jeremiads with appeals for funds and "a sufficient number of
zealous, devoted, and active missionaries."[15] Nearly all of these
reports concluded that "the missionary operations of this
Synod have not been attended with the successes which might
have been expected."[16]

Beginning in 1819, the denomination moved the location of
its mission operation from the northern Albany Synod to the
southern-based New York (City) Synod. Much more than a shift
in geography resulted from this decision. Situated at the center
of traffic between the modified Calvinism of the Presbyterian
and Congregational Churches to the east, and the democratizing
influence of the expanding frontier to the west, the Albany
Dutch had become less purist than their kinsmen in the south.
As a result, the northern and southern sections of the church
had occasionally disagreed on matters of theology, ecumenicity,
mission policy, and the propriety of accepting ministerial candidates from non-Reformed Church seminaries.

Consequently, when the denomination shifted its mission
operation from Albany to New York City in 1819, it portended
that the Reformed Church would develop a substantially new
mission strategy, one generally more provincial and conservative
that that which preceded it. It also portended that the northern
and southern sections of the Church would clash over mission
policy and denominational goals. That eruption came in 1830.

An indication of this new strategy came in 1822, when the
mission committee concluded that the previous policy of sending itinerant missionaries to widely scattered frontier areas "can
be productive of little . . . good." To replace that policy, the

committee recommended that the Church create *"permanent establishments . . .* under our care; . . . by *planting* the gospel down in *one spot,* where a prospect presents itself of collecting together *one church."*[17] Given the shape of the denomination at that time, *"its want of missionaries, and want of funds,"*[18] the proposal was perhaps necessary. But its consequences were far reaching. In effect, the committee conceded the burgeoning frontier to other denominations, and proposed that the Reformed Church concentrate on rebuilding itself. In short, the committee recommended renewal "among our own," rather than evangelism "among the destitute masses."

This new policy began to be implemented the same year, 1822, when the Reformed Church reorganized its mission program and established the Board of Managers of the newly formed "Missionary Society of the Protestant Dutch Church" as its "Standing Committee on Missions." Headquartered in southern-based New York City, this society consisted of a number of well-endowed Reformed Church notables who desired to increase the missionary spirit of the denomination. The society directed the denomination's mission program for nearly a decade, with impressive accomplishments. It supplied a number of "feeble churches" with funds and graduates from New Brunswick Seminary. It also published a monthly journal, *The Magazine of the Reformed Dutch Church,* to inform the Church of the society's mission enterprise. And it formed "auxiliary missionary societies" in nearly every congregation, a program which greatly increased the benevolent giving of the denomination. In the first four months of its efforts, nearly two thousand dollars was contributed to the missionary cause, and the amount increased to more than three thousand five hundred dollars annually by 1828, a substantial increase over previous missionary contributions in the Church. From 1822 to 1832, the society collected more than thirty thousand dollars and aided about one hundred churches and one hundred thirty missionaries.[19]

Despite these impressive accomplishments, however, by the mid-1820's the Albany Synod became overtly critical of the society's mission policy, and in 1830 the General Synod voted to terminate its formal relationship with the society's Board of Managers. Several factors caused this situation. First, the cultural and geographical differences between the northern Synod and the southern-based Missionary Society inevitably brought about distinctive points of view and, therefore, disagreement, on important issues. In the years following 1822, for example, the Albany Synod had urged the society to unite with the newly-formed and ecumenical American Home Missionary Society, believing it to be a more effective way to meet its own needs in the northern frontier. The denomination's Missionary Society, however, was situated in a more settled and provincial region in southern New York and, as a result, was unfamiliar with the exigencies in the north. Moreover, the society had been organized to guarantee a strictly Dutch and Reformed missionary program, and had determined "that [we] will send out none but men honestly attached to the doctrines of the cross." [20] Consequently, the southern-based board had resisted the overtures from the Albany Synod, convinced that the American Missionary Society had been influenced by the "liberal" theology of New England Congregationalism. Accordingly, the board had retorted: "We are strongly opposed to Hopkinsianism. We can never amalgamate with them. We can never go as a church into this Eastern Theology and Eastern policy. We are no half-way men!"[21]

There was, however, a much more practical reason for the Albany Synod's criticism of the society's missionary policy. It complained that it was being neglected by the society. The church in the north needed both ministers and money to support its own "feeble churches" and to expand into new frontier settlements. But, so it claimed, the society did not meet these needs. It was a legitimate criticism, because much of the board's resources were directed toward programs of church renewal in the south. Consequently, in June, 1827, the Albany Synod recommended that the Church establish a "northern agency,

which may tend more effectually to occupy the Missionary ground and excite a common interest throughout the congregations belonging to [the Albany Synod] in the cause of Missions.[22]

The General Synod acted favorably on this recommendation in June, 1828. In the same year the society established a "northern agency" and appointed the Reverend John F. Schermerhorn as its full-time missionary agent.[23] It was an important appointment, the first such position in the history of the Reformed Church. Two years later, however, in 1830, the society summarily fired Schermerhorn and abandoned the "northern agency."[24] That provocative decision catalyzed the northern and southern sections of the Church into serious conflict. It also brought about the society's demise within the Reformed Church.

The rationale for the board's action in 1830 is difficult to determine. Its published reason for dismissing Schermerhorn was "because far less money than [his] salary was returned into the treasury."[25] This appears strange, however, particularly because during the period Schermerhorn worked for the board he annually raised far more money for benevolent causes than in any previous year. Schermerhorn gave two other reasons for his dismissal. The more important of these concerned his theology. He claimed that he was "rudely assailed" by members of the board "on the score of the want of orthodoxy."[26] The "conservative" controlled mission board apparently identified Schermerhorn with its adversary, the northern "liberal" wing of the Church in the "Civil War"[27] of 1830. Schermerhorn, of course, defended his orthodoxy, and called the attacks by the board "Indian warfare . . . assaults in the dark . . . by the straitest sect in our church," which were unfounded and untrue.[28]

The second reason Schermerhorn gave for his dismissal concerned the board's mission policy. It was well known in the Church that Schermerhorn wanted to extend its borders into the burgeoning frontier regions of the United States. He proposed this in sermons before congregations and in the form of resolutions before classes and synods, urging the church "to occupy the important central stations of our country." [29] Schermerhorn claimed, however, that the board consistently rejected this policy. In a published statement following his discharge, he asserted that the board was "alarmed at the [idea] of the extension of our church, to which they were opposed, and are still opposed, and if possible are determined to prevent."[30]

Following Schermerhorn's dismissal in 1830, the battle lines between the northern, Albany Synod and the southern-based Missionary Society became tightly drawn. Both pulpit and press in the Reformed Church referred to it as the conflict between the "extreme liberals"[31] in the north and the "high ultras" [32] in the south; or, "the friends of innovation"[33] in the north and "the little aristocracy"[34] in the south. And, in effect, this deep controversy between the north and south in the Church focused on Schermerhorn.

The north declared him "the St. Paul of America,"[35] an "active, laborious, indefatigable . . . fast friend of the church,"[36] indispensable for the future of the denomination. The south, on the other hand, spoke of him opprobriously as the "Pope's legate" and indeed, even "his supreme holiness himself,"[37] and thus a man whose influence must be stilled. When the smoke of this conflict began to clear in 1831, the Reformed Church terminated its relationship with the mission society and established a new mission board under the General Synod. And this new board employed Schermerhorn as its first missionary agent.[38]

This new board, later renamed "The Board of Domestic Missions," directed the mission program of the Reformed Church from 1831 to 1850. This was an important era in American history, one characterized by expansionism and nationalism as the young nation set about putting its house in order "to show the world . . . of what man is capable if given freedom."[39] Stirred on by the refrains of the "National Anthem," the *laissez faire* policies of Jacksonian democracy, and an improved transportation system, new waves of pioneers, joined by a large influx of European immigrants, crossed the Misssissippi River and moved into the Western Territory during this period. These acquisitive settlers conquered every "hazard" in their path—Indian, Mexican, forest, and mountain—and soon carved out new states as they pushed the continental frontier to the Pacific Ocean.

Americans were optimistic during this period and believed it was possible to create the perfect state within this continent. And this optimism was not unfounded, because down to the 1850's all of the nation's problems except one—slavery—seemed easy of solution. Several groups established utopian communities, the forerunner of the contemporary communes, to serve as models of what society can be. In addition, numerous humanitarian societies were organized—temperance, penal reform, education, women's rights,—to ameliorate social problems caused in part by the rise of the city. The church, too, joined in the excitement of this perfectionist milieu, determined to confirm and maintain the rightness of America's "destiny under God" in the eyes of the world. Charles Finney, the great evangelist of the era, organized revivals among the middle class throughout the East coast. And, during the same period, Baptist and Methodist missionaries, and to a lesser extent Congregational and Presbyterian clergy, excited religious passions in the West. In addition, Joseph Smith discovered the missing Golden Plates buried in New York's "burned over district," from which he wrote his "Book of Mormon." And William Miller took his Adventist followers to a mountain top in the same state to await the Second Coming of Christ which, so the books of Daniel, Ezekiel, and Revelation told him, would take place on October 22, 1844.

The mood and character of America during this period naturally influenced the life and mission of the Reformed Church. The emerging nationalism of the young republic, for example, was matched by a self-conscious parochialism within the denomination. Significantly, this was common among all of the more churchly Protestant traditions—Lutheran, Presbyterian, and Reformed—during the second quarter of the nineteenth century. The ecclesiastical counterpart of a strong national union became the well-organized and self- conscious denomination, proud of its unique heritage, which it was determined to maintain, and having little interest in ecumenical associations. Following years of crisis and insecurity, such parochialism was very important to the Reformed Church, enabling it to recover its unity and its identity. As a result, an "era of good feelings" pervaded the church "such as was never before exceeded, perhaps never before enjoyed by us."[40]

Interestingly, moreover, the Reformed Church became *American* during this period, and began to identify part of its mission with what it determined were the nation's goals and ideals. The Domestic Missions Board, for example, urged the denomination to "plant new churches as extensively as can be done," not only "for the sake of Zion," but also because "there is a claim upon our Christian patriotism to enter this wide field."[41] This "wide field" held two fronts during the second quarter of the nineteenth century. On the one hand it comprised the unchurched and uncivilized masses on the frontier, whose rumored excesses threatened "our civil institutions and religious rights."[42] The other front was an "insidious but powerful . . . Romanism" and the "malign influence" of other non-Calvinist sects, which were attempting to control "the mind . . . of our Republic."[43] The summons to "Christian patriotism," therefore, was no small responsibility for evangelical protestants

who knew "the truth as it is in Jesus."[44] The salvation of the
nation's "social and political institutions"[45] and, indeed, the
"destiny of the whole human race"[46] were at stake in both the
Christianizing and civilizing influence of the denomination's
mission enterprise.

Finally, the excitement that characterized American religion
during this period also reached into the Reformed Church,
causing an occasional "quickening of the Lord's people."[47] In
1843, for example, nearly three thousand "souls" were added
to the church by confession of faith, a number double "that
reached in any one year during the whole previous history" of
the denomination.[48] Between 1830 and 1849 the Reformed
Church organized nearly one hundred twenty five new
churches. Most of these congregations were established among
Dutch and Dutch-speaking settlements in the East, although the
denomination also formed several congregations among Ger-
man-speaking immigrants. Significantly, moreover, the Church
followed a number of Dutch pioneers across the Allegheny
Mountains and organized new churches among them: Fairview,
Illinois in 1837, several preaching stations in Indiana beginning
in 1844, and by 1849 ten congregations among Dutch frontiersmen in Wisconsin and seven in Michigan. This work became so
promising that in 1843 the denomination expanded its missionary operation and established a "western department" to complement its program in the East. By 1849 these western
churches had organized themselves into two Classes, Illinois and
Michigan.

Consequently, at the mid-point of the nineteenth century,
the Reformed Church was a united and self-conscious denomination, firmly rooted in its Dutch Calvinist heritage and proudly
American. Although small in comparison with other eastern-
based churches, the denomination grew from one hundred thirty-nine congregations and fifty nine ministers in 1800, to two
hundred eighty-two parishes and two hundred ninety-nine
clergy in 1849. During this period, moreover, the church moved
west of the Allegheny Mountains, establishing several congregations among Dutch settlers in frontier regions. And finally, in
1849 the Reformed Church again reorganized its missionary
operation, and for the first time in its history appointed a
Corresponding Secretary to direct the total mission program of
the denomination. As the Reformed Church looked to the
second half of the nineteenth century, therefore, it seemed in

good shape to "take her full part in the world's regeneration."[49]

Beginning in 1850, the shape of the Reformed Church was dramatically changed by the "Second Dutch immigration." The events surrounding this migration are examined in another place in this volume.[50] It is sufficient here to note that near the end of the 1840's, three Dutch immigrant groups left the Netherlands for America and established what became Holland and Zeeland, Michigan and Pella, Iowa. These migrants were pious Calvinists, estranged from the Netherland's Reformed Church, who left their home-land primarily for religious reasons. They were the first wave of thousands of orthodox Dutch who migrated to America during the last half of the nineteenth century.

These "Protestant Hollanders" offered the Reformed Church an unprecedented opportunity for expansion across the Allegheny Mountains. In 1848, the Board of Domestic Missions reported that "other denominations are using active measures to bring [the Dutch] under their influence, while we, who are of the same origin, springing from the same branch of the Reformation . . . are doing nothing but exposing them to be swallowed up by men of every name and every creed."[51] Consequently, the board recommended that the denomination "give especial attention" to the needs of these immigrants, "with a view to bringing them into connection with our own church."[52] Two years later, in 1850, the Holland and Zeeland, Michigan churches united with the northern, Albany Synod of the Reformed Church, and in 1856 the Dutch congregation in Pella, Iowa, did the same. Subsequently, as new Dutch Calvinist immigrants came to America, and as the descendents of the three original colonies moved westward, the Reformed Church established congregations among them. By 1875 the denomination had organized seventy-nine new churches among this "second Dutch immigration," totaling nearly ten thousand members.[53]

This was expensive business for the Reformed Church, however, because most of these immigrant congregations were poor and required financial assistance. Consequently, the Board of Domestic Missions created a program whereby an eastern-based benefactor could directly assist a struggling immigrant church. This program proved to be unusually successful, matching up numerous individuals and organizations in the East with destitute migrant congregations in the Mid-West. A few representative notices from the Domestic Missions Reports for the years 1857 to 1879 illustrate the point:

Otley, Iowa . . . is the precious seed which two Sabbath schools, Flatbush, L. I. and North Newark, N. J. united in planting.[54]

Norris, Illinois, was reared and the Pastor is supported by the Christian liberality of a lady of Philadelphia.[55]

South Pass, Nebraska, with the generous aid furnished them by two ladies of New York . . . is on the point of completing a church edifice and parsonage.[56]

By such means, these and many other midwestern immigrant congregations were able to survive their earliest financial crises.

Between 1850 and 1900 the primary source of Reformed Church expansion was among these midwestern Dutch immigrants. But the Church also expanded in other areas and among other groups during this period. For example, in 1850 the denomination began a mission among German/Dutch-speaking Calvinists from East Friesland, Germany, who had settled in northwestern Illinois. One year later, in 1851, the denomination organized a church among these German immigrants, the first of a number of East Frisian congregations in the Mid-West.[57] In addition, the denomination organized more than one hundred new churches in the East, primarily among "American" Dutch.

Throughout this period, moreover, the Board of Domestic Missions consistently challenged the Reformed Church to establish congregations among non-Dutch frontiersmen in the "opening sections" of the continent. "There are now 10,000,000's of people in the North West," the Board reminded the Church in 1860, "and millions of them accessible to us."[58] Again, in 1871, the Board urged the Church "to plant, to build, to break the fallow ground," among these English-speaking settlers, adding, "it can never be done so long as our *Home-work* is made a secondary thing."[59] And this report left no question concerning the "appalling responsibility" involved in this "home-work"; the Reformed Church was called to mission in order to "enlarge the borders of Zion," and to keep America's destiny in the world on target.

And we ask, is it assumption to claim, that American ideas are this day influencing human society to its very extremities? Where is the nation that is not at this moment working up towards our standard; . . . And we report it to the General Synod, as the teaching of all history, as the lesson imparted by the failure of other nations ... that the maintenance of our free institutions, depends under God, upon the thorough *religious*, as well as intellectual education of our people.[60]

Throughout the last half of the nineteenth century, however, the Reformed Church did not expand among these indigenous "millions accessible to us," choosing instead to remain decidedly Dutch. This policy was determined primarily by a scarcity of economic and human resources—the Reformed Church was constantly in need of money and clergy for its Domestic Missions program—although ethnocentricism also seemed an important factor. Acting on a mission policy established in the early nineteenth century—"to keep on main lines of railroad already constructed," or "to plant stations within supporting distance of each other"[61] —the denomination followed Dutch Calvinists wherever they happened to build tracks and organized new congregations among them. This point was accurately stated in 1882 by the Reverend Abraham Thompson, in an address commemorating the fiftieth anniversary of the Board of Domestic Missions:

Not wholly, nor *chiefly*, perhaps is our Church designed to care for the Hollanders, but yet *largely* and *specially*. Providence has made it our special work.

We cannot separate ourselves from our history. Of our 500 churches now existing, it will be safe to say that [nearly all] of them ... have sprung almost directly from those originally speaking the Holland language. The instances are rare—exceedingly rare—where churches have been organized without a nucleus of those who had been trained in these churches. ...

The Church *has* not grown outside the limits of Holland immigration. That it *cannot*, I will not venture to affirm or even to suggest. But I do say that all its past history shows that where the Hollanders settled, *there* has been growth and strength.[62]

Not until well into the twentieth century, did the Reformed Church demonstrate that it could do what Thompson would "not venture to affirm or even to suggest"; namely, establish churches among non-Dutch speaking Calvinists. Until that time, the Church acted on Thompson's principle that "where the Hollanders settled, *there* has been growth and strength." As a result, in the East the Reformed Church established congrega-

tions among Dutch pioneers who moved to settlements generally contiguous with their kinsmen. In the West, the denomination organized churches in and around the three principal Dutch
immigrant "stations" in Michigan and Iowa, and then followed
their descendants into Illinois, Minnesota, Nebraska, Kansas,
South Dakota, Colorado, Montana, and, in the early twentieth
century, as far West as Washington and California. By 1900
nearly four-fifths of the denomination's churches were Dutch
congregations, many of these Dutch-speaking. Consequently,
at the end of the nineteenth century, the Reformed Church
naturally gained the reputation as a Dutch Church—"a little
garden walled around, chosen and made peculiar ground"[63] —
a factor which seriously affected its mission among the millions of English-speaking Americans "accessible to us."

Near the turn of the twentieth century the Reformed Church
left its "garden" long enough to work among several minority
groups scattered throughout the nation. The Board of Domestic
Missions considered this as benevolent work, rather than church
expansion; church growth would continue within the Dutch
"garden." Such benevolent programs were common in America
during the first part of the twentieth century. It was an "Age of
Crusades," when

there was a superabundance of zeal, a sufficiency of good causes, unusual
moral idealism. . . . The [American] people were ready to cry 'God wills
it' and set out for world peace, prohibition, the Progressive Party, the
'New Freedom' or 'the World for Christ in this Generation.' The air was
full of banners and the trumpets called from every camp.

The churches shared the general crusading zeal and inaugurated enterprises of their own.[64]

There were, of course, reasons for this crusading spirit within
America during this period. The confluence of the Industrial
Revolution and the rise of the city during the last quarter of the
nineteenth century had created unimagined social problems. In
addition, the growing disparity between the few who were rich
and the masses who were poor seemed to call for some modification of the capitalistic system. And the forgotten minorities
within the nation—the Native American, the Appalachian hill
people, the "colored," and the "hordes of aliens"—needed benevolent care. These were all serious problems which required

some response from concerned Americans. Equally important, however, these problems tarnished the nation's image in the world, a factor of great significance to crusading Americans at the turn of the twentieth century. Appropriately, therefore, the Board of Domestic Missions challenged the denomination to work in new fields because

We cannot but believe that God means us to be a light to the entire world. As goes the United States, so goes the world. This seems to be the destiny that God had marked out for us as a nation. . . . Our plea is not 'save America for America's sake,' but 'save America for the world's sake.'[65]

The Reformed Church responded to this passionate patriotic challenge beginning in 1895, when it launched mission programs among several Native American settlements. In that year, the newly formed Women's Executive Committee of the Board of Domestic Missions (later renamed the Women's Board of Domestic Missions) commissioned the Reverend Frank Hall Wright, a Choctaw Indian, to work near two reservations in what is now southwestern Oklahoma. Wright began his work immediately, and organized churches among Cheyenne Indians near Colony, Oklahoma, among Comanches near Lawton, Oklahoma, and among Apaches imprisoned at Fort Sill, Oklahoma. This latter congregation included Geronimo, the famed leader of the Apache terrorists who had plagued settlements throughout the South-West until 1886, when he and his men were captured by the United States Army. Geronimo "found the Jesus road" in 1907, and Wright baptized him the same year. Subsequently, in 1914, the Reformed Church organized congregations among Apaches at Mescalero, in south central New Mexico, and in the same year among members of the same tribe settled near Dulce, in northern New Mexico. In addition, the Women's Board of Domestic Missions funded two other Indian programs in Nebraska, one at Winnebago, beginning in 1907, and a second among the Omaha's at Macy, in 1934. With the exception of the work at Fort Sill and Colony, Oklahoma, which were abandoned in 1911 and 1932 respectively, each of these Indian congregations still remains within the Reformed Church.[66]

The Women's Board began a second benevolent program among a minority group in 1899, this time among "the moun-

tain people" in Jackson County, Kentucky. In that year the
Board sent three young women, Cora A. Smith, Nora L. Gaut,
and Mary G. Baker to teach among the children of the Appalachian poor in that region. Subsequently, the Reformed Church
purchased a large section of land in the area and opened a
boarding school, named Annville Institute, providing opportunity for vocational and academic training for the "hill country" youth. Local women's organizations throughout the denomination contributed scholarships for this program, enabling
the young people to attend the school. In addition, beginning in
1905, the denomination commissioned ordained missionaries to
Jackson County, who established churches within several isolated communities in that mountain region. In 1942 the denomination reorganized its Kentucky mission program under one
director, and both the Institute and the congregations still
remain within the Reformed Church.[67]

The Reformed Church started another benevolent work
among an American minority group in 1919. In that year the
General Synod agreed to purchase and maintain the Southern
Normal and Industrial School—"a colored institution"—situated
on nearly two hundred fifty acres in Brewton, Alabama. This
institution had been founded some years before by Mr. James
Dooley, a negro educator from the area, and since 1917 it
had been partially supported by a number of Reformed
Churches in the Chicago Synod.[68] In addition, several Dutch
farmers from Iowa had stocked the Brewton farm with cattle,
"far superior to that owned elsewhere in the county . . . white
or colored."[69] When the denomination assumed responsibility
for this program in 1919 there were two teachers and about
thirty students, and the lone classroom building was a converted
"Odd Fellows Hall."[70]

The Reformed Church supported this program with inordi-
nate enthusiasm, and before long there were sufficient funds to
launch an extensive building program on the Brewton grounds:
dormitories for boarding students, a dining hall, recreational
facilities, a new classroom building, a barn, and a chapel. In
addition, as the enrollment increased, the Church engaged more
and better teachers. Beyond that, numerous churches throughout the denomination provided clothing, bedding, books, toys,
and school materials for black families in the Brewton community "who come to us for this kind of help."[71] By 1945
"8,000 black boys and girls" had been given a "concrete experi-

ence in Christian living" at the Brewton institute.[72] Equally important, whereas in 1919 "2 negroes in 10 in the community" could read and write, by 1945 "a totally illiterate negro [was] a curiosity."[73] Moreover, in the same year the school's director could report that

Our mission, more so than any other agency . . . has helped to cement the relations of the two races who must live together under all the barriers to Christian brotherhood which are so characteristic of the South.[74]

This benevolent program still remains within the Reformed Church.

Beyond these several programs, the denomination also worked a number of other fields outside its own "garden" during the first half of the twentieth century. These included mission enterprises among white "cowboys and ranchmen" in southwestern Oklahoma, beginning in 1900,[75] and among Japanese, Italian, and Hungarian immigrants in and around New York City, beginning in 1908.[76] Neither of these programs was permanently successful, however; the denomination abandoned the Oklahoma field to the Presbyterians in 1911 "because the Reformed Church was unknown" in the area,[77] and in effect stopped the immigrant work at the end of World War II.[78] Other fields worked during this period and still maintained by the Church included the Jew, the migrant, the immigrant Chinese and, beginning in the 1950's, among black and Latin American communities in New York City. Each of these programs has a fascinating history of its own, packed with Christian concern, adventure, and sacrifice, which one day must be told.

In addition to all of this field work, the Reformed Church continued to tend its own "garden" during the first half of the twentieth century. This essentially meant helping numerous struggling churches to become self-supporting. By 1938 "two-thirds of the denomination's 787 churches"[79] had received such assistance, and the Church maintained this percentage through 1950. Throughout most of this period, moreover, the "Thompson Principle"—"where Hollanders settled, *there* has been growth and strength"—determined the denomination's Church expansion policy. Despite the persistent challenge that

the times call for . . a widening outlook that sees not only a ministry to people of our own particular background but to all men of whatever nationality, race, color, or creed,"[80] the Reformed Church remained essentially Dutch. Nor did the "Domestic Missions Year" of 1941 effectively change this situation. Between 1900 and 1950 the denomination organized one hundred twenty new congregations, listing a total of seven hundred sixty-three churches at mid-century. Only rarely, however, was a new church formed without a nucleus familiar with the Dutch Reformed tradition. Church retention, therefore, rather than church expansion, characterized much of the denomination's home mission program during this period.

It may be instructive at this point to make several observations concerning the mission program of the Reformed Church, from 1776 to 1950. Most obviously, throughout this century-and- three-quarters the denomination remained essentially a Dutch Church, choosing to expand primarily among its own kind. This, of course, was not a unique trait among ethnic religious groups in America, and the same pattern can be observed among the Orthodox Churches and the various branches of Lutheran and Reformed bodies. In each case, the cultural factor was a positive source of strength, providing these largely ethnic denominations with a necessary identity in the face of the developing religious "melting-pot" within America.

Second, during most of this period the Reformed Church uncompromisingly maintained its theological standards in its mission program. Consistently the mission reports applauded the fact that neophyte congregations were served by an educated clergy who properly catechized, preached the "pure" gospel, and conducted worship "decently and in order." Like the ethnic factor, the liturgical and theological dimension of the denomination's mission program was also reinforcing, providing the Church with a peculiar *raison d'etre* within America's capricious religious situation. On the other hand, however, this factor handicapped the denomination's mission program, particularly among the more unlettered and ebullient American.

Third, the Reformed Church generously provided benevolent assistance to numerous less privileged groups in America. The mission board did not develop a specific strategy for this. Rather, the Church responded to various needs as these were brought to its attention—the Indian in Oklahoma and Nebraska, the mountain people in Kentucky, the blacks in Brewton, Alabama and New York City, and others. Significantly, these benevolent programs were socially conservative by the standard of the 1920's; they provided gifts and services from concerned and generous "haves" to the needy "have-nots." The denomination never proposed funding radical mission programs aimed at bringing about social change.

Finally, throughout this century-and-three-quarters the mission program of the Reformed Church was influenced by the ebb and flow of America's social and intellectual history. This was natural, of course, for the denomination's life and mission did not exist in a vacuum. The frontier movement, immigration, capitalism, nationalism, individualism, the rise of the city, secularization, manifest destiny, Fundamentalism, the nation's wars—all of these and more decisively affected the shape of the denomination's mission program.

Such was the case in 1950, when the Reformed Church launched a significantly new program of Church expansion. Several factors apropos of the postwar period in America influenced this change. Most important was the dawn of an "age of affluence." Following nearly twenty years of depression and war, the nation's insatiable desire for the things of this world could now be satisfied. The industrial expansion begun during the war increased afterward, making it possible for Americans to earn far more money than ever before. In addition, there was the equally decisive transformation in the population balance. By 1950 two-thirds of the American people had moved into metropolitan regions. Forests and farms were bulldozed in order to accommodate an expansion of a suburban population that became three times greater than the central cities. Moreover, technological developments in transportation and communication, tended to bring vast areas which were still statistically "rural" into a quasi-suburban environment. Finally, the trend in industry to organize its business on a national basis, and to substantially increase its management personnel, made geographical mobility as important as social mobility. The "man in the grey flannel suit," the "lonely crowd," and the suburban "status seeker" became new features of the religious situation.

The international counterpart of this domestic situation was the cold war; the postwar confrontation between the "Communist Bloc" nations headed by the USSR, and the "Free World" countries, led by the United States. Between 1950 and 1953, moreover, the United States was deeply involved in a hot war in Korea. The chief religious consequence of this international situation was that consciously or subconsciously the patriotism of this "nation with the soul of a church" was aroused. Being a church member and speaking favorably of religion became a means of affirming the "American way of life," especially since the USSR and its communist allies were formally committed to atheism. It was not surprising, therefore, that a Supreme Court Justice wrote in the 1950's that "we are a religious people" and that our institutions "presuppose a Supreme Being."[81]

As a result of these factors the Reformed and other Churches were confronted with important new mission possibilities beginning in the 1950's. The burgeoning suburbs, with their ever-present problems of adjustment and loneliness, made the church the sort of family institution that the social situation required. And the awesome international scene produced a type of "Civil Religion," which made church membership both respectable and patriotic. In 1957 the Census Bureau reported that 96 percent of the American people cited a specific affiliation when asked the question: "What is your religion?"[82] And the statistics of church membership revealed that this always religious nation was in fact becoming affiliated at an increased rate.[83]

Appropriately, therefore, the Board of Domestic Missions reported in 1950 that "Today a great Door . . . is open unto the Reformed Church in America," and challenged the denomination to contribute five hundred thousand dollars for a vigorous new program of church expansion.[84] In addition, the denomination's Minister of Evangelism moved throughout the Church urging "every individual believer" to help make "America for Christ."[85] And Synodical Field Secretaries, in comity with other denominations, began securing options on farm land that would "one day be a field of homes white unto harvest for His kingdom."[86] And seminary enrollment increased, providing clergy for these new fields. The Church responded to all of this by contributing several millions of dollars to the denomination's program of church expansion. As a result, in the ten years from 1949 to 1958, the Reformed Church organized one hundred twenty new churches, a total equal to that of the previous half-century. Significantly, many of these new congregations were established in suburban areas among Americans unfamiliar with the Dutch Reformed tradition.

Subsequently, from 1958 to 1974, the denomination established sixty additional churches. This reduced pace in church expansion reflected the new climate of opinion within America during the turbulent 1960's. Three political assassinations, a prolonged war in South East Asia, racial and other riots, campus unrest—all of this and more marked the inexplicable socio-political milieu of this period. And in religion, this decade-and-one-half saw the emergence of a secular intrepretation of biblical authority, as well as a questioning of all the established structures of Christendom, including the parish church and traditional morality. Consequently, the Reformed Church confronted a more "secularized" and "permissive" American during this period, a factor which seriously affected its program of church expansion.

This final quarter century, however, roughly 1950 to 1975, was especially important in the developing history of the denomination's home mission program. Numerically, the Reformed Church organized nearly two hundred new congregations during this period, a number far exceeding that of any comparable era in the history of the Church. Significantly, many of these churches were established among "Gentile" Americans, those whom the Reverend Peter Stryker in 1800 urged upon the denomination, adding, they "open an unbounded prospect for usefulness in the Gospel ministry."[87] The past twenty-five years have proved Stryker to be a prophet. In 1975, the "Gentile"-and-Dutch Reformed Church appears in good shape to begin a new century of mission work within America.

Immigration

Elton J. Bruins

The influx of millions of immigrants into the United States during the nineteenth and early twentieth centuries significantly altered the contours of life and thought in this country. Whether pushed by burdensome socio-political conditions within their native land, or pulled by the lure of attractive possibilities in this nation, these immigrants swelled the population of America in unprecedented numbers. Nearly 5,000,000 Europeans settled here from 1820 to 1860. Between 1860 and 1900 about 14,000,000 arrived, and between 1900 and 1920 that many more. Less than one-third of these settled on farms; the rest migrated to the growing and already overcrowded cities. Here they began by carrying out the usual tasks of new immigrants at the lowest level of the social and economic order. Many of them lived together in congested quarters and, generally, spoke in their native tongue and carried on their traditions in close proximity to old-country friends. As such, they challenged the absorptive powers of the city and added other problems to the many that were already plaguing the older social and governmental structure.[1]

This century of immigration, roughly from 1820 to 1920, had a profound impact on religion in the United States. This was evident at several levels. Theologically, the in-put of tightly held Old World ideas into existing American church patterns resulted in serious debate and conflict, particularly for denominations with longstanding confessional roots in Europe. Socially, assimilation of European habits, biases, piety, and language into American denominational structures resulted in decisive consequences for some American Churches, particularly the Reformed, Lutheran, and Roman Catholic.

The most obvious consequence of immigration on American religion, however, was numerical. Here the Atlantic migration of the nineteenth century was particularly decisive, enabling some Churches to move from numerical weakness to strength in a few decades. In fact, denominational growth in the nineteenth century proved to be numerically determinative for American religion in the twentieth century; denominations holding the largest membership today are those which surged forward in the nineteenth century, either by assimilating large groups of immigrants with similar ethnic and theological backgrounds, or by winning converts through enterprising mission programs. Between 1820 and 1870, for example, 2,400,000 German immigrants entered the United States. The Germans had a profound effect upon the Lutheran Church in America, which grew from an estimated 15,000 members in 1800 to about 400,000 in 1870. The Presbyterian church also gained substantial numbers during this period, advancing from 40,000 in 1800 to 713,000 by 1870. Other Protestant bodies which had significant gains during this period, in part because of strong missionary programs to the immigrant, were the Baptists, from 103,000 in 1800 to 1,500,000 in 1870; the Methodists, from approximately 65,000 to about 2,500,000 during the same time frame; the Congregationalists from 75,000 to 306,000; and the Disciples of Christ, which was non-existent in 1800 to 450,000 in 1870. In addition, the Roman Catholic Church, under the impact of the nineteenth century European migration, grew from 100,000 members in 1800 to over 4,500,000 in 1870.[2]

By comparison, the numerical growth of the Reformed Church in America during the decisive century, from 1820 to 1920, was small. During that period, the Reformed Church grew from 58,000 in 1820 to approximately 87,000 in 1870, and about 184,000 in 1920. The reasons for this are varied and complex, and are given elsewhere in this volume.[3] It is sufficient here to point out that the problematic shape of the denomination following the Revolutionary War, the persistent scarcity of clergy as well as the requirement for an educated clergy, ethnocentricism, an undersubscribed and trouble-filled missionary program, theological controversy, and a mid-century schism, are all instructive for understanding the Church's comparatively small gains during this century.

Beyond these factors, moreover, one of the most important elements in determining both the growth of the Reformed Church during the nineteenth century, as well as the shape of the denomination in the twentieth century, was the interaction between the Church and immigration, which is the principal focus of this essay. Chronologically, this story began in the nineteenth century with the Reformed Church and German immigration, but it also included the Hungarians, Italians, Japanese and, of course, most decisively the Dutch.

Beginning in the early nineteenth century the Dutch worked closely with the German Reformed Church in assimilating German immigrants into their respective Churches. The relationship between the two denominations was naturally cordial, because both were daughters of the Reformed Church in the Netherlands. Moreover, at the start of the nineteenth century the German immigrant comprised about one-third of the membership of the Dutch Church. In 1834 the German Synod requested that the Dutch provide assistance in reaching the "destitute immigrants," particularly in the West. In the same year the Dutch increased its efforts among the German immigrant, and recruited ministers who could establish and serve German speaking congregations.[4]

As a result, in 1838 the Reformed Church organized the German Evangelical Mission Church of New York City, the first German immigrant church established by the denomination. It was an important event, because that congregation mothered many other German communions, and also because it served as the host church for numerous German immigrants who arrived at the Hudson Bay harbor. The Reverend John C. Guldin, who was minister of the church from 1841 to 1863, and concurrently a missionary agent to the German immigrants under the Board of Domestic Missions, was the principal force in these developments.[5]

During this period, moreover, the Dutch and German Churches continued to work closely on the German immigrant situation, incorporating this concern with discussions on Church union. Meeting in Harrisburg, Pennsylvania, in 1844, twelve delegates from each Church passed the following resolution:

That vigorous efforts be made by the Dutch Reformed Church to extend her missionary operations in the destitute parts of the German Reformed Church . . . and that the immigrant join whichever denomination is nearest.[6]

This resolution, as well as others pointing toward union, were subsequently approved by both denominations.

All of this, however, came to an abrupt end in 1847 as a result of the so-called Mercersberg controversy.[7] Consequently, beginning in 1848 the Dutch Reformed Church carried on its

ministry to the German immigrants without the close cooperation of the German Reformed Church. Numerically it was an
unfortunate dissolution, because subsequent events showed that
the Dutch Church was ill-equipped to minister alone to the
growing influx of German immigrants.

In June, 1857, Dr. John Garretson, Corresponding Secretary
of the Board of Domestic Missions, reported to General Synod
that the denomination's work among German immigrants was
progressing well. To substantiate this claim, he noted that in
1847 the Reformed Church could count only one German
congregation, but in 1857, the number was "about thirty."[8]

Apparently, however, the leadership of the German constituency in the Reformed Church read the progress differently.
In October, 1857, Guldin assembled a German ministers convention in New York City which drafted a memorial to General
Synod on the subject of the German mission churches. The
Synod referred the document to the Board of Domestic Missions for study and action. Secretary Garretson gave the Board's
response to the memorial at the 1858 meeting of General
Synod.

"We sympathize deeply with our brethren who send this
memorial," Garretson began,

> yet it is to be regretted that such a convention should have been held. The
> precedent is an unhappy one, as it opens the way to other foreign na-
> tionalities to do the same, and thus bring agencies to bear on the General
> Synod apart from the established order of the church.[9]

Garretson continued by making a defense of the Board's policy
and tartly reminded Guldin and the German pastors of the
assistance already given them by the Reformed Church:

> During these ten or twelve years we have expanded our efforts among our
> German brethren, and are now almost entirely sustaining seventeen minis-
> ters—during the year now closing we have appropriated five thousand and
> eighty-five dollars for their support.[10]

The appropriation cited by Garretson appears small, and in
comparison with the need it was inadequate, but it represented
one-third of the Board's total budget for 1857.

The major issue in the memorial was the scarcity of well-
trained German speaking ministers. Guldin, in fact, was pressing
the denomination to allow "foreign German ministers" to trans-

fer their ordination, preach, and administer the sacraments within the Dutch Church. It was a risk-taking and daring proposal which to Guldin seemed a prudent means for the denomination to keep pace with the expanding German immigrant population. The denomination, however, was invariably without funds or clergy to either encourage or implement the dreams of its ecclesiastical entrepreneurs. Consequently, Garretson's response was inevitable:

> The proposed plan of introducing foreign German ministers is received by your Board as one of more than doubtful expediency. While we might undoubtedly receive some choice men, even they must enter upon an American work under many disabilities; being strangers to all our habits, usages, and to an extent to the wants of their own countrymen in this land of their adoption. We are more and more confirmed in the conviction that we must raise our own German ministers, and that we may look to our American-German Churches for an adequate supply. . . . In the great problem to be settled with the rapidly increasing German element, these are the men to meet the exigencies of the case, both as respects our country and Christianity.[11]

Garretson's decision proved shortsighted, albeit expedient, and, as a result, the Reformed Church lost out with the German immigrant in the burgeoning eastern cities. A few congregations in and around the metropolitan New York area, descendents of the Guldin era still remain, but the Church's missed opportunity in the nineteenth century was never regained.[12]

The denomination had better success with the German migration to the farmlands of the Mid-West. In 1847, a large number of German/Dutch speaking Calvinists from East Friesland, Germany, settled what became known as German Valley in northwestern Illinois. Subsequently, many of these Germans migrated westward to Iowa and South Dakota, and also into Minnesota.

The Reformed Church made contact with these Germans through Mr. Jan Vander Las, an employee of the American Bible Society. Vander Las petitioned the Reformed Church to begin a mission to the Germans, and his suggestion was pressed by the indefatigable Guldin. Subsequently, the Board of Domestic Missions acted on the proposal and commissioned several pastors to the German Valley region. In 1851, the Reformed Protestant Dutch Church of Silver Creek, Illinois, was organized, the first of a number of East Frisian congregations in the Mid-West.[13]

The development of German speaking stations in the Mid-

West proved useful to the denomination in several significant and unexpected ways. For example, in 1894, the East Frisian churches founded the Pleasant Prairie academy in German Valley, which they planned, unsuccessfully, to develop into a college. In addition, in 1916 the churches helped to establish and fund a German department at Central College, Pella, Iowa, in order to teach the language to students who came from the German speaking churches. And, finally, a few enterprising East Frisians published and widely circulated the periodical, *Der Mitarbeiter*, which printed denominational news.[14]

Although the Reformed Church gained far fewer German immigrant adherents than it might have with a better funded Domestic Missionary program, the contribution of the Germans to the life and thought of the denomination has been significant. They have added to the existing diversity of the Church, extended its geographical boundaries, and provided important and challenging leadership. The German influence upon the Reformed Church is a story that is just now beginning to be recognized and begs for the pen of some careful historian.

Unlike the German narrative, the story of the Reformed Church and Dutch immigration in the nineteenth century has often been told. And for good reason, because the Dutch migration was uniquely decisive for the life and growth of the denomination. The story is retold below to highlight that influence and to critically interpret it.

In comparison with the massive exodus of other Europeans to the United States in the nineteenth century, the Dutch migration was small. For example, during the two decades, 1820-1840, fewer than 2,500 Dutch arrived at the Hudson harbor. From 1840 to 1860, about 20,000 more came to North America. This number increased after the Civil War, reaching a peak during the decade of the eighties, when about 55,000 Dutch immigrants reached the United States.[15]

Only a small percentage of these Dutch immigrants became members of the Reformed Church. The reasons for this are related to the causes of the migration; the question of whether it was "the hunger of the souls of the Dutch folk or the necessities of their bodies that chiefly motivated their mass migration to America."[16] An objective evaluation of the data suggests that both "souls and bodies" must be taken into account, but that economic causes quickly superseded the religious motives.

The religious factor developed primarily from the repressive

policy of King William I to force conformity on a small number
of his subjects who refused to submit to certain royal decrees
concerning the State Church, principally the Church Reorgani-
zation Law of January 7, 1816. This law changed the name of
the State Church from the *Gereformeerde Kerk* to the *Hervormde Kerk*. Both terms can be translated to mean Reformed
Church, but in the minds of the critics, *Hervormed* meant
"reorganized" rather than "reformed"— reorganized, that is, to
suit the wishes of the King. Under the new law, church bodies
such as synods, classes, and consistories were maintained, but
were supervised more closely by the State. The training and
examining of ministers were also placed under stricter governmental control.

Other factors added insult to injury in the minds of some of
the more orthodox Calvinists. For example, some resented the
introduction of evangelical songs as a supplement to the Old
Testament Psalms customarily sung during the church services.
Dissenters showed their displeasure with such substitutions by
wearing their hats during the singing of the pietistic hymns or
by waiting outside the church until the singing ended. Some
critics also felt the government was trying to keep the Bible out
of the public schools, thereby making religious education a
"mere general moral one, offensive to neither Jew nor Roman
Catholic."[17] Finally, a religious awakening, known as the *reveil*
and participated in primarily by intellectuals, was especially
critical of ministers for being too rationalistic in their preaching.
Supporters of the *reveil* advocated a return to the fundamental
theological ideas of the early Dutch Reformed fathers and
chastized the national Church for becoming too formalistic and
complacent.

Influenced by these religious developments, a nucleus of
theological students at the University of Leiden began meeting
together for support, worship, and mutual exchange of views.
The group became known as "Scholte's Club," after the name
of its most zealous member, Henrik Pieter Scholte. Following
their ordination into the ministry, several of the group's members became determined opponents of the Church Reorganiza-
tion Law of 1816. They included in addition to Scholte, the
Reverends Albertus Christian Van Raalte and Anthony Brum-
melkamp. Subsequently, Scholte and Van Raalte were each
responsible for leading several hundred Dutch immigrants to
Iowa and Michigan, respectively.

The controversy finally resulted in the so-called secession of 1834, when the Reverend Hendrick De Cock, together with his entire congregation at Ulrum, in the province of Gronigen, publicly seceded from the *Hervormde Kerk*. De Cock's action prompted Scholte, who was serving a church at Doeveren in North Bradant, and later Van Raalte, who was ministering to two small congregations in Overijssel, to do the same. By 1835, sixteen congregations had seceded from the State Church.[18]

The state reacted harshly against the Seceders and imposed fines and, on occasion, imprisonment on those who worshipped in disregard of the new regulations. This repressive policy, however, must be set in the context of the post-revolutionary temper of Europe at that time. Given the prevailing *sitz im leben*, the King's demand for uniformity—which extended to politics as well as religion—was consistent with the policy of other European states. Unfortunately, however, a number of Seceders were severely persecuted. Scholte, for example, claimed that during a period of about a decade, he had paid thirty-two hundred dollars in fines.

In spite of this harrassment and persecution, the Seceders refused to be deflected from their course. And subsequently, the government relaxed its harsh policy against religious deviance. Following the abdication of William I in 1840, religious persecution in the Netherlands gradually declined, and was almost non-existent when a new liberal constitution was adopted in 1848.

During this transition period, however, roughly 1840 to 1848, a number of Seceders emigrated from the Netherlands. By the time the Government had relaxed its policy of harrassment against religious dissent, a prevailing emigration psychosis had penetrated the Seceder's camp with such power that it would have been difficult to reverse the trend. Van Raalte expressed this opinion to a fellow Seceder shortly before he left for America in 1846: "You will not be able to stop this emigration any more than you can stop the Rhine in its course."[19] In a few instances, almost entire congregations of Seceders, together with their ministers, decided to leave for the United States where they could worship as they pleased.

But religious problems represented only one set of causes leading to Dutch emigration in the nineteenth century. Poor economic conditions were also important and eventually became the dominant factor. In fact, Seceders never constituted a majority among the Dutch emigrating to America during the 1840's; even Roman Catholic emigration exceeded that of the Secessionist group. Moreover, because Dutch emigration continued in significant numbers after persecution had nearly stopped in 1848, it is obvious that religion was not the only factor influencing the emigration of the Hollanders.[20]

The adverse economic situation stemmed from many causes. Because the Netherlands was a small commercial nation, it suffered more than most countries from the wars of the French Revolution and the Napoleonic Era. In the late 1840's roughly twenty-seven percent of the Dutch were unemployed or on relief. Moreover, taxes were very high, falling most heavily on those least able to bear them. High rents, small farms, and a limit to how much land could be reclaimed from the sea also brought on an agricultural crisis.[21]

In addition, other problems aggravated the Netherlanders' adverse economic situation. Periodic floods ruined farmlands that had been claimed from the surrounding ocean, and diseases among the livestock added to the hardships of the rural people. A cholera outbreak in 1832 carried off thousands of townsmen and farmers. The Winter of 1844-45 was the most difficult in Holland's history. Finally, a potato disease, that reached its height in 1845-46 caused a serious shortage of Holland's most important staple, resulting in famine conditions in parts of the country.

The confluence of religious, economic, and political factors, therefore, induced the Dutch to migrate to the United States in the mid-nineteenth century. Significantly, only a small percentage of the total number of these immigrants were Seceders who later joined with the Reformed Church. And, in the late nineteenth as well as the twentieth centuries, when other waves of Dutch Calvinist immigrants settled in the United States, most of these entered the newly formed Christian Reformed Church and not the Reformed Church in America. Consequently, the Dutch migration, which was the most natural source of immigrant growth for the Reformed Church, proved less numerically fruitful than it might have been.

Three Seceding associations were particularly important to the story of the Reformed Church and Dutch immigration in the nineteenth century. These were known as the Utrecht, Arnhem, and Zeeland associations, and were headed respectively by the Reverends Scholte, Van Raalte, and Cornelius Van der Meulen, each of whom was a secessionist minister. In 1846, Van Raalte led most of his party to western Michigan and settled what became known as Holland, Michigan. Shortly thereafter, Van der Meulen settled his group about six miles east of Holland at Zeeland, Michigan. And, in the same year, Scholte's colony disembarked at Baltimore, Maryland, and travelled cross-country to the prairies of south central Iowa, where they organized a village they called Pella, meaning "refuge," after the town to which some of the Christians had fled when Jerusalem was destroyed by the Romans in 70 A. D. The total number of these three immigrant groups was no more than twenty-five hundred.

These midwestern immigrant communities, solidly Dutch and fervently Calvinist, were carefully observed and assisted by the Reformed Church in America, which for over two centuries had experienced a successive series of frustrations in trying to broaden its base and reach a new constituency across the Alleghenies. In 1847, The Albany Synod was informed that "a body of Pilgrims has reached our shores from Holland," and a request for aid was made.[22] One year later, in 1848, Garretson, the Secretary of the Board of Domestic Missions, reported that "other denominations are using active measures to bring [the Dutch] under their influence, while we, who are of the same origin, springing from the same branch of the Reforma- tion . . . are doing nothing but exposing them to be swallowed up by men of every name and every creed."[23] That autumn, the churches in and around Holland, Michigan, which were already organized into a Classis, were invited by the Reformed Church to attend the next Synod meeting, and in 1849 Doctor Isaac Wyckoff of Albany visited these immigrants on behalf of the Board of Domestic Missions. During Wyckoff's visit the Classis prepared a request for admission into the Reformed Church:

Considering the previous and blessed unity of the Church of God and the plainly expressed will of our Savior that all should be one, and also the need which the separate parts have of one another, and especially remem- bering how small and weak we ourselves are, therefore, our hearts have longed for intercourse with the precious Zion of God ever since our feet first pressed the shores of this new World . . . all God's children, of what- ever denomination, are dear to us; but in the management and care of our own religious affairs we feel more at home where we find our own stan- dards of faith and principles of church government. . . . We have, therefore, resolved to send one of our brethren, Rev. A. C. Van Raalte, a minister of the Church of God, as a delegate to your church Judicatory, which is soon about to meet in Albany or vicinity. We authorize him in our name to give and to ask all necessary information which can facilitate the desired union.[24]

In 1850 the Albany synod voted to receive the Classis of Holland, Michigan, into the membership of the Reformed Church. This action gave the denomination its most significant foothold in the West, one which proved deep and decisive for the future of the church.

The Reformed Church also courted Scholte's colony in Pella, Iowa, and encouraged its union with the denomination. The Church sent financial support to the Iowa immigrants through Wyckoff and Doctor Thomas De Witt of New York City, who also petitioned the congregation there to unite with them. But Scholte, the senior minister of the Pella church, thought differently than Van Raalte. His experience in the Netherlands made him suspicious of all established Churches, and he remained independent. In the early 1850's, however, a number of Scholte's members broke from his church to form the First Reformed Church of Pella, Iowa. This congregation joined with the Reformed Church in America in 1856, the first of many Dutch immigrant churches in Iowa to unite with the denomination.

During the following decades, until the end of the nineteenth century, a number of Dutch immigrants who were settled in the principal Mid-West centers of Holland-Zeeland, Michigan and Pella, Iowa, moved out to form other communities in new areas. For example, small colonies of Dutch from the Michigan center migrated to Grand Rapids, Kalamazoo, Muskegon, and Grandville, Michigan. Other Dutch immigrants went to Illinois and established Low Prairie, founded in 1847, and High Prairie, organized in 1849.[25] These two communities were located six miles apart and about twenty miles south of the center of present-day Chicago. This area is now part of Metropolitan Chicago, and the communities are known respectively as South Holland and Roseland. In addition, in 1870 Henry Hospers led a number of colonists from Pella, Iowa, to northwest Iowa and formed the community of Orange City, a colony which later spilled westward into North and South Dakota, and northward into Minnesota. Beyond all of this, moreover, a new colony of

Dutch immigrants crossed the Atlantic in the mid-nineteenth century and established villages in Alto, Waupon, Sheboygan, and Cedar Grove, Wisconsin. In each case, these solidly Dutch Calvinist communities organized churches which later united with the Reformed Church in America.[26]

Finally, it must be noted that not all of the Dutch Seceders who migrated to America in the nineteenth century settled in the Mid-West. Some remained in the East, particularly in Paterson and Passaic in New Jersey, settling near relatives or friends who had emigrated earlier. These Seceders were quickly assimilated into the Reformed Church, and they were of great assistance in advising other Hollanders who migrated to America after the Civil War.

The impact of the nineteenth century Dutch immigration upon the Reformed Church has been profound. Numerically, these immigrants not only added new numbers to the denomination, but they also provided bases in the Mid-West from which the Church subsequently launched mission programs into the Far West. In 1882, for example, only twenty five years after the Van Raalte migration, the Secretary of the Board of Domestic Missions reported that "one-sixth of the churches and one-eighth of the membership of the Church was in the Holland Classis."[27] In 1974, more than one-half of the denomination's churches and membership lay West of the Alleghanies. Equally significant, the benevolent giving of the midwestern churches for 1974 was nearly three times more than that of the older eastern branch of the denomination.

In addition, the midwestern Dutch immigrants have made important contributions to the educational life of the Reformed Church. They quickly established and financed academies, or preparatory schools, three of which subsequently evolved into four-year Liberal Arts colleges which continue to be supported by the Reformed Church. These three institutions are Hope College, in Holland, Michigan, Central College, in Pella, Iowa, and Northwestern College, in Orange City, Iowa. Moreover, with the approval of the General Synod, these midwestern churches established theological education at Hope College, beginning in 1866. This action led to the founding of Western Theological Seminary in 1884.[28]

Beyond this, the immigrant churches gave support and impetus to the denomination's already impressive foreign mission program. Indeed, by the end of the nineteenth century, these midwestern Calvinists, most of whom were either spiritual or actual descendants of the Seceders, assumed the leading role in the missionary enterprise of the Reformed Church, providing the denomination with the major share of the financial and human resources for this program. At present, the vast majority of the men and women who serve in ministry of the Reformed Church can trace their roots to the nineteenth century Dutch Seceders.

The impact of these Dutch immigrants on the Reformed Church has also surfaced in other, more ambiguous ways. The Seceders were estranged from the State Church in the Netherlands, and they came to the Mid-West primarily to escape religious harrassment and to establish pious Christian communities. They also embraced an extreme form of Calvinist piety and theology, patterned after the supralapsarianism of Voetius, a seventeenth century Dutch theologian, and they held little brief for ecclesiastical or theological pluralism. Moreover, the Seceder's rural setting in the Mid-West gave them opportunity to implement their principles, preach their theology, practice their piety, and nurture their youth in a protective, congenial environment. In short, there were nuances in the history, theology, biases, geography, and piety of the Dutch immigrants which were manifestly different from that of the eastern based Reformed Church which they joined, beginning in 1850.

Consequently, since 1850 the older, eastern section of the Reformed Church and the immigrant, midwestern sector of the denomination have often clashed on substantive issues. One such issue has been ecumenicity. In 1893, for example, the denomination rejected the proposed merger with the German Reformed Church primarily because the Dutch immigrant group voted unanimously against it.[29] And more recently, in the 1960's, the Reformed Church defeated a proposal to unite with the Presbyterian Church in the United States, the eastern Classes voting for merger, and the midwestern churches voting overwhelmingly against it.[30]

There were, moreover, other issues that caused tensions between the older, eastern section and the immigrant, midwestern sector of the Reformed Church since the union of 1850. These included Darwinism and Higher Criticism, which surfaced in the late nineteenth century, and the Social Gospel, the "Adam" question, Barthianism, and the role of women in the Church, which emerged in the twentieth century.[31] Although the breakdown on these issues was not always precise, the East tended to espouse a more liberal position, and the Mid-West generally held to a conservative view. The denomination has learned to live with this tension, however, rejecting extremism for compromise, and preferring periodic controversy to schism.

During the century, 1850 to 1950, the primary source of Reformed Church expansion in the Mid-West and the Far-West was the Dutch immigrant and his descendants. Building on a mission policy established in the early nineteenth century, the denomination followed Dutch Calvinists wherever they happened to plant roots and organized new congregations among them. As a result, Reformed churches were spotted among Dutch colonies in Nebraska, Kansas, Colorado, Montana, and as far West as Washington and Orange County, California. By 1900, nearly four-fifths of all the Reformed Churches in the Mid-West and Far-West were Dutch speaking congregations, the remaining one-fifth consisting of German and indigenous American communions. Many of these immigrant congregations remained Dutch speaking until well into the twentieth century. Because the Reformed church was so manifestly Dutch, particularly in the Mid-West, it lost its opportunity with the English speaking American in the city, the emerging suburbs, and the farm during this period.

The denomination worked almost exclusively with the Dutch immigrant in the Mid-West and the Far-West, from 1850 to 1950, because it was successful at it. Indeed, until about 1950, with the exception of the German immigrants in Illinois and Iowa, the Reformed Church gave little effort to establishing churches in the Mid-West among either non-Dutch immigrants or indigenous Americans, and was generally unsuccessful when it did. This point was noted in 1882 by the Reverend Abraham Thompson, in an address commemorating the fiftieth anniversary of the Board of Domestic Missions:

Not wholly, nor *chiefly*, perhaps, is our Church designed to care for the Hollanders, but yet *largely* and *specially*. Providence has made it our special work.

We cannot separate ourselves from our history. Of our 500 churches now existing, it will be safe to say that (most) of them . . . have sprung almost directly from those originally speaking the Holland language. The instances are rare—exceedingly rare—where churches have been organized without a *nucleus* of those who had been trained in these churches. . . .

The Church *has* not grown outside of the limits of Holland immigration.

That it *cannot,* I will not venture to affirm of even to suggest. But I *do* say that all its past history shows that where the Hollanders settled, *there* has been growth and strength.[32]

Thompson's remarks may have overstated the total mission picture in the Reformed Church, but there is little doubt that the Board of Domestic Missions emphasized expansion among the Dutch immigrant. In order to implement this program, in the late 1880's the board appointed the Reverend Rense H. Joldersma as missionary superintendent to the Dutch for the Synod of Chicago, the judicatory to which all the churches in the Mid-West were responsible. In addition, the board appointed a number of Dutch-speaking ministers to meet Dutch immigrants arriving in New York and New Jersey ports, considering it "wise to meet as many of them as possible with some sort of welcome immediately upon their landing."[33]   One of these appointed ministers, the Reverend Helenus E. Nies of Patterson, New Jersey, reported in 1890 that he annually contacted more than six thousand Hollanders at Hoboken and Ellis Island, adding,

Besides, endeavoring to answer a thousand questions and repeated almost as often, about railroads, time of departure, tickets, checks, baggage, etc., your missionary found opportunity to give, here a word of information about the Church, there a note of introduction to a brother minister out west, and in other ways to be useful to these strangers in a strange land.[34]

A subsequent report portended ominous consequences for the Reformed Church and its relationship to the Dutch immigrant. Nies noted that the attitude of the Reformed Churches in the Netherlands toward "our Church" has dramatically changed, a fact which "speaks volumes for our work among the immigrants in the future."[35] Nies was referring to the open policy of the Reformed Church in America in regard to membership in secret societies, particularly the Free Masons. The Separatist Church in the Netherlands rejected this policy and refused membership to anyone who belonged to a secret order. Consequently, the Reformed Church in the Netherlands urged their emigrating members to join the Christian Reformed Church in America, a denomination carved out of the Reformed Church in the 1870's primarily on this issue. This policy significantly reduced the number of Dutch immigrants for the Reformed Church after 1900 and seriously affected the work of the denomination among Dutch immigrants in Canada following World War II. This development, however, may have proved to be a mixed blessing: although it modified the denomination's work among the Dutch immigrant, it enabled the Church to turn some of its mission resources toward the indigenous American as well as other non-Dutch immigrant groups.

With the exception of the Germans, the Reformed Church was not involved in any mission program among non-Dutch immigrants before 1900. This policy was determined primarily by a scarcity of economic and human resources, although ethnocentricism also seemed an important factor. At the turn of the twentieth century, however, this policy began to change as the Board of Domestic Missions challenged the Reformed Church to support a program of evangelism to "the hordes of aliens pouring into our country."[36] The Board did not intend that these "aliens" would become a new source for church extension for the denomination; church expansion would continue to come through the Dutch. Rather, the Board reported the "alien" program to the denomination as a foreign mission venture, and it couched its appeal to the Church in the rhetoric of a Foreign Mission Board.

More than a million immigrants come thronging into our country every year. Vast hordes of these are without any religious faith or connection whatever. 230,000 coming in the past year could neither read nor write. . . . It is high time we were doing Foreign Missionary work within our own borders. America is being heathenized as fast as we are Christianizing Asia. . . . [These aliens are] settling in colonies in all our cities, Russians, Serbians, Hungarians, Poles, Bohemians, Italians, Chinese, Japanese. Why should not some of our young men and women who wish to be missionaries acquire one of these languages and get to work in a foreign colony, without going more than a half-hour's trolley ride from their own home?[37]

The Reformed Church responded favorably to this appeal, and began its first "foreign mission" program to the "alien" Japanese immigrant in New York City in 1908. This was followed with a mission to the Italian immigrant in Newark and Raritan, New Jersey, in 1909, and to the Hungarians at Peekskill, New York, in 1910. By 1920 there were six Italian missions, four in the East and two in Mid-West Chicago, and by 1929 there were seventeen Italian mission stations and eight Hungarian churches and missions. The Women's Board of Domestic Missions, which was organized in 1882, took a leading role in this enterprise, particularly with the Japanese in New York.

The denomination's mission to these non-Dutch/German "aliens," however, never fully developed. Whatever the motives that initiated the program, they were not maintained. Moreover, the program was costly; the "alien" mission stations were unable to become self-supporting. Finally, although a few of the "alien" clergy proved themselves outstanding—the Italian, Pietro Moncada, the Hungarian, Louis Hamory, and the Japanese, Ernest Atsushi Ohori were especially notable—and were warmly received by the denomination as devoted "foreign missionaries," the overwhelmingly Dutch Reformed constituency found it difficult to accept a non-Dutch congregation as an equal.

Already by 1913 the Board of Domestic Missions became aware that the denomination's early enthusiasm for its "alien" mission program was waning. Consequently, in an attempt to reestablish support for the program, the Board reminded the Church of the basic difference between that "foreign mission" venture and its continuing work among "our own" Dutch immigrants:

... it is manifestly unwise to consider this service in the light of Church Extension. If our reason for commissioning men to preach the Gospel to Italians and Hungarians is anything other than evangelistic, we are wasting both time and money.[38]

In 1929, the Board again clearly explained the philosophy for its work among the "aliens."

The purpose of work among foreign language groups has been to evangelize and Americanize. It is still considered worth while to have a missionary at the Fort to meet Hollanders with a greeting in their own tongue and to extend friendly help to the stranger. But we never have listed Hollandspeaking churches as alien-work—these are our own people.[39]

By the end of World War II the Reformed Church had terminated its mission to the "alien." The denomination's work among the Hungarians was taken over by the German Reformed Church "which makes more of a specialty of service among Hungarians than we do."[40] And, following the deaths of the first generation ministers to the other non-Dutch immigrant groups, the work ended. In 1974, less than one-half dozen Reformed Churches can trace their origin to this "foreign mission" program.

The story of the Reformed Church and immigration, from 1776 to 1976, concludes appropriately with the Dutch—however, this time in Canada. Following World War II, the Canadian government opened that country's doors to vast numbers of immigrants, many of whom were Dutch. These Hollanders were primarily from the working class—farmers, laborers—who departed the Netherlands because

a series of unsettling experiences—the economic depression of the 1930's, the rise of Nazism, and the Second World War—together with a concern about the future helped create a psychological climate conducive to extensive emigration.[41]

The Dutch Government encouraged this emigration, regarding it as a means for relieving population pressure, reducing unemployment, and solving the alarming housing shortage, and in 1949 it began granting transportation subsidies to persons wishing to leave the country. From 1945 to 1974 nearly 500,000 Dutch emigrated from the Netherlands. Approximately fifteen percent of this number were Calvinists, many of whom settled in Canada.[42]

The Reformed Church in America was interested in assimilating these Canadian Dutch immigrants into its Church, and in 1948 the General Synod instructed the Board of Domestic Missions to study the situation. The Board's study, which was reported the following year, was significant because it recommended that the denomination undertake the work "without the regular funds of the Board," in cooperation with the United Church in Canada, the Reformed [Hervormde] Church in the Netherlands, "and other evangelical churches."[43] Twenty-five thousand dollars "in special gifts" was to be raised for the program.[44] In short, the Board approved the plan to minister to "our own" Dutch immigrants in comity with other evangelical churches in Canada.

It was decided to organize Reformed Churches, and that when the people have become "acclimated to the country and language they will be given the opportunity to unite with other denominations or to continue as Reformed Churches."[45]

This interesting decision requires some explanation. There were two distinct Reformed Churches in the Netherlands at this time, the *Hervormde Kerk*, which was the official State Church, and the more orthodox *Gereformeerde Kerk*, which was organized out of the Secession of 1834. For the most part, the older eastern branch of the Reformed Church in America was a theological legacee *of the Hervormde Kerk*, while the midwestern constituency of the denomination traced its roots to the *Gereformeerde Kerk*. Since the late nineteenth century, however, the Reformed Church in America and the *Gereformeerde Kerk* were formally out of touch with each other because of the "Secret Societies" issue and also because of subsequent theological developments within each communion.[46] To further complicate this already complex story, moreover, nearly all the members of the Christian Reformed Church, which seceded from the Reformed Church in America in the 1870's, were also descendents of the *Gereformeerde Kerk*. And since the late nineteenth century, the Christian Reformed Church and the *Gereformeerde Kerk* were working out a harmonious program on the immigrant and other issues.

When Dutch Calvinists began arriving in Canada following World War II, the vast majority of these immigrants were from the *Gereformeerde* rather than the *Hervormed Kerk*. The Christian Reformed Church quickly capitalized on this situation, and budgeted large sums of money for Canadian immigrant work, set up immigration centers, and established ecclesiastical machinery to facilitate the easy transference of membership from the *Gereformeerde* Church to its own.

The Gereformeerde Kerken in the Netherlands have now appointed *'Deputaten voor Emigratie'* with whom we are working together in unity especially for the purpose of transferring membership certificates from one country to the other and for making contacts with the dispersed before they drift away, and lose spiritual contact.[47]

The efficiency of the Christian Reformed Church in Canada was not matched by the Reformed Church in America which, by comparison, seemed uncertain of its policy, hesitant, and reluctant to use its resources for this potentially fruitful source of Church Expansion. The reasons for this are unclear, although it appears that several factors were at issue—the politics of the long-standing tension between the eastern and midwestern sections of the Church, the friction between the Christian Reformed Church and the Reformed Church, and a lack of sufficient funds. Whatever the reasons, however, in 1953 the Board apparently decided to concede the *Gereformeerde Kerk* migrants to the Christian Reformed Church and to concentrate on the comparatively fewer number of *Hervormde Kerk* immigrants, noting, "our church is the logical church to serve them."[48] It was a decisive policy, one which determined that the Reformed Church would have little numerical success among the Dutch Calvinists in Canada.

Following that decision, the Board began pressing its work among the *Hervormde Kerk* immigrants with more vigor, increasing its budget substantially, and soliciting Dutch- speaking Reformed Church ministers to serve the eighteen new churches. In 1953, the Board reported to General Synod that "the work with the Dutch immigrants in Canada has grown mightily, with many additional settlers coming overseas because of the recent floods in Holland."[49] Most of these "additional settlers," however, were from the *Geerformeerde Kerk* and they affiliated with the Christian Reformed Church.

Although there were several attempts during the 1960's to unite the Reformed Churches in Canada with the Presbyterian Church of that country, the denomination has preferred to continue its Canadian work as an American denomination.[50] In 1973, there were twenty-seven Reformed Church congregations in Canada, organized under the Classis of Ontario, and a total of 7,907 members.[51] By comparison, the Christian Reformed Church in 1973 listed one hundred sixty-two congregations, organized under nine classes, and a total membership of 75,000.

For all practical purposes, the period of immigration in the United States is over. Although this fact is hardly newsworthy, if understood and taken seriously it does have some implications for the future life and growth of the Reformed Church. Most obviously, it means that the Reformed Church can no longer depend on massive waves of new immigrants for Church growth; the era of the Van Raaltes and Scholtes leading large colonies into the Reformed Church will not be duplicated in the future. It also means that the period of Dutch hegemony in the denomination will slowly come to an end. In addition, it means that the Reformed Church will be free to *de-alienize* its present "foreign" constituency, appreciating its ethnic and racial diversity, celebrating the contributions of its varied ethnic groups, and accepting all of these groups as full participants in the life of the Church. And finally, it means that Church growth will be realized only by vigorous programs of evangelism and church expansion among the variety of races and nationalities that comprise the American "melting-pot."

World Mission

Herman Harmelink III

The Reformed Dutch Church did not engage in any world mission programs during its first one hundred fifty years in New York and New Jersey after its founding in 1628. Throughout that period the Reformed congregations in America were themselves a "world mission" field of the mother Church in the Netherlands. In addition, many of these Dutch colonial congregations were "handelskerken," churches intended to serve merchants and traders living in colonial outposts.[1] And during this century and one half the American Church was busy trying to establish and maintain its own existence in a relatively unfriendly environment. There was, consequently, no zeal for or interest in launching a world mission enterprise.[2]

Beginning in the 1790's, however, after the Reformed Church achieved independence from its parent Church in the Netherlands, a number of persons within the denomination caught the vision of the world as a mission field. This vision was partly influenced by the new situation within America at that time. Fresh from its victory over the British, many in the new Republic were determined to have the nation become a "model of Christian charity," and to export its Christian and democratic principles to the entire world. In addition, the millennial mood that enveloped the Christian Church at that time heightened this resolve, challenging a number of Christians to serve as foreign missionaries. And the Second Great Awakening in New England also influenced this vision.

As a result, in 1796 several individuals in the Reformed Church joined with Christians of other denominations to form the New York Missionary Society, "to propagate the glorious gospel of Christ in places which are destitute of it."[3] The intention was to see the whole world as its mission field, although its work was mainly with Indian tribes in North America. John H. Livingston, minister of the Dutch church in New York City, served as an early officer of this society.

Livingston, who has long been known as the "Father of the
Reformed Church," might also be called the "Father of World
Mission" in the denomination. Livingston consistently challenged the young men who received theological instruction
from him to consider the foreign mission enterprise. He also
took an active part in the establishment of the Berean Society
(later the Society of Inquiry) at New Bruhswick Theological
Seminary, an organization for promoting among students an
enthusiasm for the missionary cause. In addition, he preached a
number of mission sermons, generally rooted in millennial expectations, which inspired wide appeal for mission concerns.
One of these sermons, titled "The Everlasting Gospel," was
reprinted in New England where it was "blessed of God more
than any other means to produce . . . the foreign mission spirit"
there.[4]

Preached in 1804 in New York City, the sermon also shows
the strong millennial and anti-Roman motive that underlay the
denomination's world mission program in the early nineteenth
century. To inspire more strenuous efforts in "propagating the
gospel" and to assist his listeners in understanding the "signs
and sitrrings of the times,"[5] Livingston based his sermon on a
"prophecy" from the book of Revelation:

And I saw another Angel fly in the midst of Heaven, having the everlasting
Gospel to preach unto them that dwell on the earth, and to every nation,
and kindred, and tongue, and people, crying with a loud voice, fear God,
and give glory to him; for the hour of his judgment is come; and worship
him that made heaven and earth, and the sea, and the fountains of
waters.[6]

Livingston interpreted the "prophecy" to mean that the writer
of Revelation foresaw a time when a zealous ministry would
arise in the midst of the churches, "with a new and extraordinary spirit . . . and be a prelude to momentous changes in the
church and in the world." He proclaimed that this "time"
would occur somewhere between the Reformation, "commonly
called the age of Revelation," and the fall of "Great Babylon, . . . the Anti-Christ," the Pope, which he put in the year
1999. The millennial age, he was certain, would then commence
"in the year 2000."[7]

Livingston thus placed the fulfillment of the "prophecy"
sometime "between the year 1500 and 2000." But he was

speaking in 1804. "Three hundred years have elapsed since the Reformation," he noted, "and instead of increasing, the church has rather diminished in purity, in zeal, and in numbers." Therefore,

we are compelled . . . to look forward for the accomplishment; and are now reduced to the short remaining space of two hundred years. Within this compass there can be no mistake. At some point of time, from, and including the present day, and before the close of two hundred years, the angel must begin to fly in the midst of the Churches and preach the everlasting Gospel to all nations, and tongues, and kindred, and people in the earth. . . . This time, we believe, is arrived.[8]

This millennial theme was also the basis for another of Livingston's sermons, preached in a barn in Dutchess County, New York, during the War of Independence. This sermon was particularly important for the future history of world missions in the Reformed Church. In his audience was a little Hessian drummer who had been taken prisoner by the American forces after the defeat of Burgoyne at Saratoga. The sermon inspired the drummer boy, Christian Bork, to enter the Christian ministry, and he later served the Franklin Street Reformed Church in New York City. Among Bork's faithful parishoners was a young physician, John Scudder, who was challenged to prepare himself for overseas service under the American Board of Commissioners for Foreign Missions (A.B.C.F.M.).[9]

The A.B.C.F.M. was one of several ecumenical mission organizations the Reformed Church related to during the first half of the nineteenth century. The American Board grew out of the vision of Samuel J. Mills, a student at Andover Seminary. Mills had first become interested in the missionary cause as a student at Union College, Schenectady, New York, a college sponsored in part by the Reformed Church. While at Union he had studied a number of sermons preached by Doctor Livingston, particularly the sermon titled "The Everlasting Gospel". He had also become a fast friend with a number of Reformed Church students at Union, especially John F. Schermerhorn, who later became the denomination's first missionary agent.[10] Subsequently, Mills had transferred to Williams College, Massachusetts, where he organized the famous Haystack Prayer Meetings. He later enrolled at Andover Seminary, where he helped to establish the "Society of Brethren," an organization comprised of students determined to serve as foreign missionaries. In June, 1810, Mills and the other "Brethren" appeared before the Congregational Association in Massachusetts, and offered themselves as missionaries.[11] In the same year, a number of laymen from the Congregational, Presbyterian, and Reformed Churches organized the A.B.C.F.M. to recruit and support missionaries for overseas work.[12]

While maintaining its fraternal relationship with the A.B.C.F.M., in 1817 the Reformed Church also joined with the Presbyterian Church and the Associate Reformed Church to form the United Foreign Missionary Society. The following year, 1818, the State of the Churches report of General Synod noted that "missionary zeal, hitherto so languid, is beginning to revive."[13] And in 1820, the General Synod sent a pastoral letter to the churches noting that "Christ's Standard" had been planted "in China, in India, in different parts of Africa, in the wilds of America, and in the islands of the sea."[14] One of those planting "Christ's Standard" overseas was Doctor John Scudder, who with several other missionaries of the A.B.C.F.M. had left for Ceylon in 1819. Scudder was ordained to the Christian ministry soon after his arrival, and combined an effective evangelistic preaching and teaching ministry with his practice of medicine. In 1838 the American Board transferred the Scudders to India, with headquarters in Madras. The first American Dutch Reformed missionary worked in that region for an additional eighteen years.[15]

In 1832 the Reformed Church established its first Board of Foreign Missions to complement its Board of Domestic Missions, organized the same year.[16] In addition, however, the General Synod negotiated a Plan of Cooperation with the A.B.C.F.M. For the most part this plan was nothing new, for individual missionaries of the Reformed Church had been sent out by the American Board before 1832, and Reformed Church members had also served on its governing council since its founding in 1810. The new factor was the formal relationship of the Reformed Church to the Board. The arrangement allowed the Church to plant its distinct mission or missions in a given region, "with an ecclesiastical organization and public worship according to [its] own view and wishes."[17] In addition, the denomination agreed to financially support the work of its own missionaries sent out by the A.B.C.F.M. The American Board, in turn, determined the region for mission work and also commissioned and supported the missionary. The Reformed

Church maintained its formal relationship with the A.B.C.F.M. for twenty five years, from 1832 to 1857. During that period, therefore, the foreign mission program of the denomination was in large measure managed by an ecumenical board.

In addition to India, the Reformed Church also began mission programs in two other areas during its long association with the A.B.C.F.M. One of these areas was the Dutch East Indies (now Indonesia). In 1829-1830, David Abeel was commissioned to that region by the Seamen's Friend Society and the A.B.C.F.M. Abeel not only convinced the Reformed Church to support work in that area, but in 1836 he also challenged four New Brunswick Seminary graduates to labor with him in that field.[18]

The Reformed Church entered this region assuming that the Netherlands Government would give its support to this mission venture. Quite the opposite happened, however. Before long clergy from the Netherlands Reformed Church in Indonesia were reporting that the American Reformed missionaries were "political intriguers" and "agents of their government," arousing the suspicion of the Dutch Government.[19] The Netherlands officials no doubt determined that the United States Government would follow the American missionaries into the East Indies, not realizing that the ties between American churches and their government were less intimate than their own. In any case, the Dutch government sufficiently discouraged the American Reformed missionaries, and they soon departed from Indonesia for mainland China.

Thus China became the other great area of interest for the Reformed Church during its connection with the A.B.C.F.M. Abeel went to Amoy, situated on the southeast coast of China, in 1842, soon after the conclusion of the Opium War when Britain opened a number of Chinese ports to Western influence. The events surrounding Abeel's first years in China were packed with sacrifice, excitement, and close bouts with death. In addition, he was racked with physical pain during these years and would not have been faulted had he returned home. His millennial vision, however, "to preach the everlasting Gospel to all nations, and tongues, and kindred, and people in the earth," kept him in the field.[20] Abeel's life, like the other pioneering missionaries sent out by the Reformed Church, reflects the commitment of the denomination to the cause of foreign missions in this early period.

Under Abeel's leadership, the Amoy region soon became the

center of operations for both the Reformed and the English Presbyterian Churches, who worked cooperatively in this enterprise. Abeel left China in 1846, and was followed by John Van Nest Talmage, who arrived in Amoy in 1847 and remained there for the next forty five years.[21] Talmage was instrumental in the preparation of an important Chinese dictionary, in Romanizing the colloquial language of the area, and in Bible translation. He was also greatly involved in the preparation of Chinese small print movable type. One of his interesting letters to the A.B.C.F.M. included an extensive discussion of the proper translation into Chinese of the words "God" and "Spirit."[22]

Beginning in 1857, and for the first time in its history, the Reformed Church assumed full responsibility for its foreign mission program. The Board of Foreign Missions had proposed the action the previous year, when it recommended that the denomination sever its relationship with the American Board and "conduct [its] Foreign Mission in an independent manner."[23] Interestingly, this decision was consistent with the mood of other evangelical Churches in America at that time. A cultural explanation for this can be found in the prevailing nationalism of the Republic during this period. The ecclesiastical response to a strong national union became the self-conscious denomination, determined to recover and maintain its distinctive witness. The mood was anticipated in the Reformed Church several years earlier when it broke off union discussions with the German Reformed Church on doctrinal issues.[24]

There was, however, a more practical reason for the recommendation of the Board of Foreign Missions. It hoped that such action would increase the denomination's support for its mission program which, in the mid-1850's, seemed plagued by "an apathy too strong to be overcome."[25] This "apathy" was reflected in the denomination's giving for foreign missions; its forty thousand communicants contributed only thirteen thousand dollars annually in the mid-1850's, less than one cent a week per member. In addition, the Board of Foreign Missions believed that the action would guarantee greater supervision of the denomination's mission enterprise. Significantly, however, there was nothing in this proposal that showed dissatisfaction with the activities of the A.B.C.F.M. Indeed, the resolution stated that

the intimate relation which has existed for a quarter century between the Reformed . . . Church and the A.B.C.F.M. . . . has confirmed our confidence in the wisdom, integrity, and the catholic spirit of that great and noble institution; nor shall we ever cease to feel a lively interest in the growth of its operations and the success of its plans.[26]

In 1857 the General Synod approved the recommendation of the Board of Foreign Missions, thereby terminating its relationship with the American Board. In the same action the General Synod created a new Board of Foreign Missions, with full responsibility for the denomination's overseas mission program. Subsequently, the A.B.C.F.M. transferred to the new Mission Board the property holdings of the Arcot and Amoy mission stations.[27]

Beginning in 1857 there have been a number of conflicts in the evolving history of the denomination's foreign mission program, where profoundly important differences emerged between the American "mother" Church and its overseas missions and missionaries. For the most part these situations have been creative, resulting in greater understanding of the meaning of mission and the nature of the Church for each age. In the American Church, this has generally resulted in a movement from extreme parochialism, where the denomination understood its task as planting foreign branches of the Reformed Church in overseas stations, to a theologically based ecumenism, where the denomination understood itself as a partner in Christ with the overseas Churches. The first of these conflicts erupted in 1857 between the newly created Board of Foreign Missions and the Amoy mission.

By 1857 the Amoy station comprised six churches, three organized by Reformed Church missionaries and three established by English Presbyterian missionaries. None of these churches, however, was formally organized under the care of its "mother" Church. Rather, the six churches formed an indigenous association, in effect a quasi-classis or presbytery, and asserted their right to ordain and discipline. The missionaries in Amoy, particularly Talmage, were satisfied that this was both a biblical and practical direction for mission churches to follow, and worked to implement the plan.[28]

The Board of Foreign Missions thought otherwise, however, claiming that the situation raised two fundamental issues: the nature of the Church, and the obligation of ordained missionaries to their Church. The board argued that by definition the Amoy congregations were not "true" churches because they were not properly organized under the government of an established denomination. It claimed that both the government of the Reformed Church, which was "instituted under . . . the Great Head of the Church," and the Gospel it preached, were part of one "evangelical system of truth." Therefore, both Gospel and government were required, "the one with the other," before a "true" church could be formed.[29] The General Synod agreed with the board's interpretation of the problem and, in 1857, passed two resolutions:

1. That the Synod view with great pleasure the formation of Chruches among the converts from heathenism, organized according to the established usages of our branch of Zion.
2. That the brethren at Amoy be directed to apply to the Particular Synod of Albany to organize them into a Classis so soon as they shall have formed Churches enough to render the permanency of such organization resonably certain.[30]

The Amoy churches refused to consent to the Synod's resolutions, however, and determined to retain their quasi-independence as a "true" Church. In subsequent years, from 1857 to 1863, numerous letters and resolutions from both Amoy and New York crossed the ocean, each side asserting its own position while at the same time searching for a compromise that might ameliorate the situation. The issue was finally resolved in 1864, when all of the Amoy missionaries threatened to resign if forced to capitulate to the board's policy. The same year, 1864, the General Synod rescinded its 1857 resolution in favor of the position of the Amoy missionaries.[31] This action moved the denomination toward greater cooperation in its overseas mission enterprise.

The Board of Foreign Missions began work in two new overseas areas during the last half of the nineteenth century. One of these new fields was started in Japan in 1859. In that year the Reverend and Mrs. Guido Verbeck began a ministry in Nagasaki and both the Reverend and Mrs. Samual R. Brown and a physician, Duane Simmons, started work in Yokohama, beginning in 1861. These were followed by the Reverend and Mrs. James Ballah who also worked in Yokohama, beginning in 1861. The efforts of these missionaries was made hazardous because the Japanese government forbid its peoples acceptance of Christianity, imposing harsh penalties on those who disobeyed. In addition, the missionaries were not familiar with either the language or the culture of the Japanese, making evangelistic work especially difficult. After several years of language study, however, the missionaries became sufficiently fluent to begin Bible translations. They also began holding Bible studies in their homes. The first known Protestant converts to Christianity in the history of Japan were won by Reformed Church missionaries, and these converts were baptized by Ballah and Verbeck in 1864. Verbeck was also instrumental in developing the organizational and institutional life of the new Church in Japan. When the first congregation was established in 1872, the members chose the name, "The Church of Christ in Japan." Five years later, in 1877, the three Reformed and Presbyterian churches from Britain and America at work in Japan united their efforts into one organization.[32]

The second new mission field opened by the Reformed Church during this period was in Arabia, beginning in 1892. Interestingly, however, this mission outreach began without the permission or support of the Board of Foreign Missions. Under the inspiration of Professor John G. Lansing of New Brunswick Seminary, three young theological students felt called to establish a mission among the Muslims in Arabia. James Cantine, Samuel Zwemer, and Philip T. Phelps frequently met with Professor Lansing in "Abraham's Bosom," the upper section of Hertzog Hall at the seminary; and, at one of the meetings they decided to petition the Board of Foreign Missions to send them to Arabia. The plan they prepared was submitted to the General Synod in 1889, but because the Board of Foreign Missions was thirty five thousand dollars in debt at that time the Synod and the Board rejected the proposal. This did not stop the determined young theologs, however, and by 1891 they had formed an independent mission organization and raised a good deal of money. As a result, by 1892 both Cantine and Zwemer were at work in Arabia.[33]

In 1894 the Reformed Church officially adopted the Arabian Mission, and thereafter gave it substantial support. Schools and hospitals were established, and many of the finest missionaries of the Reformed Church served in the Arabian field. Zwemer became a world-famous leader in the missionary movement, and the story of the "desert doctor," Paul Harrison, who worked in Arabia from 1909 to 1954, had an impact far beyond the bounds of the Reformed Church. Although few converts from Islam were made, the success of the mission in medicine and education was very substantial.

During this period, roughly 1857 to 1900, the Board of Foreign Missions was consistently in need of funds to support the denomination's mission program. This was particularly true in the years following the Civil War, when the nation's economy caused a near-panic among the American people. This point was well noted by a Reformed Church pastor writing on this topic a century ago: "For the last ten years we have fought to hold our own against fluctuating rates of exchange, which have reached, at times, a fearful height." He paid tribute to the Board of Foreign Missions, however, for its modest administrative costs, noting that only seven and one-half percent of all money raised was used for administration. But he lamented that the number of missionaries overseas remained steady or declined since the separation from the American Board. He concluded with an appeal for greater generosity on the part of the Church for world missions.[34]

The Women's Board of Foreign Missions was organized in 1875 as a direct result of the denomination's sagging efforts in the world mission enterprise following the Civil War. Until this time the role of women in the leadership of the Church had been almost non-existent. Women were allowed to accompany their husbands to foreign fields, and several single women were sent abroad, but only as "assistant missionaries"; their role was strictly limited, even though their functions might be extensive. Women did not serve in any official capacity in the Church, however, either on the local or the national level. Thus it was a major moment in Reformed Church history when the General Synod allowed the women of the denomination to organize and administer their own "foreign board," even if its role was "auxiliary" to the denomination's Board of Foreign Missions.

This new Women's Board proved to be eminently successful. It quickly established numerous mission societies across the denomination, urging these organizations to support the mission programs of the Reformed Church. As a result, between 1875 and 1900 the Women's Board raised nearly one half million dollars. This total increased substantially during subsequent years, and in the decade before the Great Depression in 1929 the Women's Board raised nearly a quarter million dollars annually for the overseas work of the Church. By the early 1940's the women collected nearly half of all the funds available to the Foreign Board. Partly as a result of this, the General Synod moved to merge the two Foreign Boards in 1946.[35] Until that union, no woman had served as a member of the Board of Foreign Missions. Miss Ruth Ransom, the Secretary of the Women's Board at that time, became the first woman executive of the denomination's Foreign Board in 1946.

Since 1864, following the decision regarding the Amoy mission, the Reformed Church has maintained a "pioneering leadership in missionary ecumenism."[36] One result of this has been that many of the missionaries of the Reformed Church have been very influential in world Christianity. Ida Scudder in India, Samuel Zwemer and Paul Harrison in Arabia, John Talmage in China, and Luman Shafer in Japan were certainly among the most prominent. But perhaps no one had a greater ecumenical role than A. Livingston Warshuis. After graduating from New Brunswick Seminary in 1900, Warnshuis went to China as a Reformed Church missionary. According to the famous Chinese philosopher Lin Yutang, Warnshuis was one of the most able foreign missionaries ever to serve in China, and it was China's misfortune that such an able person was removed from basic missionary service to other spheres of leadership. Following his years of work in Amoy, the great mission leader, John R. Mott, named Warnshuis executive secretary for the China Continuation Committee, a position he held from 1914 to 1920. His task as secretary was to promote evangelistic outreach for all Christian churches and missions in China, and also to further the movement toward Christian unity. Warnshuis helped to promote the union of three missions in South Fukien which, in 1919, resulted in the Synod of South Fukien, and led in 1922 to the First Assembly of the Church of Christ in China.

In 1910 the World Missionary Conference was held in Edinburgh, in large part through the work of John R. Mott and John H. Oldham of Britain. It was the first substantial effort at bringing some kind of communication, coordination and planning to the work of the foreign missionary boards and societies of the Churches of America and Europe. The Continuation Committee in China, which Warnshuis served, was one of several committees established in various parts of the world to follow up the intentions and decisions of the Edinburgh Conference. A further result of the Edinburgh conference was the establishment in 1920 of the International Missionary Council (IMC). Warnshuis, together with Mott and Oldham, comprised the triumvirate that launched this new organization.

Warnshuis was situated in London from 1921 to 1924, and

from then until his retirement in 1942 he headed the New York Office of the IMC. Among his many responsibilities were preparation for and leadership in the meetings of the IMC at Jerusalem in 1928 and at Madras in 1938. He did much to further good relations between the American mission boards and missionaries and those of Britain and the Continent. In a time of theological confusion, Warnshuis stood firmly for the Biblical Gospel and thus was better understood by the Europeans than were some Americans more closely identified with the Social Gospel.

Two of Warnshuis' most important contributions to world Christianity came near the end of his career. One was his concern for "orphaned missions," those overseas efforts of British, Dutch, German, and Scandinavian Churches which could no longer be aided by their home base because of World War II. Through the IMC, Warnshuis helped to raise more than eight million dollars to assist these orphaned missions, over eighty percent of which was given by the American Churches. His other contribution was his leadership in helping to establish Church World Service, the relief arm of the Churches which did so much to help the needy in Europe immediately after World War II, and which continues today to help people wherever famine and other disasters strike. Warnshuis was not only a Christian ambassador, as Norman Goodall called him; he was one of the ecumenical pioneers of the world missionary movement shared with the rest of the Christian community by the Reformed Church in America.[37]

Another result of the denomination's "pioneering leadership in missionary ecumenism" has been its historical involvement in cooperative mission programs in each of its overseas stations. The unification of Reformed and Presbyterian work in China, first in Amoy and then in the South Fukien United Synod, has already been noted.[38] The South Fukien Synod became a part of the United Church of Christ in China. As a result of the Chinese Revolution in 1949, however, all Western missionaries were forced to withdraw, and the Church of Christ in China, insofar as it still exists, has little contact with the Churches formerly related to it. The Reformed Church missionaries in China were transferred to work with overseas Chinese in cooperative programs in Singapore, Hong Kong, Taiwan, and the Phillippines.

In Japan, the Reformed and Presbyterian missions worked

together for a united indigenous Church almost from the start. In 1876 the Reformed Church, together with the American and Scottish Presbyterians, organized the Union Church of Christ in Japan. Later, other Protestant groups affiliated, but it was not until 1940 that the Church of Christ in Japan (Kyodan) came into being. Under strong pressure from the Japanese government forty two denominations entered the union; those who refused had their organizational life disrupted. At the close of the War the Nazarenes, Anglicans, and Lutherans again withdrew, but most of the other bodies remained together in the United Church.[39]

The Church in South India developed in a more comprehensive direction than that of China or Japan. Jacob Chamberlain, a Reformed Church missionary in India, was a pioneer worker for Reformed-Presbyterian cooperation. Union of the Presbyterian Churches in India was discussed as early as the 1860's, and in 1875 the Arcot Classis of the Reformed Church, which had been formed in 1854, became a part of the Presbyterian Alliance in India. Subsequently, the Arcot Classis invited the Free Church of Scotland and the Church of Scotland to consider merger with it. And, in 1902 the Free Church and the Reformed Church united to form the Synod of South India, with Chamberlain as the first moderator. The final report of the Classis of Arcot to the General Synod of the Reformed Church, submitted in 1902, reported a membership of nearly two thousand four hundred families.

In 1908, the British and American Congregational missions joined this new Synod to form the South India United Church with a communicant strength of twenty four thousand. A decade later, in 1919, this United Church began an historic discussion with the Methodists and, for the first time, the Anglicans, pointing towards a comprehensive united Church to include those communions. The discussions and negotiations were long and involved, and were delayed because of World War II. Finally, in 1947, the year of India's independence from Great Britain, the United Church of South India was formed, the first in the world to include both episcopal and non-episcopal Churches. The membership of the United Church was about one million in 1947, and negotiations with other groups, including the Lutherans, continue to take place.[40]

One final overseas area where the Reformed Church began a cooperative venture with another denomination was in Africa.

This new work started in 1947 among the Anuaks in the Upper Nile region near the Ethiopian-Sudanese border. By 1956 the "Church of Christ" was established in that region, comprising a union of churches organized by Reformed and United Presbyterian Church missionaries. This young united Church continues to be supported by both of these American bodies.[41]

The history of the denomination's mission program, therefore, supports the thesis that the Reformed Church has maintained "a pioneering leadership in missionary ecumenism." Many of the denomination's missionaries have become renown in world Christianity. And the Church has consistently cooperated with other denominations in every overseas field it has entered. This ecumenical interest, however, should not be viewed as the exclusive focus of the Reformed Church in its world mission enterprise. The highly skilled and often heroic work of the denomination's missionaries in education, medicine, agriculture, translation, literacy, food relief, and evangelism, represents a story deserving the highest praise, and could equally have been the emphasis of this part of the essay. Historically, however, ecumenism has provided an important theological framework for the denomination's missionaries, who have worked cooperatively in non-Christian cultures in order to manifest the unity of Christ's Church.

Out of this process, moreover, the Reformed Church was challenged to reexamine both its theology of mission and its purpose in sending missionaries overseas. By the twentieth century, neither the millennialism of Livingston nor the American "mother"-foreign "daughter" polarity seemed adequate. In addition, increased secularization forced the Church to ask what was constitutive of mission work. And the advent of new and independent Churches overseas begged questions concerning the relationship between those communions, the missionaries who served in those Churches, and the Reformed Church. A significant decrease in both the denomination's missionary personnel and its giving for mission made such questions particularly urgent in the first quarter of the twentieth century.

As a result, in the 1930's the Board of Foreign Missions participated in an intensive reexamination of its world mission program with the Laymen's Inquiry into Foreign Missions. Funded by John D. Rockefeller, Jr., this study was sponsored by the mission boards of seven denominations: Baptist, Congregational, Reformed, Presbyterian, United Presbyterian, Methodist Episcopal, and Protestant Episcopal. Professor William Ernest Hocking of Harvard was the chairman of the committee. Among the useful recommendations made in the report were greater use of nationals in the leadership of younger churches, and a unified administration in the United States of the mission boards. F. M. Potter, an executive of the Reformed Church Board of Foreign Missions, supported these recommendations.

The Laymen's Inquiry report as a whole was severely criticized, however, because of certain emphases and presuppositions which were contrary to the prevailing convictions of the sponsoring Churches and boards. The report, for example, called for a greater appreciation of Asian religions, and an alliance of all of the great religions against the forces of secularism and materialism. Professor Hocking's chapter stressing the uniqueness of Christianity was harshly criticized because it seemed to neglect the redemptive factor. The same was true of the chapter by Rufus Jones on the scope of mission, which praised educational and medical mission as evangelism in and of itself, but not as a *means* of proselytising.[42] A copy of the Report was sent to each missionary serving under the Reformed Church, most of whom rejected it.

By the mid-point of the twentieth century, however, the Reformed Church did reach some conclusions concerning its relationship with overseas Churches. These were articulated in 1953 by Barnerd M. Luben, an executive of the Board of Foreign Missions. Addressing an audience at the Arcot mission, which was celebrating its centennial in that year, Luben spoke about relationships, not between the Reformed Church in America and the Arcot Mission, nor between the Arcot Mission and the Church of South India, but between the Reformed Church in America and the Church of South India. "As a denomination," Luben said, "we are entirely out of sympathy with the notion that we have so distinct a witness and so pure a faith, and other communions so lacking in such faith and witness, that to cooperate with them would seriously compromise our faith.... " And again, "in no country are we attempting to build 'The Reformed Church in America.' We will have no part in ecclesiastical colonialism. It is our aim to direct all efforts toward the establishing of a free, self-respecting 'Church of Christ' in the several countries." The focal point of all correct relationships, he concluded, comes down to this:

"the Church of South India is recognized by the Reformed Church in America as a sister communion, a free and independent Church in a free and independent nation."[43] When contrasted with the denomination's attitudes a century earlier, Luben's remarks represented a dramatic shift in the mission theology of the Reformed Church.

Beginning in the 1960's the General Synod made several changes within the Board of Foreign Missions, intended to reflect the denomination's "reformed" mission attitude in that decade. For example, the Foreign Board was renamed as the Board of World Missions, giving substance to the belief that sister Churches overseas were equal partners in mission. In addition, the overseas Churches became initiators in the recruitment of missionaries. As a result, less stress was placed on recruiting career missionaries, and more emphasis on short-term and special-talent ministries needed by overseas Churches. And the Board increasingly emphasized the importance of ministering to the whole person through educational, medical, agricultural, technical, and social forms of activity as well as through the preaching and teaching of the Gospel. Finally, in 1968 the General Synod placed the Board of World Missions, together with the Board of North American Missions and the Board of Education under the denomination's newly created General Program Council. Modelled on the corporate structure, this new organization symbolized that the mission of the Church in the world is one, wherever and however it is being presented in the name of Christ.

During the 1960's and early 1970's, moreover, there was a sharp decline in the number of overseas missionaries supported by the Reformed Church; between 1955 and 1975 the number decreased from one hundred sixty to eighty.[44] Several factors caused this situation. The prolonged war in Southeast Asia caused a serious economic situation in the nation, particularly among middle-class Americans. As a result, the denomination's giving for missions decreased substantially in this period. In addition, the nation's inability to resolve its racial problems made white American missionaries unaccepted in some nonwhite cultures. And an increased secularism in America during the 1960's, resulting in a questioning of all the established structures of Christendom, affected the missionary spirit of the Church. Finally the emergent nationalism in a number of overseas countries, together with a heightened maturity of the

Churches in those countries, caused some leaders in those Churches to bluntly urge a hiatus in all American missionary efforts.

Such was the advice, for example, of the Reverend John Gatu, General Secretary of the Presbyterian Church of East Africa, who spoke at a Mission Festival sponsored by the Reformed Church at Milwaukee, Wisconsin, in 1971. Speaking on the topic, "Missionary Go Home," Gatu criticized Western missionaries for importing American values, for their assumption that the American way of life was superior to Third World nations, for their arrogance in directing and controlling the life of Third World Churches, and for using money as a "carrot" to exercise that control. For these reasons Gatu proposed an indefinite withdrawal of missionaries, and a moratorium against their return.[45]

Gatu's remarks received a mixed response within the Reformed Church. Nor does it appear that his comments represented the thinking of the majority of overseas Church leaders. But his poignant message, together with the issues referred to above—the decrease in missionary giving, the declining number of missionaries, the stigma of racism in America, secularization, overseas nationalism, increased maturity of overseas Churches— did move some within the denomination to again reexamine the Church's theology of mission. Anticipating this reexamination, in 1970 Professor John Piet of Western Theological Seminary wrote *The Road Ahead*, which is the denomination's most promising study on the subject.[46]

As the overseas mission program of the Reformed Church moves on "the road ahead" into the third century of the nation's life, there is much on the road it has already travelled of which it can rightfully be proud. The denomination was a pioneering missionary Church in American religious history, and was the first to plant Protestant Christianity in several countries around the world. In addition, it was among the first Churches in America to recruit and send medical and educational missionaries into Third World regions. With strong financial support from the Reformed Church, these missionaries established hospitals and schools which are still among the finest in those countries. The Reformed Church also pioneered in agricultural and linguistic missionary work, substantially improving both the food production and the literacy of Third World people. Finally, from the start the Reformed Church was a leader in overseas ecumenism, cooperating with other Christian bodies around the world in enlarging the Church of Christ.

What shape the denomination's theology of mission will take on "the road ahead" into the twenty first century is an open question. Surely the experience gained on the "road" to the present will be instructive for what is "ahead." But other factors must also be considered: the impact of the technological revolution on world consciousness, the devastating problems of over population and world hunger, energy and food consumption, the disparity between the rich and poor nations, the meaning for the Church of the term "global village," the emergence of Third World nations as world powers, the declining image of the United States in world affairs, an increasing acceptance of other world religions in America and other places, the awesome possibilities of nuclear disaster. In short, the theology of mission that will carry the Reformed Church on "the road ahead" in the next century should include studied consideration of the meaning and message of Jesus Christ in the new world situation. In this travel the previous history and dynamic of the Reformed Church in mission can provide a helpful map.

Theology

Eugene Heideman

The central theological strands in the history of the Reformed Church in America have been woven by a church determined to hold together two orientations. On the one hand, the church has insisted that the Church of The Netherlands correctly interpreted the Scriptures when it accepted the Heidelberg Catechism, the Belgic Confession, and the Canons of Dort as "Standards of Unity." On the other hand, in accepting the doctrine that God rules over all, it has been confronted with the problem of how to live under the sovereignty of God in America.[1] Despite the fact that many have asserted that "patriotism and piety are thus blended together,"[2] the two orientations have never completely coalesced; they often have resulted in considerable tension, as this essay will attempt to make clear.

The Dutch who came to New Amsterdam in 1624 and thereafter were theologically related to the Puritans who settled in Massachusetts. Not only had there been English representatives at the Synod of Dort in 1618-19, but the Dutch and English Puritan theologians mutually influenced each other during the 17th century.[3] In both colonies, it was expected that, under the sovereignty of God, not only were individuals to experience their faith, but the new settlement as a whole was to be a community under God. While maintaining a clear distinction between Church and State, in New Amsterdam it was an article of order that "it is the duty of Christian Magistrates to countenance the worship of God, to recommend religion by their example, and protect the members of the community in the full and regular exercise of religious liberty. . . ."[4] Until 1664, the Reformed religion was the established faith in New Amsterdam, with governors enforcing its provisions while pastors faithfully preached the Word.[5] During this first period, the settlers experienced little tension between the theology of Dort and their attempt to live the faith in New Amsterdam.

With the coming of the English in 1664, the situation changed. Politically, the Reformed religion lived precariously as the English governors began to press for the establishment of

the Church of England after 1674. The Dutch Reformed managed to maintain their rights to worship according to the treaty
of 1664, but unlike their Massachusetts counterparts, they were
not expected to take responsibility for the morality or life of
the colony as a whole; those matters now were in the hands of
the English. Ecclesiastically, the Dutch Reformed, in emphasizing the provisions of 1664 also committed themselves to
maintaining their ties with the Classis of Amsterdam in The
Netherlands. In the eighteenth century, when many believed it
to be expedient to allow ministers to be ordained in the New
World in order to avoid the long ocean voyage to Amsterdam,
this connection with the Classis was to be the occasion of a
stormy conflict.[6] From a long-range point of view, however, the
fact that all agreed on maintaining the jurisdiction of the Classis
of Amsterdam was decisive in affirming that the Dutch Reformed desired to locate their theological and cultural identity
in the tradition of Dort rather than with the English. Moreover,
because the New World church was eager to convince the Classis
of Amsterdam of its mature orthodoxy during the Conferentie-
Coetus conflict, the ecclesiastical combined with the political
factor to place a decidedly conservative theological stamp upon
the church.

By 1792, two men, Theodorus J. Frelinghuysen and John H.
Livingston, had in decisive ways shown the way for the Dutch
Reformed to remain true to their traditions while participating
in the life of the New World. Both had studied at Utrecht, the
center of Dutch Voetian experiential theology; each was profoundly influenced by the warm personal tone and theological
content of the Heidelberg Catechism.

Frelinghuysen arrived in New York from the Netherlands in
1720 and served until 1741/2 in the Raritan valley of New
Jersey. While formally accepting the orthodox theological
stance of Dort, in his preaching and pastoral activity he placed
the new birth and sanctification of the believer at the center.
Believing that true faith demands experiential knowledge, he
attacked all formalism and called for the individual to surrender
himself to God and his service.[7] In spite of initial opposition to
his work, Frelinghuysen's emphasis upon the conversion and
piety of the individual became a permanent fixture in the
theology of his denomination as well as in the whole revival
tradition in America.

Livingston (1746-1825) led the Dutch Church into its role as a participant in the building of a new country while remaining faithful to its theological heritage. His theological legacy can be summarized in three general areas. First, he continued the emphasis of Frelinghuysen and others on the personal experience of the faith. In his report of his conversion, he points up two doctrines which became central for him and which have continued to occupy that role in the theology of the Reformed Church—the one being the divinity of the Lord Jesus Christ, and the other being justification by faith. In pointing up these two, he also indicated the central role of Scriptures, emphasizing that for a period of several months he consulted no book but the Bible. In his emphasis upon the experimental knowledge of the Triune God implanted in the soul, Livingston set the Reformed Church's theological studies, including the formal training for the ministry at the seminaries, within the arena of faith and pastoral work rather than of philosophical speculation.[8]

Livingston's second contribution was an emphasis on the unity of the Church. He was responsible for bringing to an end the Conferentie-Coetus controversy and was the primary author of the "Explanatory Articles, 1792," which enabled his denomination to work independently of the Classis of Amsterdam. An examination of the "Explanatory Articles" shows their author to have a firm grasp of presbyterian principles of church government, with an emphasis upon an educated ministry, careful statement of doctrine, and clear delineation of authority and responsibility.

It was Livingston's third great contribution which pointed the Reformed Church in a new theological direction as a basis for its full participation in American society, as well as in the foreign missionary movement. In a sermon preached before the New York Missionary Society in 1804, he stated that the millennial period was drawing near, with a distinct possibility that the fall of "great Babylon" would be immediately before the year 2000. Before that event, this world will see the signs of its approach, namely the punishment of the nations who aided anti-christ in murdering the servants of God, the conversion of the Jews, the gathering of the gentiles into the church, and the destruction of the anti-christ (i.e. the Pope at Rome). The magnitude of the event arrests our attention.

In the physical order of things the event is possible; agreeably to the moral system it can be effected; and devoutly to be wished. When all nations receive the Gospel, and become real Christians; when men of every rank, 'from the least to the greatest, shall know the Lord', and devote themselves to their redeemer, than all will be happy. Individuals will be happy, society will be happy, and peace, joy and holiness prevail throughout the whole earth.[9]

The sermon concluded with the conviction that in clearly preaching the gospel the Church was participating in the events leading up to the millennial period.[10] He included the thought that America was the place with the most favorable conditions for vigorous missionary endeavors as well as efforts of charity.

By the beginning of the nineteenth century, the Reformed Church had made a theological transition from Dort to the United States of America. Every minister in the Reformed Church signed the formula of adherence to the Standards of Unity as affirmed by Dort. Subtle adjustments had been made to account for American conditions.[11] With Frelinghuysen the experienced faith of the Heidelberg Catechism rather than the doctrine of election as stated in the Canons of Dort was at center stage. Through Livingston, the Reformed Church recognized that God's sovereign will in public life was not exercised so much through a Christian magistrate as through the preaching of the gospel in this period before the millennium.

The Theology of Dort in Nineteenth Century America

The Belgic Confession and the Church Order of Dort had stated the doctrine that the church is independent from the state in its government, while limited to the exercise of ecclesiastical rather than political authority. In its "Preface to the Entire Constitution, 1792," the Reformed Church accepted the American Puritan principle of voluntary membership.

In consequence of that liberty wherewith Christ has made his people free, it becomes their duty as well as privilege, openly to confess and worship him according to the dictates of their own consciences. . . . Wherever such explanation constitute a bond of union wholly voluntary. . . . The unerring Word of God remaining the only standard of the Faith and Worship of his people, they can never incur the charge of presumption, in openly declaring what to them appears to be the mind and will of their divine Lord and Savior.

The Church is a Society, wholly distinct in its principles, laws and end, from any which men have ever instituted for civil purposes. It consists of all, in every age and place, who are chosen, effectually called, and united by faith to the Lord Jesus Christ.[12]

The "Preface" was apparently accepted without debate and has remained unchallenged as a fundamental principle of Reformed Church faith and life. Yet its effect upon the theological stance of the denomination has become ever more important. It forms the milieu in which the theological decisions since have been made; it is a decisive American element in the doctrine of the church which introduces tensions into the theology of Dort. Among the issues raised would be the doctrines of election and limited atonement, the church and the sacraments, especially infant baptism, and the nature of the ministry.

During the first three decades of the nineteenth century, the acceptance into its theology of the denominational voluntary church structure opened the door to full participation in the great mission of the Church in America, while providing just enough distance from others to allow continued loyalty to Dort. The Dutch Reformed participated in the coming of the Kingdom of God by joining the inter-denominational voluntary societies organized to promote missions, the Bible cause, morality and Sabbath observance, African Colonization, etc.[13]

Yet some feared that Dort was being neglected. Interest in cooperation with other denominations in the cause of missions and revivals was particularly strong in the Albany area. Evangelists in America, often embarrassed by the doctrine of election and limited atonement when calling upon sinners to repent, had received theological encouragement from Samuel Hopkins (1721-1803) a congregationalist theologian. Although Hopkins himself remained within the realm of Reformed orthodoxy while modifying the doctrine of the imputation of Adam's guilt, his followers were less careful.[14] In 1818-19, the consistory of the Church of Owasco, New York, appealed to the Classis of Montgomery to investigate the charge that the Reverend Conrad Ten Eyck "did not believe that Christ had atoned for any man . . . but for sin." Eventually the matter reached the General Synod.

At the meeting of the General Synod in October, 1820, Mr. Ten Eyck answered six questions posed by the Synod's committee. Three of the answers being deemed unsatisfactory, Ten Eyck made additional clarifications, the key statement being:

In answer to the second question, I did not mean to convey the idea that Christ died for sin in the abstract, but that the evil nature of sin rendered an atonement indispensably necessary, and that without such an atonement, it was impossible for God to extend mercy, even to the elect. By the words, he obeyed in the room and stead of his people, I meant and do mean to convey the idea of substitution; which doctrine I fully believe.

This statement satisfied the Synod, which proceeded to approve the stance of Ten Eyck while disapproving his "former opinions on the doctrine of atonement." That Ten Eyck's "former opinions" may have enjoyed support from others at the Synod is clear from the further resolution that

Whereas, it has been repeatedly alleged, on the floor of this Synod, that some of its members have denied the infinite value and suffering of the death of Jesus Christ, to expiate the sins of the whole world. . . .

Therefore the Synod resolved that

the Word of God and the standards of this church teach us, that the Lord Jesus Christ died as an atoning sacrifice, only for those whom the Father has given him; for whom in the divine love and wisdom, he became the substituted victim.[15]

The Synod had decided, but the issue was not closed. In 1822, a small number of dissenters left to form the "True Dutch Reformed Church in the United States of America," believing that the Synod had been too lenient. In 1830-31 the issue again arose when *The Christian Intelligencer* charged the Reverend John F. Schermerhorn, Synodical Missionary, with "Hopkinsian" leanings.[16] The doctrine of the atonement continued for decades to be a focal point of exposition and discussion.[17]

The Ten Eyck dispute not only virtually foreclosed any chance of cooperation or union with any denomination suspected of tolerating "Hopkinsianism," but it also made the leadership of the Reformed Church much more concerned about theological purity, with the result that the denomination forfeited its opportunity to expand its influence westward.[18]

A further effect of the dispute, however, was to chart a course for the Reformed Church in matters of theological controversy. On the one hand, by re-affirming the theology of Dort, the Reformed Church maintained its heritage. On the other hand, by being more quickly satisfied with the answers of Ten Eyck than full theological precision may have demanded, the Reformed Church allowed for more local and individual interpretation than some of the "orthodox" wanted to give. As a result of this moderate stance, the Reformed Church has not experienced the fierce theological controversies or schisms which have rent certain other Reformed and Presbyterian bodies.[19]

American revivalism presented another challenge to the theology of Dort in the early nineteenth century with the arrival first of the Baptist and Methodist preachers and then with men such as Charles Finney, who used "means" such as the "anxious bench" and the "protracted meeting."[20] With the advent of Finney, revivals changed their character. The earliest revivals in the Reformed Churches, led by men such as Frelinghuysen, had been regarded as the outpouring of God's Spirit upon his elect people. That outpouring came in God's own time as a by-product of faithful preaching. The later revivals, consciously using evangelistic techniques, came to be regarded as "the divine blessing upon measures conceived and executed by man."[21]

The Reformed Church met this challenge from full-blown Arminian revivalism without official controversy. Its long experience in Dutch experiential pietism and the traditions of Freylinghuysen,[22] as well as the chastening experience of 1822, guided the denomination's leadership to a clear position: the ministers of the denomination stood by Dort, while accepting the extraordinary work of the Spirit without promoting "enthusiasm" (i.e. emotionalism).[23] The editors of *The Christian Intelligencer* stated clearly:

With regard to doctrinal truths, and the principles of practical godliness, we, as a church, have settled landmarks, and rules by which we judge, but as it respects the measures by which to promote or cherish revivals we have none. Ministers, with the advice of their own counselors, must be left to their own discretion. If even in certain cases or congregations, certain measures might be inexpedient, it does not follow that they must be equally so in others. We must not confine the work of God within *ordinary* limits.[24]

This rule stated by the editor is reflected for the next century as the progress of local revivals and the Fulton Street Prayer Meeting are reported;[25] the General Synod takes the same attitude as it rejoices over and promotes the work of revivalism from year to year. The doctrines of Dort were maintained, but local ministers and consistories were left free to follow the leading of the Spirit of God.[26]

The foregoing discussion of the Ten Eyck case and revivalism has given two examples in which the Reformed Church was apparently willing to soften the doctrine of election as stated in the Canons of Dort, at a time when the Presbyterian Church was facing the possibility and then the actuality of division. Apart from the dominant personalities and cultural factors facing the two churches, one can find theological roots for the standpoint of the Synod which differed from those in the Presbyterian Church.

It is possible to locate the difference in the fact that the Westminster tradition had placed the statement on election in the doctrine of the decrees,[27] while the Belgic Confession and the Heidelberg Catechism had related election more closely to God's work in Christ.[28] Thus the Dutch tradition remained closer to Calvin who had located the discussion in Book III of the *Institutes* after the discussion of the work of Christ rather than in Book I where he discusses the doctrine of God.[29] The effect of the differing approaches is to allow the tradition of Dort to give more weight to God's sovereign work in the processes of history while the Westminster tradition places the weight on the sovereign decision of God before the foundation of the world.[30] One must not overemphasize the distinction between the two traditions, for during the middle decades of the nineteenth century the leadership of the Reformed Church had great admiration for the theological views of the Francis-Turretin-Charles Hodge Old School thought. However, the fact that the great mediating theologian-historian in the Old School-New School controversy, Henry B. Smith, espoused a position closer to Calvin and Dort on election is a sign that the difference is important in the attitude of the church towards historical events.[31]

Where the revivalist movement had tempted the Reformed theology to "Americanize" in the 1840's there appeared a movement from the other side—the so-called "Mercersberg theology"—which asked whether the Reformed Churches in America had not already departed far from their true theological and liturgical roots. The leaders of the movement, John W. Nevin and Philip Schaff, were professors in the German Reformed Seminary at Mercersberg, Pennsylvania. Influenced by German romantic historians and theologians, Nevin reacted against both his Puritan origins and the enthusiasm and sectarianism of the revivalists. Together with the church historian Schaff, he developed a theology centered on the Incarnation and the Mystical Presence of Christ in the church, with a further emphasis upon more formal liturgical usages.[32]

In the 1840's the relationship between the Dutch and German Reformed Churches was close, with the Synods exchanging delegates and proposals for merger on the horizon. Nevertheless, there could scarcely have been a worse time chosen in which to consider the ideas proposed. It was the time of the beginning of the great Roman Catholic immigration to America; Reformed Churchmen stood in the vanguard of those who desired to maintain America as a fortress against "popery."[33] In 1844, *The Christian Intelligencer* opened the attack, objecting that the Mercersberg men held views of apostolic succession which were hierarchial and that they were guilty of "Puseyism" with affinity to popery. It also charged that Schaff placed an emphasis on the church and its sacraments in preference to personal, individual piety.[34] The Mercersberg theology had little immediate effect upon the theology of the Reformed Church, apart from the fact that it caused a breach in relationships. It may also have encouraged the Reformed Church in America to strengthen its defenses by aligning itself a little more with the theology of Charles Hodge, with whom Nevin had several debates through theological journals.[35]

Nevertheless, the Mercersberg theologians had raised issues which could not be easily thrust aside; among these the nature of the church, sacraments,[36] and liturgy were to be discussed again in the twentieth century. Perhaps even more important, however, was the fact that Nevin and Schaff introduced the theory of historical development into theological activity. Men like Joseph Berg and Charles Hodge, like almost all Protestant Americans of their day, used the church history of Mosheim, who conceived of Christian doctrine as a fixed and unalterable system. In their conception, orthodoxy was stable, a system of divinely revealed truth which could be mined from Scripture. If the theologian is expert enough, he would discover there God's perfect truth, complete and admitting of no improvement.[37] A reading of lectures in theology by the seminary professors of the Reformed Church in America in the nineteenth century reveals that, for them, like Berg and Hodge, "the past was an armory of theological tenets, and a man had a right to pick and choose as he would."[38]

Schaff pointed out that the modern historiography is distinguished from that of rationalism in two respects:

On the one hand, it is far more disposed to take the lives of other generations at their own valuation, to respect their individuality, and not to measure them so obviously by the standards of the historian's society. At the same time, the new history finds a principle of continuity and unity in the idea of the progress of humanity conceived as an organic development.[39]

On the basis of Schaff's theory of history, the Mercersberg men published detailed historical studies on the Reformed concept of the church, sacraments, and liturgy, as well as other doctrines, showing that the Reformed and Presbyterian churches had departed from the teachings of Calvin and even from the Heidelberg Catechism and the Belgic Confession.[40] The historical approach was a foretaste of the future, but for the moment the older methodology held its ground. In 1884, Samuel Woodbridge rejoiced that the American Church and especially New Brunswick Seminary still stood firmly within orthodoxy.[41]

The solid orthodoxy of the Reformed Church was attested in the 1850's by the arrival of Van Raalte and his followers in western Michigan. The new immigrants, spiritual descendents of seventeenth century Dutch pietists, felt a kinship with the Dutch Reformed in America and united to it.[42] The long-term effect of Van Raalte's followers was to reaffirm the tie with the orthodox Dutch tradition at a moment when the Dutch language was being lost in the older areas, as well as to reinforce the denomination's interest in personal and national piety and morality. They saw themselves as the followers of a new Joshua, a chosen people with a call from God to build a new Canaan to the glory of God.[43] The last half of the nineteenth century thus bears witness to a church secure in its inheritance from Dort, now living in harmony with its environment, building the kingdom in preparation for the millennium,[44] prepared even to consider a merger with other Protestant bodies.[45] Secure in its theology, the Reformed Church confidently went forward in the tasks of building up the flock, promoting missions, the Christian Sabbath, temperance, and moral uplift. The Board of Domestic Missions was confident that we are exerting an incalcuable influence upon the social and political condition, as well as upon the spiritual destiny of the whole human race. The tyrant feels the restraining power of free America. The oppressed look longingly for the day when God shall grant them the blessings of a free government, and of an unshackeled Gospel. And the pagan views with wonder, a civilization for which climate, soil and productions do not account, but which takes in higher elements,—*light, truth and God.*[46]

The hopes of Livingston were being fulfilled; the voluntary principle was being proved to be a happy amendment to the Belgic Confession, Article 36, and the traditions of Dort.

From Predestination to Eschatology

In December, 1952, Dr. Milton Hoffman, Professor at New Brunswick Seminary, commented with true insight on the state of the Reformed Church:

In our seminaries our theological studies are still Bible-centered. Today a return to the Bible is characteristic of theological schools in America and Europe. For us it is nothing new. We are not ashamed of our confessional position.[47]

A careful study of the literature of the period 1900-1950 confirms this statement. Nevertheless, during those years, many things had happened which had brought about fundamental changes in the orientation of the Reformed Church. The tradition of Dort and the concern for America remained, but the crucial theological word had become "eschatology" rather than "predestination." Professor Elton Eenigenberg of Western Seminary summed up the new attitude:

The Lordship of Christ will be fully manifest in his return. Christians, who find in the resurrection of Christ the source of their hope, must live unconformed to this world, sharing in his passion, in the fellowship of his suffering. 'It is only from the foot of the cross where love goes down to meet the misery of men that hope can be proclaimed.'[48]

Space allows only a brief survey of how the Reformed Church moved from the optimism of the Board of Domestic Missions in 1871[49] to the more sober outlook of 1953. The survey will show that the key factor was a change in climate in which the church began to feel that the historical approach of Nevin and Schaff fit better in the twentieth century than the *a priori* and rational method of Berg and Nodge. The change was not so much a conscious choice as an almost subconscious mood.

One feels the change in 1923 when Edward S. Worchester was elected professor of theology at New Brunswick seminary. At that time the eastern section of the Church, feeling the pressures of secularization and urbanization, was losing confidence in the words of the sixteenth and seventeenth centuries. It felt the need of help from someone who could state the Old Gospel in contemporary language. Challenged by some of the Synod delegates as to his views on various statements in the Canons of Dort, Worchester frankly stated his objections. In spite of his position, the Synod elected him to the Seminary position. In his inaugural address, he stated his approach to theology:

Oh! if we want a formula written out once for all, from which to deduce by mere syllogism a whole philosophy of being, I grant you I know not where to find it. But if we are willing to sit down reverently with the material that is at our hand in this Bible of ours and in the continuing Christian life in which we share, and prayerfully give ourselves to the guidance of promise, it is not the poverty of the revelation that will stagger us, but the wealth of it.[50]

A second area where the change of climate began to be felt related to evolution. Where Hodge, consistent with his rationalistic approach to theology and his doctrine of the decrees, insisted that the concept of evolution was inconsistent with God's "Design" in creation,[51] Reformed writers were much more cautious. Evert J. Blekkink, at Western Seminary, devotes twenty pages of careful lecture notes to the subject and finally accepts "Christian evolution" while rejecting all other forms.[52] John E. Kuizenga, also at Western, at about the same time adopted a cautious acceptance of certain forms of evolution.[53] Finally, Albertus Pieters, also at Western, set forth a full-scale defense of long ages of evolutionary development as being consistent with Genesis.[54]

The third area of change came as the United States became increasingly pluralistic and secular. Protestantism lost its dominant position; prohibition came to an end, and the Sabbath was no longer a day exclusively for rest and worship.[55] Somewhere around 1935-40, the Reformed Church in America realized that the dream of a Protestant Christian America prepared for the millennium was not being fulfilled.[56]

Finally, the change was felt in the use of the Bible. At the turn of the century, the Synod had to deal with a conflict about the doctrine of inspiration, in which the Classis of Holland objected to a book in which Dr. John De Witt of New Brunswick had rejected verbal inspiration in favor of a pious, but scholarly historical and higher critical approach to the Bible.[57] The controversy continued on through the period of Fundamentalist-modernist debate in America, but the coming of the conservative Old Testament scholar, John H. Raven, to New Brunswick in 1899 apparently pacified the critics of De Witt for the time being.

It is significant that in spite of the Reformed Church's emphasis on the Bible, the two seminaries throughout their history were always dominated by pastoral systemic theologians, who quoted from the Scriptures as a source book much as Hodge quoted from here and there in history. The first breach in that dominance at Western Seminary (with the possible exception of the Beardslee's) came in 1926 with the appointment of Albertus Pieters. Pieters represented a traditional position, with a nineteenth century view of science and a polemical stance over against the modernists, the dispensationalists, the Federal Council of Churches, the Christian Reformed Church, and Reformed legalism. One of his students, Lester Kuyper, went on to do graduate study and mastered the techniques of contemporary Old Testament study. He served as professor of Old Testament from 1939 to 1974.

Joined in 1941 by his New Testament colleague, Richard Oudersluys, Kuyper quietly but persistently became the first Biblical scholar in the Reformed Church to conduct a careful study of the Biblical roots of some of the important concepts of the Standards of Unity. In a series of articles appearing over two decades, Kuyper showed that the language of the Standards needed modification to recognize that mercy and justice are closely related rather than two contrary concepts,[58] and that God is not the impassive sovereign of the decrees, but the Holy One who "repents" and "grieves."[59] At the same time, he rejected an understanding of Adam and Eve rooted in "federal theology" in favor of a literary-historical approach to Genesis 2-3.[60]

After 1960, John Piet, using the same methods of Biblical research, attacked the Belgic Confession in its statement of the three marks of the church, maintaining that it had gone astray

because it had failed to recognize the concept of "mission" and
the relation of "election" to "mission," as well as in recognizing
a non-Biblical distinction between the "visible" and "invisible"
church.[61]

Had the above reservations been written during the nineteenth century, they would have been subjected to heavy attack
and scrutiny by others within the Reformed Church. The fact
that they received only isolated opposition reflects the changes
which had been taking place. Following the Worcester controversy of 1922, it was clear that the General Synod would no
longer enforce strict theological precision regarding the Canons
of Dort. By 1931, a number of Classes were officially protesting
modernistic tendencies in the Federal Council of Churches and
suggesting that the Reformed Church no longer be associated
with that body.[62] By 1937, The Special Committee on Curricu-
lum suggested ten normal experiences as defined by American
theological liberals as a basis for a Religious education curricu-
lum, but the Synod could not agree on the subject.[63] In the
same year, a minister in Washington State provoked wide controversy in an article accusing many in the Reformed Church of
having modernist tendencies, including the denial of the basic
doctrines of the faith as defined in the Creeds.[64]

After World War II, the Reformed Church found itself
heavily involved in Foreign and North American Missions, social
issues, and evangelism. Feeling that the Church Order of Dort
was in need of extensive revision, the church, leaning on American Corporation structure as a model, developed a more central-
ized bureaucratic structure. While it attempted to avoid the
theological issues involved, it was clear that the tradition of
Dort was becoming less relevant to the Church Order.[65] With
changes in the Church Order, the Synod's lack of interest
in strict enforcement of doctrinal precision, and Biblical
scholars increasingly ready to question the classical definitions,
it seemed to many that the tradition of Dort was on the verge
of collapse.

Nevertheless, in the 1950's through the leadership of seminary professors and the Board of Domestic Missions which was
serving the needs of immigrants in Canada, contact was renewed
with the Hervormde Kerk in The Netherlands after a gap of
almost a century.[66] There a number of church leaders and
theologians such as H. Berkhof, A. A. van Ruler, Th. L. Haitje-
ma, and Hendrik Kramer, had emphasized an eschatological

interpretation of the traditions of Dort in bringing about church renewal in The Netherlands after the War. Through their work, a number of Reformed Church pastors and theologians recognized that while many of the detailed concepts of Dort could be open to question, the tradition as a whole continued to represent a central landmark for the Reformed Church in America.[67]

The first impact of the re-discovery of Dort in the 1950's was in the sphere of liturgy and the sacraments. Under the leadership of Gerrit Vander Lugt, Richard Oudersluys, Howard Hageman and others, The Committee on the Revision of the Liturgy read the provisions of Dort in the light of the older Strasbourg liturgy as well as contemporary New Testament studies. The result was a new liturgy with a more eschatological dimension, accepted in 1966. The new liturgy, accepting the basic structure of the whole Western Church tradition, looked toward more frequent celebration of the Lord's Supper, provided for congregational responses, suggested the use of traditional prayers, etc.[68] The effectiveness of the Liturgy Committee's opposition to both Zwinglian views and American neo-gothic sentimentalism was reinforced by a study in Church architecture by Donald Bruggink and Carl Droppers, whose views on the importance of an architecture true to the Reformed tradition were incorporated into many of the new church buildings.[69]

In the field of theology and church order, there were some who continued to believe that Dort must continue to function and be strictly interpreted by the Synod from the orientation of predestination. The Society for Reformed Publications, located in Grand Rapids, Michigan, issued a number of pamphlets and books re-affirming the nineteenth century interpretation of Dort.[70] While the Grand Rapids group continued to play its role, the theological leadership passed to those who were more closely related to developments in The Netherlands. The work of John Beardslee III and Eugene Osterhaven in the study of the seventeenth century theologians has been particularly noteworthy.[71] Hageman, John Hesselink, and Justin Vander Kolk went behind Dort and showed that the Strasbourg Liturgy and John Calvin's thought had a freshness and vitality for American life which later writers of the traditions had missed.[72]

In the doctrine of the ministry, the Theological Commission has carefully studied the traditions of Dort, and re-affirmed traditional structures. However, it has suggested major changes by recommending the ordination of women, allowing elders to

administer the Lord's Supper, and defining the ordained ministry in terms of "function" rather than "status."[73] Combined
with a change in 1972 in the "subscription formula" signed by
ministers at the time of ordination or installation,[74] Dort
remains the landmark rather than the legal code for Reformed
ministry in America.

Many of the recent developments have been summed up in the
efforts of the denomination to write an additional confessional Standard. After fifteen years of work, the 1974 Synod
adopted a new provisional Standard, entitled *Our Song of Hope*,
to be voted on finally in 1978. This confession combines a
re-affirmation of Dort with an ecumenical concern and openess
to the future, with a concern for evangelism and for social
justice. By its title and contents, it indicates that "eschatology"
has taken priority over "predestination." It concludes with a
prayer of expectation, thereby summing up the present theological stance of the Church:

"Come, Lord Jesus:
    We are open to your Spirit.
    We await your full presence.
    Our world finds rest in you alone."[75]

Social Concerns

John De Jong

We are part of the forces that must struggle for the great victory of perfect evangelization. Our aim and motto must be, 'The whole for Christ.'
There is an aspect in which every man's influence is national. It is direct
upon his neighbors; and the aggregated mass, the nation, receives its
character and color from the individuals composing it. Much more is the
influence of a denomination national. We ought to feel it more deeply,
and labor and give, not as if aiding scores of feeble churches, but as if we
designed to bear our part in the great enterprise of making this whole
great country a truly Christian country.[1]

These words express a commitment to the building of a
Christian America that the Reformed Church shared with many
evangelical churches in the nineteenth century. As outlined in
the 1876 report to the General Synod on the state of religion,
the goal was "to make this country the land of the School
house, of the Bible, of the Sabbath, and of the Sanctuary."[2]

At the close of the American Revolution a century earlier,
few but the most clairvoyant could have anticipated the early
achievement of these goals. Church members were a numerically
insignificant part of the population. The American Revolution
had severely tested many denominations, particularly the Reformed Church. Enlightenment rationalism had spread secularism and infidelity. For those who could not conceive of a
Christian society without state support of religion, the new
practice of separation of church and state portended bleak
times for the churches.

Despite these gloomy prospects, it was possible one hundred
years later for evangelicals to assert that amazing progress had
been made toward making the United States a truly Christian
land. Church membership had increased significantly, and society bore the stamp of Christian influence. The task of Christianizing the nation had not been completed, but the progress
experienced in the first one hundred years of the nation's
history inspired hope for future triumphs in the United States
and around the world. The report of the Board of Domestic
Missions in 1872 exulted, "God has made our land the teacher

of nations. We are literally a city set upon a hill, whose light cannot be hid. . . . American institutions and ideas are to day sending their beneficent and ameliorizing influences to the extremeties of human society."[3]

All of this suggests that the Reformed Church shared with other nineteenth-century evangelicals a compelling concern for society as a whole. Contrary to the stereotype that regards evangelicals as so consumed by a passion for saving individual souls that social concerns are neglected, they insisted that Christ calls men "not only to personal salvation, but to duties in society."[4] Recent scholarship, represented most impressively in Timothy Smith's *Revivalism and Social Reform*, has richly documented this concern.[5] The purpose of this essay is to outline briefly selected manifestations of this concern in the Reformed Church through the first two hundred years of the nation's history. It will be shown that although the goal of making "this whole great country a truly Christian country" still beckons the Reformed and other evangelical churches, twentieth-century conditions have made its realization as envisioned in 1876 increasingly doubtful and in need of revision in ways that are still not entirely clear as the Reformed Church prepares for another century of ministry in this nation.

At the outset it is important to note that the confluence of social and evangelical concern that characterized the nineteenth-century churches was a function of both theological commitment and the peculiarities of American religious experience. On the theological side, the Calvinistic heritage that shaped the Reformed Church and others was a major force. Calvinists believed that God's sovereignty extended to all facets of life. Accordingly they have best represented those Christians who seek what H. Richard Niebuhr has called the transformation of culture.[6] The Puritans of New England were the most important bearers of this tradition in early American history, but it flowered in Calvinistic churches in other areas as well.

As these churches emerged from the period of the American Revolution they were convinced that success or failure on their part would determine whether the United States was to become a Christian or pagan country. It was apparent, however, that conditions in the young nation required new measures. There was, for example, the newly established practice of separation of church and state that precluded the use of political instruments in the building of a Christian America. At no time had churchmen, not even the Puritans, conceived of the state as the primary force for bringing a Christian society into existence; but they had frequently assigned to it an important role, and they realized that the force of Christian laws and magistrates could do much to restrain evil and guide both the redeemed and the unredeemed to proper behavior.[7] With this instrument no longer available it appeared that the transformation of society now had become almost entirely dependent on the successful conversion of individuals. The growth of democracy in early nineteenth-century America forced similar conclusions. Democracy implied a voluntaristic society in which majority will determined affairs. Successful evangelistic effort appeared to be the only way to mobilize such majorities.

The immensely successful evangelistic efforts that followed employed a warmly emotional pietism, a simplified theology, exciting millennial expectations, challenging perfectionism and systematic revivalistic techniques. All were calculated to appeal to a broad spectrum of people whose educational and cultural opportunities were limited and who generally preferred action to contemplation. This was particularly true in frontier areas, but revivalism was not simply a frontier phenomenon. It also swept the settled communities of the East where the Reformed Church had most of its members.

The Reformed Church participated extensively in this evangelistic effort. The Church's theological caution would not permit it to embrace all the strategies noted above, and it did not evangelize extensively on the frontier; but even a cursory review of the Reports on the State of Religion presented to the General Synod provides a revealing overview of the ebb and flow of revivalistic activity during the nineteenth century. Furthermore, the Dutch immigrants of the middle decades of the nineteenth century quickly joined this important activity. As Eugene Heideman has shown, the Dutch immigrants had their roots in a pietistic reaction to the rationalism and modernism of their state church. As their ties with traditional Dutch theology weakened, they readily adopted American revivalism.[8] Although their pietism and "ethnic isolationism" inclined them toward escapism and withdrawal, these tendencies did not prevail completely. Both Van Raalte in Michigan and Scholte in Iowa were active in social and political affairs, and their example encouraged their followers to do likewise.[9]

In casting about for the means to make their concern for

society concrete, evangelical Protestants did not make use of the denominational social action agencies that are familiar to us today. Instead, they created voluntary societies that undertook a variety of moral, benevolent and missionary activities. These societies proved to be particularly appropriate instruments in democratic America since they relied largely on persuasion to achieve their objectives. In addition, they were free from direct denominational authority and not dependent upon the mobilization of denominational majorities before they could act. They also offered members from small denominations, such as the Reformed Church, the opportunity to exercise a greater impact on society than might otherwise have been possible.[10]

Throughout the nineteenth century, the Reformed Church commended to its members participation in or support of a number of these voluntary societies. In a paper of this length it is impossible to describe all of these societies and the causes that they promoted, but some demand special consideration. One prominent cause was Sunday observance. Much of the Reformed Church's support for this cause was channeled through the American Sabbath Union and the Lord's Day Alliance. Regarding Sunday observance as one of the marks of a Christian nation, nineteenth-century Protestants promoted it not only for fundamental religious reasons but also for the social benefits that accrued to a society that respected the Lord's day. One highly valued benefit was the improvement of morality. A Sunday free from secular distractions enabled the church to exercise its moral influence more effectively. Depriving society of this influence could only lead to increased crime and immorality. Health and happiness were also tied to Sunday observance.

We believe there never was a time when students of sociological and economic subjects were more thoroughly agreed that the weekly rest day must be protected; and we are sure there never was a time when the Sabbath was so appreciated by a thoughtful Christian public as the only safeguard against encroachments of selfishness and greed on the part of competing corporations; the only safeguard against lawlessness and anarchy on the part of organized labor.[11]

The violations of the Lord's day with which the Reformed Church was most concerned included the Sunday operation of public transportation facilities, the carrying of mail, Sunday newspapers, various forms of recreation (including the new pastime of bicycle riding) and all unnecessary labor. The Reformed Church also spoke out strongly against employers who threatened workers with dismissal if they did not work on Sunday.

Although the Reformed Church and voluntary associations generally preferred to gain their objectives through persuasion, it was frequently necessary to resort to the force of law for final success. This raised problems. Could legislation really be effective in matters of morality? Was the resort to law an admission that the conversion of individuals was not sufficient to effect important changes in society? Sunday observance legislation in particular raised questions about church and state separation. A solution to the latter problem was to assert that Sunday rest was not simply a religious matter but one of the civic institutions of the land and part of the common law. Thus to uphold Sunday observance by law was constitutional and no violation of anyone's right of conscience.[12]

Moderation in the use of alcohol was another cause that nineteenth-century evangelicals widely supported. Disturbing increases in consumption coinciding with an apparent decay in morality brought this problem to the attention of the churches. Accordingly, the General Synod encouraged its ministers to promote total abstinance "by example and precept." Church members were urged to join temperance societies, particularly the American Society for the Promotion of Temperance and the Anti-Saloon League. Days of fasting and humiliation for the cause were also celebrated, and members were encouraged not to sign license applications for taverns in their communities.

As with the cause of Sunday observance, the churches eventually turned to the law for final resolution of the problem. This encountered some resistance in the Reformed Church, partly because of doubts over the effectiveness of such laws and also because recent Dutch immigrants were fearful that prohibition would prevent the use of wine for the Lord's Supper.[13] Such reluctance diminished in the twentieth century. In 1914 the General Synod appointed a Committee on Temperance and endorsed the movement toward prohibition.[14]

Almost immediately after the goal of prohibition had been realized, the problem of enforcement became a major concern. In the face of widespread violations of the law, the General Synod urged that there be "no open or surreptitious stills in the homes of Reformed Church families, and no condoning of such practices."[15] Although the Reformed Church opposed the mounting pressures for repeal, the "noble experiment" was doomed. However, since repeal the temperance cause has continued to rank high on the list of the Reformed Church's social concerns.

The effort to rid American society of the evil of slavery was the most important and most tragic in its implications of all nineteenth-century reform movements. Early in the century most churches were not actively concerned with the issue. The General Synod, however, quickly endorsed the American Colonization Society, which compensated slave owners and sent freed blacks to Africa. By mid-century most churches in the North were against slavery, but abolitionism was widely opposed. The views of Samuel B. How, who was later elected president of General Synod, reflected a strongly held position. He argued that although slavery was an evil, it was no sin and was clearly upheld in the Bible.[16] In the West, H. P. Scholte also criticized the abolitionists and charged them with radicalism and failure to consider the fundamental interests of the slave owners.[17]

These ideas were by no means universally shared, but they were widespread enough to trigger the charge that the Reformed Church was pro-slavery. The *Christian Intelligencer* denied the allegation and in turn accused the abolitionists of a radicalism that threatened to disrupt the churches and American society. The Reformed Church, it asserted, was conservative in that it adhered steadfastly to the principles of "freedom, law, and Christian fraternity."[18]

Further defenses of the Church's stance appealed to its evangelical character. This was a significant strategy because in later years it would be employed again and again in discussions of the Reformed Church's social responsibilities. Essentially the argument was that clergymen who embraced abolitionism were "pseudo-divines" who strayed from their true commission—the preaching of the gospel. On the other hand, it was asserted that Reformed clergy, with few exceptions, adhered strictly to their task and preached a gospel of peace and love. Their message was that "the worst slavery in the world is the *slavery of sin*, and the best freedom that 'glorious liberty wherewith Christ makes people free.' " In short, the true Christian response to the evil of slavery was to preach the power of the gospel in the hearts of both slaves and slaveowners.[19]

Civil war came and it apparently confirmed the charges against the abolitionists. But wartime was no time for recriminations, and the measure of the Reformed Church's concern over the tragedy of war was the General Synod's appointment of a committee to draft its sentiments on the crisis. The burden of the Synod's counsel was that secession was unjustified rebellion and that loyalty to the Union and constitutional government was part of each church member's obligation. In the same vein, the *Christian Intelligencer* advised its readers that the war should not be made into a war against slavery but should remain a war to preserve the Union.[20]

This brief review of the Reformed Church's role in the slavery controversy suggests two observations. First, the Reformed Church had quite obviously developed a deep attachment to the values and institutions of the nation, particularly democracy and constitutional government. Samuel B. How went so far as to suggest that the abolitionists who advocated policies that threatened the Union were guilty of ingratitude to God for the blessings of the government under which they lived.[21] This enthusiasm for national values was made explicit in the 1863 Report on the State of Religion which indicated that while the Reformed Church was proud of its Dutch heritage and unwilling to ignore it, she had found a congenial home on American soil. "She is American," the report stated, "in her calm assertion of human rights in opposition to injustice and prescriptive tyranny."[22] Some years later the Reverend T. B. Romeyn was to claim that the key to the Reformed Church's influence on American life was the remarkable harmony that existed between its ideals and practices and those of the nation.[23] All of this suggests a drift toward what H. R. Niebuhr has called "Culture-Protestantism"—a willingness on the part of the church to embrace prevailing social values and institutions and assign to them a religious significance.[24]

Second, the counsel that the Reformed Church should not be distracted from preaching the gospel into abolitionist adventures reflected the commitment of nineteenth-century evangelicals to personal conversion and individual moral nurture as the most effective instruments for dealing with social problems. They found in this an easy release from the need to work for fundamental changes in the structure of society despite their vital concern for society as it found expression in the idea of a truly Christian country. In short, both the evangelical outlook and the leaning toward Culture-Protestantism worked to create a general reluctance to engage in far-reaching programs of social change.

This is not to deny the success that nineteenth-century evangelicals had in putting a Christian stamp on American society, but later generations would come to question whether they might not have placed too much confidence in these tactics. This indeed became the complaint of the social gospellers—those laymen and clergymen who in the late nineteenth century became concerned that the churches were not dealing effectively with the problems that accompanied the rapid industrialization and urbanization of American society. It is common for students of American history to see in the social gospel a radical departure from the evangelical tradition, but despite its new elements, it actually represented a continuation of the evangelical search for a Christian America. Where it differed most markedly was in its participants' perception of the problems that demanded the immediate attention of the churches and in the methods to be employed in attacking them. To the social gospellers, the most urgent problems were not intemperance or transgressions of the Sabbath but labor conflict, corrupt politics, substandard living conditions, exploitation of consumers and the massive economic and political power of business. These were problems that demanded new tactics. Instead of relying on individual conversion, moral nurture and benevolence, the social gospellers launched direct attacks on inhumane social institutions and practices.

Although the movement was well underway by the beginning of the twentieth century, the Reformed Church was not deeply involved initially. This, however, was characteristic of many denominations since the social gospel was originally a non-denominational endeavor and was not taken up by denominational agencies until after the turn of the century. The Reformed Church nonetheless nurtured two of the foremost exponents of social Christianity in the twentieth century— Graham Taylor and A. J. Muste. Both were graduates of New Brunswick Seminary and at one time served as Reformed Church ministers. Both, however, left the Reformed Church early in their careers because it did not provide them with wide enough scope for their social concerns. Taylor became the founder of the Chicago Commons Social Settlement, and Muste became one of the outstanding leaders of the peace movement.[25]

A variety of reasons may be suggested for the Reformed Church's reluctance to take up the social gospel in its early years. Judging by the editorial policy of the *Christian Intelligencer*, there was much hesitancy about the social gospel's attack on business. Commenting on the anti-business stance of William Jennings Bryan and the Democrats in 1896, a writer asserted that the majority of businessmen were benefactors of their communities and implied that there were no citizens "more patriotic, more benevolent, more valuable in every sense than the owners of property. . . . "[26]

Without hard evidence it would be fruitless to speculate at length on the reasons for this alignment on the side of business. But comments such as the one quoted above invite the opinion that we have here another evidence of Culture—Protestantism. Business was a prestigious force in American society in the late nineteenth century, and it was closely linked in many minds with the progress of the nation—a linkage that made it difficult to mount a far-reaching criticism of it.

There also seems to have been a reluctance within the Reformed Church to abandon nineteenth-century individualistic social attitudes and accept the social gospel contention that many social problems were due to causes that transcended individual responsibility and consequently could not be solved by individual effort alone. Thus the *Christian Intelligencer* found it necessary to warn against paternalism, which it defined as the effort to solve social problems by removing them from the individual's hands and placing them in the hands of the state. Christ's example was to liberate individuals; individual responsibility was his guiding principle. Moreover, the testimony of history was that true progress had always been through individualism rather than paternalism.[27]

Many other factors undoubtedly entered into the Church's caution in embracing the social gospel, but in the final analysis theology appears to have been one of the most important. Although it would be inaccurate to equate the social gospel with theological liberalism, the connection frequently existed, and it invited suspicion of the social gospel. The problem was given an extended airing in the 1920's and 1930's as the Reformed Church tardily developed a modest interest in the social gospel. John E. Kuizenga, writing in the *Leader*, succinctly summarized the major issues. He attributed to the social gospel a list of errors that included denial of God's transcendence, denial of the reality of the fall, failure to take the Bible as a final and authoritative revelation and indifference to personal salvation. He concluded his analysis with the familiar evangelical insistence on the importance of the individual's relationship with God.[28] This emphasis also characterized John Beardslee, Jr.'s analysis of the idea of the Kingdom of God, one of the social gospel's most important themes. Beardslee insisted that the Kingdom was not a society or a social plan but the reign of God in the life of the individual.[29]

Despite this suspicion of the social gospel, evangelical critics insisted that they were not hostile to social Christianity. In fact they asserted that it was a form of evangelism. However, much of what they described as social Christianity was essentially benevolent activity or crusading for traditional moral causes like temperance, Sunday observance, clean entertainment and others. A questionaire sent to Reformed Church pastors in 1921 indicated overwhelming interest in such causes.[30] But spokesmen for the evangelical tradition were capable of forceful statements in behalf of broader social concern. Thus Siebe C. Nettinga, writing at a time when many warm debates occurred over the Reformed Church's participation in social causes, insisted that the church's primary concern with the regeneration of individuals did not absolve it from delivering a social message. Christians, he said, are not only called to be evangelists but "ministers of the Word" as well, and the Word most clearly speaks to social issues.[31]

One must not ignore the pressure of events in strengthening the Reformed Church's resolve in this direction, particularly the depression of the 1930's. The depression brought home to many Americans of the middle class, as no previous experience had, the lesson that insecurity and hardship can strike anyone in a complex urban and industrial society. It demonstrated painfully that hard work, individual initiative and moral rectitude did not insure one against economic hardship. Undoubtedly this made many more receptive to the idea that the church must deal with the structures of society in a serious way.

Implementation of this heightened sensitivity to social concerns was taken up by the Committee on Public Morals. This committee had been founded in 1918 through the amalgamation of two older committees that had dealt with temperance and Sunday observance. These causes continued to rank high among the new committee's concerns, but it gradually expanded its activities as it saw it was not getting at the roots of social problems. Accordingly it requested that the General Synod recognize its broadened concerns by changing its name to the Committee on Social Welfare. Although there was some balking, the Synod complied with the request. In so doing it concurred with the committee's determination to deal with contemporary social problems by "correcting those conditions in our social life which are immediately responsible for them."[32]

In expanding the scope of its concerns the Social Welfare Committee and its successor organized in 1955, the Christian Action Commission, investigated such problems as unemployment, child labor, labor unions, woman's rights, crime, penal reform, minimum wages, pornography, homosexuality, family life, divorce, marriage, communism, abortion, amnesty and many others. Other agencies of the Reformed Church, most notably the Board of Domestic Missions, also exhibited broadened social concern. Evangelism was obviously the primary concern of the Board, but nearly everywhere it sent its missionaries it also sought to meet the needs of the whole man. Among the hill people of Kentucky it met educational, medical and other social needs. Similarly in Brewton, Alabama it served the cause of education. It also ministered to migrant workers and sharecroppers, some of the most deeply hurt and neglected victims of the depression. It was also at work in the cities among various immigrant groups and later among blacks. The Board's reports to the General Synod in the late 1930's were impressive documents of social concern. The participation of the Reformed Church in the Federal Council of Churches and later in the National Council of Churches also brought social gospel thinking and activity into the Church's life.

Of the many social problems that the Reformed Church has dealt with in the twentieth century, two are of particular interest both from the standpoint of their importance and the amount of attention given to them. The first was the question of peace and international order. Interest began to develop in this subject in the late nineteenth century. This interest increased in the early months of World War I as the Reformed Church endorsed the neutralist policy of Woodrow Wilson. After the United States entered the War, the Reformed Church supported the war effort, but this did not dampen its concern for peace. In June of 1922 the General Synod established the Committee on International Justice and Goodwill.[33]

In the ensuing years this Committee confronted the Church with a steady stream of statements on such matters as the Washington Conference on arms limitation, The Kellogg Peace Pact, the League of Nations and the Court of International Justice. In the 1930's these concerns reached a peak as disillusionment with the results of World War I fueled a potent anti-war spirit. For many Americans, World War I no longer was a noble crusade but a terrible tragedy in which neither side had been totally right and both sides had been guilty of much wrong. Others saw behind the United States' involvement the operation of a monstrous conspiracy of greedy munitions makers. Still others attributed it to the continued existence of international anarchy in a world in which nations had in reality become interdependent.

The conclusions to be gained from all of this were clear; the churches must redouble their efforts for peace and international order so as to avert another tragedy. The leadership of this effort in the Reformed Church was distinguished. Lawrence French was chairman of the Committee on International Justice and Goodwill throughout much of the 1930's and was an important advocate of a larger role for the Committee. Bernard Mulder, editor of the *Intelligencer Leader*, helped to keep the issue before the Church. Many drew inspiration from A. J. Muste, who in the late 1930's was Secretary of the Fellowship of Reconciliation.

Even with peace sentiment widespread in the 1930's, the lot of the peace advocates was not always easy. Many were distressed with the lack of response to their efforts, especially from the western churches.[34] An additional burden was the suspicion they frequently came under for being too closely associated with theological liberalism. Much of this was carping criticism, but some of it was perceptive and responsible. An important example of the latter came from Albertus Pieters, who found the increasingly frequent and doctrinaire expressions of peace sentiment sent out by the General Synod and some classes to be unrealistic and unbiblical. He charged that many of the peace advocates failed to recognize the hard truth that liberty had more than once been won with the sword and might on occasion again need to be defended with the sword. He also charged that they did not take seriously the Biblical teaching on war that recognized it as "a grim and terrible necessity in the hands of God for the restraint and punishment of sin." In view of this, uncompromising statements to the effect that the Reformed Church was done with war forever were both unrealistic and irresponsible.[35]

The approach of World War II revealed how premature such statements were. Although peace and neutrality continued to be supported, many in the Reformed Church recognized the need to stand against totalitarian threats. However, in assuming this stand steps were taken to avoid repetition of errors that many felt had been made in World War I. The *Intelligencer Leader* editorialized that the Church must not become a recruiting agency for war and that patriotism and religion must not be equated. The irrepressible pacifist voice of Broer D. Dykstra was given frequent access to the pages of the *Intelligencer Leader* to warn against the militarization of Christianity. The first wartime report of the Committee on International Justice and Goodwill reminded the Church that national survival was not the cause with first priority for Christians.[36]

Since it was widely believed that one of the causes for World War II was the failure of the United States to join the League of Nations, there was strong support for the creation of new machinery for maintaining peace after the War. An important figure in this effort was Luman Shafer, who became Secretary of the Board of Foreign Missions in 1935. He was author of *The Christian Alternative to World Chaos* (1940) and a member of the Department of International Justice and Goodwill of the Federal Council of Churches. He also served as the Secretary of the Commission for a Just and Durable Peace of the Federal Council. Shafer wrote a series of articles in the *Intelligencer Leader* which are interesting not only for their support of the cause of international organization but also for their plea to the churches to concern themselves with social and political structures. This represented a line of thought that was typical of the social gospel viewpoint. Shafer argued that the idea that Christian individuals will make for better institutions failed to recognize that Christians living in a system that rests on principles foreign to Christianity will follow the principles of the system. Thus Christians must work for more than the transformation of individuals, they must work to transform systems— specifically the system of international anarchy.[37]

Generally the Reformed Church welcomed the establishment of the United Nations, but at the same time caution was expressed that reflected the continuing tension between a social gospel emphasis and the evangelical tradition. Louis Benes, editor of the *Church Herald*, asked that Christians keep in mind the limitations of secular institutions and recognize that only institutions and men that are God-fearing can really insure peace.[38]

After World War II it became difficult to pursue the cause of peace with the same intensity that had characterized the decade of the 1930's. A major inhibition was the spread of communism, which was perceived as a threat to both nation and church. Defense of the nation and Christianity frequently assumed a higher priority than support for international organizations or peace. The Committee on International Justice and Goodwill warned against this, and it sought to spread the idea that the most effective methods of combating communism were non-military. These efforts led to nearly annual resolutions against universal military training, nuclear testing and the arms race. But inevitably there was division over these issues, and the General Synod received many overtures in the 1950's to strengthen its stand on resistance to communism.

An additional burden for the peace advocates was the success of the communists in exploiting the peace issue. This placed many of the supporters of the peace cause under suspicion as communist collaborators or dupes. The traditional identification of the peace movement with theological liberalism also haunted its advocates. Critics frequently charged that in their reduction of Christianity to "a mere system of ethics," the liberals were vulnerable to the high-sounding rhetoric of the communists and easily became unwitting collaborators with them.[39]

As involvement in the war in Vietnam increased in the 1960's and caused bitter controversies, it brought to the attention of the Reformed Church an important issue related to its concern for peace—the problem of dissent and conscientious objection to war. The record of the Reformed Church in behalf of peace prepared it to be understanding of war resistors. An important precedent was set early in World War II. As conscription became a possibility in 1939, the General Synod laid out procedures whereby it would recognize and minister to those who became conscientious objectors. In 1941 a fund was set up to support conscientious objectors in the Civilian Public Service Corps who could not pay the required costs. After World War II the General Synod favored amnesty for those who for reasons of conscience could not bear arms. These precedents had an important bearing on the resolution of this issue during the war in Vietnam. However, a new element in the 1960's was the effort to gain recognition for the principle of selective objection to war. The General Synod did not endorse this, but it adopted a policy of sympathetic and supportive counseling for war resistors.[40]

Another major social concern of the Reformed Church in the twentieth century has been racism. It did not occupy the Church's attention as long as the peace cause did, but in the years that it was a major concern it aroused intensive interest. Immediately after the Civil War there was only passing concern for the freed blacks. A short-lived evangelistic effort was started in South Carolina, but it was soon passed on to the Southern Presbyterians.[41] Late in the nineteenth century the rise in the number of lynchings brought protests from the General Synod, but at best the interest of the Reformed Church in the plight of blacks was slight before World War I. What interest there was was frequently expressed in painfully paternalistic tones:

> If these people are not to become a menace to our body politic the white man must not attempt to shift this burden. We have the positive conviction that the only means for their salvation is the Gospel given under the guidance and supervision of the churches of the white race.[42]

At the beginning of World War II the Social Welfare Committee designated the race problem one of the major issues in American life, but little was recommended to solve the problem. More intensive concern became apparent in the 1950's and 1960's as the Christian Action Commission kept the issue before the attention of the Reformed Church with a series of resolutions and pronouncements including an important Credo on Race Relations that was adopted in 1957. This was followed in 1961 by the promulgation of a Covenant on Open Occupancy, which committed those who signed it to eliminate race as a factor in housing. Throughout the 1960's the Christian Action Commission attempted to stimulate action on the local level that would achieve the implementation of these statements. Further evidence of the concern for the race issue was the Synod's establishment of a special Commission on Race. [43] Finally, the pages of the *Church Herald* contained extensive coverage of the problem.

Although these actions expressed a forceful stand in principle for racial justice, there was frequent disagreement over how the evils of racism might best be combated. Opinions differed over the wisdom of marches, sit-ins and demonstrations and the participation of ministers and others in them. Efforts to have the General Synod indicate support for the National Association for the Advancement of Colored People met defeat in 1960 and 1961. However, in 1963 it commended and encouraged the Southern Christian Leadership Conference and the work of Martin Luther King. In 1969 the General Synod received and gave consideration to the demands of the Black Manifesto. It rejected the Manifesto's major economic demands, but the rejection was accompanied by expressions of understanding for the conditions that had prompted these demands.[44]

Although the Reformed Church's expressions of opposition to discrimination, segregation and other manifestations of racial prejudice were encouraging, there were those who were dismayed that behavior did not always square with words. A particularly disturbing instance of this was the flight of congregations from the inner city where the problem of race was most severe. A number of articles in the *Church Herald* roundly criticized this exodus and the neglect of the inner city that it entailed. In an effort to deal with these criticisms various ministries were undertaken in such cities as New York, Chicago and Cleveland. But there was disagreement on what the exact nature of these ministries should be. The Reverend Don De Young has by example and in articles in the *Church Herald* issued a noteworthy appeal to avoid paternalism and to deal with black churches in the cities as equals rather than as mission stations. Howard Hageman has described the evangelical and social gospel approaches to inner city problems in an article that reveals that this, too, has been an area in which the ancient tensions between these two approaches to social problems persisted.[45] To conclude on a somber note, the judgment of Elton Bruins on the Reformed Church in the Mid-west still holds today for the whole Church with few exceptions:

The mid-western church has demonstrated a great love for foreign mission enterprises and it has generously supplied funds and personnel for it, but its attitudes toward minority groups within its own bounds consisted often of suspicion quite inconsistent with a loving concern for their needs. It has shown interest in a Negro mission school in Alabama but the Reformed churches in the cities of Milwaukee, Chicago, Grand Rapids and Detroit usually found it easier to move away from, rather than face racial problems.[46]

Despite the extensive broadening of the Reformed Church's social concerns that had taken place since the beginning of the twentieth century, its social role has continued to cause debate. An instance of this occurred in 1957 when a proposal came before the General Synod to delete that section of the Constitution that stated, "Ecclesiastical matters only shall be considered and transacted by ecclesiastical bodies." Deletion seemed to many to be in order since a literal interpretation of that section made unconstitutional much of the involvement in social concerns that was taking place. But an editorial in the *Church Herald* opposed deletion and bemoaned the willingness of the General Synod to address itself as widely as it did to social issues. The editorial claimed that most of the social action pronouncements were ineffective, they did not reflect the general thinking of the Church and they diverted the attention of the Church from its primary task—the conversion and nurture of individuals. The latter, insisted the writer, offered the only effective means to the transformation of society. "Let the Church be the Church" was the final plea of the editorial.[47]

This editorial and the responses to it indicated that there was continuing confusion over the Reformed Church's role in society. Curiously, both sides agreed that it had a social role and that it should speak out on social issues, but there was wide disagreement on what issues should be spoken to and how the speaking should be done. In short, the terms of the debate had not changed appreciably since the Reformed Church first confronted the issues raised by the social gospel movement at the beginning of the twentieth century.

It must be noted, however, that this rehashing of old issues has taken place under circumstances that have been drastically altered by the rapid pace of secularization in the twentieth century. Twentieth-century history is replete with instances of social institutions that have sought to eliminate religious control or influence. As a consequence society has become increasingly fragmented into autonomous provinces—business is business, politics is politics, war is war, scholarship is scholarship, etc. Perhaps it has ever been thus in practice if not in theory, but in the twentieth century the practice has become the determiner of theory. To the extent that the churches have conceived their mission to be to transform and shape society and provide guidance, the phenomenon of secularization has afforded them a shrinking arena for action and diminished their prospects for influencing the course of events.

This has been the case most obviously for those still committed to nineteenth-century conceptions of a Christian America. At one time it seemed realistic for American Protestants to expect that the civil governments in this country would operate in accordance with evangelical moral and religious precepts and that political offices would be filled from the ranks of Christians. At one time it seemed perfectly legitimate for Christians to insist upon having the Bible read and prayers said in the public schools. At one time it was possible to claim confidently that the Christian Sabbath was one of the civic institutions of the nation. But as the nation approached its two hundredth anniversary, these claims and expectations no longer appeared to be realistic.[48]

The problems that the secularization of society placed before those pursuing social gospel concerns were no less perplexing. Paradoxically they found themselves urging the churches to broaden their social concerns at the very time that the secularizing process was gaining momentum. As the churches sought to speak to the problems of race, labor, international affairs, poverty and economic justice they were confronted with the fact that very few involved with those problems could be persuaded to accept solutions that were proposed on the grounds that they were Christian or that they had the sanction of the churches or their agencies. Indeed, it became increasingly difficult to formulate Christian solutions to problems in these areas. During the 1960's the Christian Action Commission frequently attempted to develop (or it commissioned others to develop) positions on various topics of concern. The task was never easy. One major source of difficulty was that in modern times one looked to scientific expertise, political negotiation or brute force for solutions to the problems of the day. The preceding discussion of the Reformed Church's efforts in behalf of international peace illustrates how difficult it could be either to comprehend what was going on in international affairs or to influence the course of events.

Despite those challenges that make the goals that nineteenth-century evangelicals laid out seem increasingly remote, the ideal of a truly Christian nation transformed through the testimony and labor of individuals and the collective action of the churches still beckons. Recently Eugene Osterhaven, while recognizing the implications of modern secularization, advocated that the Reformed Church continue its commitment to the ideal of social transformation. To abandon that goal would to him be a tragic mistake.[49] There are undoubtedly many in the Reformed Church today that share that conviction. But it is also probable that the need to revise if not substantially relinquish the goals laid out one hundred years ago may present the Reformed and other churches with an opportunity to fashion a more realistic and at the same time theologically sounder conception of their role in modern, secular society. It may be noted that in addition to the challenge and exhilaration contained in the idea of a Christian America, there was also a pitfall in the form of easy slippage into Culture-Protestantism. Careful rethinking of its goals in the light of contemporary challenges could mean for the Reformed Church the freedom to be more discriminating, more demanding and more truly prophetic as it speaks on social concerns both to its members and the society in which they live. The counsel of Reinhold Niebuhr, who devoted so much of his brilliant career to clarifying the church's social role has much relevance for the Reformed Church at this milestone in its ministry to the nation. "The task of any movement devoted to 'Social Christianity' must be . . . not so much to advocate a particular nostrum for the solution of various economic and social evils, but to bring a full testimony of gospel judgment and grace to bear upon all of human life. . . ."[50]

Education

Norman Kansfield

Whenever the Reformed Church in America has reflected upon its experience in education, she has most often delighted in rehearsing tales of institutional hard times. The fact that is most familiar from the early years of Rutgers College is the long list of financial crises which forced the school to be closed more than it was open. And from Hope College's early years the most vivid picture is that of Domine Albertus Van Raalte accepting cabbages and potatoes as donations to keep the struggling school alive. As the result of such images, coupled with accounts of teachers going long periods without receiving payment on their salaries and emotional descriptions of buildings falling into decay because of imbalanced budgets, it is possible for a reader to begin to wonder if the Reformed Church in America was ever really interested in or committed to education.

Those of our forefathers who were deeply involved in the educational task have become better known to us in their struggles and failures than in their successes. This memory is unfair. It is true, of course, that there were missed opportunities. On numerous occasions the chance to provide educational leadership was presented to the Reformed Church in America. Often, in these moments, she discovered herself to be short of cash or lacking in manpower or unable to scare up the resolve to take advantage of the opportunity. On these occasions the moments passed, and others took up the cause. And the Reformed Church's involvement in education was altered from what it might have been.

But this research cannot be overly concerned with what might have been nor can our present era stand in harsh judgment of the commitment of our forefathers to education. In time's long perspective our forefathers may have made mistakes and occasionally (for reasons we now fail to appreciate) allowed their educational institutions nearly to starve to death, but they did have a real and abiding commitment to education. The purpose of this research has been to discover and to understand

the pattern of that commitment in the Reformed Church in
America.

I. A Theology of Education

In order to appreciate the commitment of the Reformed
Church to education, it is necessary to understand at the outset
that the Church has been involved in education not so much
from a sociological as from a theological ideology. This becomes
clear when we look at the earliest years of the Church's life in
America. Before 1664 (when the British captured the Colony)
New Netherland comprised the territory today represented by
most of New York, New Jersey and Delaware, and the Dutch
West India Company was primarily responsible for the shape
and purpose of its corporate life. The West India Company
(along with its more famous and successful sister company, the
East India Company) was a trading conglomerate and expected to make a profit from its ventures in America. Such a
company, trading primarily in beaver pelts and timber, could
expect no direct benefit to the company from an involvement
in education. And yet, if the records of the Lords Directors are
to be believed, the Company's concern for and involvement in
early educational functions were of the most significant
nature.[1] The Reformed Church, represented by the Classis of
Amsterdam, selected, examined and certified schoolmasters for
service in New Netherlands,[2] but the West India Company was
responsible for paying their salaries.[3] Neither the Lords Directors in the Netherlands nor the Directors General in America
greatly questioned this arrangement. Their background had long
suggested to them that education was an area of special concern
and province for the Church, and the West India Company
simply saw its role as that of providing the Church with the
means by which an educational ministry could be adequately
carried on among the Company's colonials.

But, we must ask, where did such a conception of the
Church's involvement in education have its origin? In part, at
least, education had always been a segment of the Church's life.
Before the Reformation, education, such as it existed in Western Europe, was carried on in the home alone, or for the select
few who did receive advanced training, in monastery schools or
ecclesiastical academies. The Reformation, with its heavy
emphasis on two doctrines in particular, greatly expanded the

Church's role in education. By stressing SOLA SCRIPTURA—
the scriptures alone—as the only rule for faith and practise and
by asserting that all within the church together were priests—
that the mission and message of grace belonged to a priesthood
of all believers—the Reformed Church took upon herself a
heavy burden in education. The Word of God could be rightly
proclaimed only by an articulate educated ministry, and correct
proclamation could only have a significant impact when the
laity was literate. The "church reformed and committed to
constant reformation" could only rightly reorder herself
"according to the Word of God" when the Church was sure that
her whole self accurately and fully understood that Word.

The writers of the Heidelberg Catechism, as they composed
that document in 1563-1564, sought to give definition to this
educational need in relationship to the Sabbath. After the
Catechism has asked "what does God require in the fourth
commandment?" (Lord's Day 38, Question 103), the following
response is given:

First, that the ministry of the Gospel and the schools should be maintained, and that I, especially on holy days [*festis diebus/feier tag*], but
on other days as well, should studiously attend godly assemblies in order
that I may diligently listen to God's Word, participate in his holy sacraments and add my public prayers to those of the rest of the congregation,
and, to the best of my ability give something to the poverty stricken. And
further, that in all my life [all the days of my life] I may be free from evil
deeds, bending my will to God's that by the Holy Spirit he may do his
work in me and thus, in this life, I may begin to weave the fabric of the
eternal Sabbath.[4]

The true keeping of the Sabbath is not so much centered in
the abstention of labor on one day a week, but is concentrated
in a manner of living. The Sabbath, for the writers of the
Catechism, was never so much profaned as when God's Word
was not rightly proclaimed because pastors were ill-trained or
when God's Word was not correctly heard, read and observed
because the body of Christ was illiterate. Nothing is closer to or
more necessary for the preservation, research and proclamation
of God's own revealed word than education. As Zacharius
Ursinus, in his Commentary on this question and answer,
stated:

if God wills to have ministers in his Church, he wills also that everyone,
according to his ability, help forward and further the maintenance of the

ministry and the schools of learning, and do his utmost to see that Ministers, Professors, and Schoolmasters be honestly provided for. For without the study of arts and sciences neither can man be made fit to teach, nor the purity and sincerity of doctrine be upheld and maintained against heretics.[5]

The Dutch Church, from her earliest years, sought to translate this theology of education into institutional actuality. At the first Dutch national synod, held "in exile" at Wezel in 1568, deacons were charged with responsibility for founding and supporting schools.[6] The second national synod, also "held in exile," at Emden in 1571, required each classis in its regular meeting to ask of each church "whether the care of the poor and the schools is maintained.[7]

Later, in preparation for the great Synod of Dordt, a pamphlet was published which sought to bring together, under several main headings, the various Acts of Dutch synods from 1568 to 1617. This pamphlet summarized synodical concern for education as follows:

1. The churches shall exercise concern that in the upper schools there are teachers who are outstanding in learning and in pious godliness [*godtsalicheyt*].
2. Each church shall have her own schoolmasters for the instruction of her young persons.
3. The church shall prescribe for schoolmasters the devotions to be observed and which books shall be most necessary for the education of the young person.[8]

Even though the great "Canons" of Dordt do not speak of education, the Church Order, approved at the 155th session (May 13, 1619) makes it quite clear that at the time of the Synod, the Reformed Church in the Netherlands felt that education was one of her special responsibilities. In the tradition of earlier synods, Dordt, in Article twenty-one of Church Order, decreed:

Everywhere the Consistories shall see to it that there are good schoolmasters to teach not only reading and writing to the children, the languages and liberal arts, but also to instruct them in pious godliness [*godsaligheid*] and in the Catechism.[9]

Under Article forty-four the "Classical Visitors"—those members of the classis who were responsible for visiting each of the congregations under the jurisdiction of the classis in order to make sure all was being done "decently and in order"—were to determine if ministers, consistories and *schoolmasters* were "faithfully administering, their offices, adhering to purity of doctrine, observing in all things the accepted order."[10]

Article fifty-four of this Church Order placed schoolmasters under the same kind of theological responsibility as ministers and professors of theology when it required:

Likewise, the schoolmasters under the immediate care of the Consistory, shall be obliged to subscribe the aforesaid articles [the "confession of faith of the Reformed Church in the Netherlands" as signed by ministers and professors of theology] or in place thereof to sign the Christian Catechism.[11]

The Church Order is not quite as specific in its concern for higher education. Still, when the whole document is read, one can feel that concern. In Article 8, for example, the fathers said that "schoolteachers, mechanics [the term that meant 'skilled professional tradesmen'], or others, *who have not regularly studied*, shall not be admitted to the office of the ministry unless the best assurances be obtained of their singular talents, piety, humility and sobriety. . . . "[12]

Article 18 defined the function of professors of theology. It reads: "The office of the Teachers or Professors of Theology is to explain the holy scriptures and vindicate the pure doctrines of the gospel against heresy and error."[13] While this says nothing about transmitting knowledge to each new generation of students, it is clear from Article 19 that Dordt's real concern at this point was with higher education, especially training for ministry. Article 19 encouraged each congregation "to raise public funds for the support of Students in Theology."[14] We know from other sources that university training for ministry was the accepted method of pastoral education. Dordt made the professors who taught theology in the national universities officers of the Church (and therefore answerable to her) and expected individual congregations to support gifted students as they prepared for ministry. But the Church Order is not inflexible in this matter. Article 20, in the same spirit as Article 8 mentioned above, reflects a high concern for thorough theological training while at the same time recognizing alternate methods to the university approach. Article 20 orders that "in churches where a number of able ministers are settled, the practice of discussing *Theological Theses* shall be instituted, that by such exercises some may be prepared for the ministry; pursuing, however, therein, the special appointment and order of the General Synod."[15]

The Reformed Church in the Netherlands, at the time of the Great Synod, was quite apparently concerned with education specifically at two levels: basic general education (for a literate laity) and university training of the highest order (for a thoroughly trained ministry). By 1620, the Catechism's theological principles relating education and the Christian life had been institutionalized sufficiently so that they could become the mode of operation which the Church and the West India Company could use and feel secure with in the New World. The Reformed Church's history in education, since its earliest years in America, has been consistent with these two clearly defined needs.

II. The American Actualization

Since New Netherlands was conceived only as a trade colony of the West India Company, it ought not to surprise us that during the early years of their American experience the Dutch colonists continued to look to the Netherlands for a supply of well-trained pastors. The same kind of dependence was, of course, not possible in regard to the practical, primary education of the laity. Even if the West India Company and the Classis of Amsterdam were committed to a careful cooperation which insured a continuous supply of well-prepared Schoolmasters for the Colony, the local consistory was still charged with the responsibility of making sure that the school was well run and the program effective.

On the basis of the best evidence available, the first recognized schoolmaster arrived in New Netherlands some time early in the fall of 1637, with certificates of approbation issued by the Classis of Amsterdam. Adam Roelantsen "having requested to go to New Netherland as schoolmaster, reader [voorlezer] and precentor [voorsanger], was accepted, as recommended upon his good testimonials and the trial of his gifts, on August 4, 1637; and was sent thither."[16] Mr. Roelantsen, and other of his successors were probably charged with the same kinds of responsibilities as was Evert Pieterson (schoolmaster at New

Amsterdam, May 2, 1661-1674 and of the "Reformed Dutch School in the City of New York", 1674 to ca. 1686).

His instructions, "drawn up by the Burgomasters of this city with the advice of the Director General and Council," included:

1. He shall take good care, that the children coming to his school, do so at the usual hour, namely at eight in the morning and one in the afternoon.
2. He must keep good discipline among his pupils.
3. He shall teach the children and pupils the Christian Prayers, commandments, baptism, Lord's supper, and the questions with answers of the catechism, which are taught here every Sunday afternoon in the church.
4. Before school closes he shall let the pupils sing some verses and a psalm.
5. Besides his yearly salary he shall be allowed to demand and receive from every pupil quarterly as follows: For each child, whom he teaches the a b c, spelling and reading, 30 st.; for teaching to read and write, 50 st.; for teaching to read, write and cipher, 60 st.; from those who come in the evening and between times pro rata a fair sum. The poor and needy, who ask to be taught for God's sake he shall teach for nothing.
6. He shall be allowed to demand and receive from everybody, who makes arrangements to come to his school and comes before the first half of the quarter, but nothing from those, who come after the first half of the quarter.
7. He shall not take from anybody, more than is herein stated. Thus done and decided by the Burgomasters of the City of Amsterdam in N.N., November 4, 1661.[17]

These tasks the schoolmasters were usually expected to carry out in a room in their home. Many of the records of New Amsterdam indicate that the schoolmaster's house was provided as part of his salary, at first by the West India Company, then by the community and later by the Church.[18]

Education concentrated on teaching very basic skills. To be able to read and to write, to know the catechism and to pray piously were the primary goals of this process. To be competent in simple arithmetic and to understand the workings of grammar were of secondary importance. All other subjects were expected only of those who intended to enter one of the "learned" professions.

Very little is known about actual teaching methods. Lists of textbooks have survived in a variety of sources, and all lists show a surprising uniformity. The Bible, along with the Catechism and the Dutch Psalter were apparently used in the course of regular education as texts for reading, as well as for religious instruction. In addition to the whole Bible, two "histories", that of David and that of Tobias, were found in each list of textbooks.[19] ABC books, such as the ART OF LETTERS, must have been common to all schools.[20]

The methods of education changed very little during the late seventeenth and eighteenth centuries. The context of that education, however, was radically altered. Following the British capture of New Amsterdam in 1664, the Dutch had slowly to adjust to life in an English Crown Colony. For a long while the Dutch continued to be the dominant force within the life of New York. But Dutch immigration had virtually ceased when the Netherlands could no longer claim trade interest in these shores, and slowly the British population assumed majority proportions.[21] More and more of life had to be lived according to British custom, and the English language slowly displaced the Dutch in the city's commerce and industry. As this happened, the Dutch schools were increasingly seen as the fortresses of Dutch language and culture.

Writing nearly two centuries later, Kilpatrick observed:

It is almost pitiable to see the blind zeal of the church leaders in resisting the spread of the English language. The closer the touch with Holland, the blinder and more vehement the zeal. If there had been an early willingness to accept the inevitable, to translate the church service into English, and to effect ecclesiastical independence from Holland, the numbers and wealth of this church at the present time would be vastly greater. But all of the strength of the Dutch character seemed rooted in opposition.[22]

Kilpatrick's judgment may sound harsh, but he had just previously cited the appointment of Mr. Barend De Forest (January 5, 1725-1726), which appointment read, in part: "all who belong to the Dutch Reformed Church and have any regard for God, and prefer the worship of the Dutch Reformed Church, cannot but see and acknowledge that . . . it is equally necessary for [the school children] to be versed in the language in which God's worship is conducted and exercised [as well as to know English]"[23] It is, therefore, hardly surprising to find that the *Articles of Union* (which in 1771 ended the unhappy rivalry between the Coetus and Conferentie parties in the Dutch Church in America), are nearly as insistent about language as about doctrine in Article 31: "Schools under the Care of Churches." That article reads:

Finally, the respective congregations shall hereafter make it their business to establish public or private schools, in which under the direction of Consistories, instruction shall be given as much in the languages as in the fundamental principles or doctrine of the Reformed Dutch Church as the same are taught in our Low Dutch Churches.[24]

The Dutch Church slowly came to terms with her environment. From 1764 there were regular English worship services, beginning in New York City and slowly becoming less and less unusual elsewhere. In 1767 the *Liturgy and Psalms* was translated into English by the Collegiate Church. In 1788 the Synod had all of the Standards of Doctrine translated into English. And in 1792, when the American Church met to chart her independent existence and to frame her institutional life as a denomination in the United States of America, her Constitution (called the "Explanatory Articles") was immediately published in English. Two years later, the Synod took the final plunge and voted to keep its minutes in English.[25]

Such radical transition could not occur without deeply unsettling effect upon the common life of a church that continued to call herself the Reformed Protestant Dutch Church. The pain of those changes is perhaps nowhere more evident than in the area of primary education. The "Explanatory Articles" reflect this in the only direct word spoken about regular education.

The zeal of the Reformed Church, for initiating children early in the truth [expressed in Article 54th of the Church Orders, where care is taken that Schoolmasters shall be of the Reformed religion], cannot be evidenced in the same manner in America, where many denominations of Christians, and some who do not even profess the Christian religion, inhabit promiscuously; and where Schoolmasters can seldom be found who are members of the church. In such situation it is recommended to parents to be peculiarly attentive to the religious education of their children, not only by instructing them, and daily praying with them at home, but by never employing Schoolmasters whose characters are unascertained or suspicious, and especially none who scoff at the holy scriptures or whose conduct is immoral.

It is also further recommmended that parents endeavor to prevail upon school-masters to make the children belonging to the Dutch Church, commit to memory, and publicly repeat in the school, one section of the Heidelbergh Catechism, at least once every week.[26]

The straightforward insistence that it was proper and expected for every Reformed Congregation to have its own school is gone by 1792. The Dutch immigrants were, by the end of the eighteenth century, curiously willing to bend to the "American way" of doing education. There is in the Explanatory Articles very little which reflects the necessity of maintaining an "us over against them" attitude. In schools, especially, there is no separatism, only concern that nothing be taught which would have a negative effect upon the religious experience of the young. In fact, if we listen carefully to Article 31, we can even hear a note of mission. Schoolmasters are to be "prevailed upon" to have the children of the Dutch Church memorize and publicly repeat *in the school* sections of the Catechism.

In 1809 the last uneasiness regarding the decline of parochial schools among the Dutch Churches surfaced at the General Synod. A committee appointed by the Classis of New York reminded all that the Church Order of Dordt expected each church to establish an extensive educational program to be administered domestically by parents, scholastically by schoolmasters of the church, and ecclesiastically by "pastors, elders, readers or visitors of the sick." The authors of the 1809 report observed:

It is the system of complete organization which promotes the unity, forms, while it preserves, the habits, combines the efforts, increases the strength, and pours moral health into the fountains of society. In the neglect of this system, it is impossible that any society can so fully preserve the spirit of one body, and preserve its infant members from corruption, indifference, or alienation.[27]

The link in "the system" for which the committee showed such concern was, of course, the parochial school. The members were rather well convinced that the other parts of "the system"—the home and the church—were carrying on their functions rather well. The disappearance of the parochial school and the uncertain religious nature of its more public replacement worried the committee. The members concluded:

Whilst, therefore, it may be difficult to carry it into effect, it is surely worthy of the attempt, and your committee would recommend the following resolutions:
1. That it be recommended to each Consistory to divide the congregation into as many districts as there may be schools required, and that respectable and influential men be associated under the direction of the Consistory, as trustees for the school, in each district.

2. That it shall be the duty of these trustees to look out for suitable schoolmasters, and examine the qualifications of such as may apply, and take all proper measures to provide such support and accommodations as will secure for these stations men of sound principles and competent attainments.

3. That the turstees, or a committee of them, visit the school of their district once every month, to carry into effect, as far as circumstances will permit, the sixth article in the preamble to this report, and that they be particularly careful to engage the teacher to instruct his pupils in the doctrines of the Reformation, confining the children of the Reformed Church to their own standard.

4. That the pastor of the congregation be *ex officio* chairman of each district committee, when he may find it convenient to attend; and that he visit the several district schools in rotation, as frequently as possible; and that at their first meeting they choose a chairman for one year, whose duty it shall be to call them together as often as circumstances require, and to pay special attention to the monthly visitation.[28]

The Committee's report met with little success within the Church. Already many of the most prominent members of the Church were deeply involved in the Free School/Public School movement,[29] determined that in a free America, education was necessary for the continued welfare of the nation and therefore, education was the right and responsibility of all citizens. The Church may not always have been wholeheartedly in the crusade for the common school, but the Reformed Church in America was very quick to accept the common school as a most effective and efficient means by which to insure the Church a literate laity. In the church Constitutions of 1833 and 1874 there is no word regarding parochial education. From 1840 to the 1870's many overtures were introduced to Synod concerning desired changes, expansions or guarantees for the common school.[30]

About 1850 another attempt was made to revive parochial schools. Mr. Samuel B. Schieffelin provided some funds for this purpose. At first there was considerable interest, "Christian School Books" published and "encouraging reports of the influence of Christian training" were sent back to Synod. "But it was found that the subject did not take hold of the heart of the Church. Sometimes such schools seemed desirable, but the Public School System seemed all sufficient.[31] With the waves of new Dutch immigrants in the middle of the century, parochial schools could bridge the gulf between their native language and their new American environment. The Germans in the Midwest benefited from the parochial school for the same reason. But by the end of the nineteenth century most parochial schools of Reformed Churches had died. The denomination was obviously at peace with the common school as long as the children of the church were adequately trained in basic reading, writing and arithmetic and so long as nothing was taught which forthrightly contradicted biblical teachings. The Synod itself "regarding our common schools as essential to our common welfare" stated:

The Common School is vitally essential to the fusing of the heterogeneous elements of our population into one nation, to the end that popular suffrage may continue to be a sure buttress of our government.[32]

What the denomination ideologically here recognized to be in the best interest of the nation, it had long before seen to be in the practical best interest of the Reformed Church in America.

The Dutch Reformed Church in America had existed under British rule for barely fifty years when some among her membership began to sense that doing things in the old Dutch fashion and depending on the Classis of Amsterdam for advice, counsel and direction might not long continue to meet the needs which the Church faced here. As year followed year, citizens of this soil sensed that to be an "American"—this "new" creature—was to be something far different from a transplanted European. Generations who had never seen Europe were born, matured and died in the colonies. Slowly the notion grew: American problems needed American solutions. With a system of lay education well established, the problem which most concerned the Church was the development of means whereby a supply of capable pastors, well instructed in the Reformed theology, could be assured for the growing number of American congregations.

During the earliest years of the Dutch experience in America it was normal for congregations in the New World to look to the Netherlands for pastors. The Holy Spirit, however, touched young lives in America also. In 1653, Samuel Megapolensis (1632-1706) responded by attending Harvard College (graduating in 1656) and then returning to the Netherlands for additional theological study.[33] Finally, at the age of 30, he was ordained by the Classis of Amsterdam and in 1664 returned to America, serving the Church in New Amsterdam from 1664 to 1668. Megapolensis more or less established the pattern that was to remain normative for American ministerial candidates

throughout the seventeenth century. By 1700, several men had
gone from America to the Netherlands for theological training
and for ordination.[34]

This system assured that Reformed pastors in the American
Churches would be as thoroughly trained as pastors serving
congregations in the Netherlands. The system, however, had
two serious shortcomings.: 1) it could not very well equip
American students for the needs and challenges of an increasingly American ministry, and 2) in both time and money the
system was extremely expensive. In fact it had high costs in life
itself. More than one candidate was lost at sea after years had
been spent in the Netherlands preparing for ministry in America.

As American situations changed, this system proved to be a
more and more serious handicap to the life and work of the
Church. Men of vision, during the first half of the eighteenth
century, labored with determination to establish some American means for training pastors as well as for ordaining them.
Perhaps no person was more dedicated to or influential in this
struggle than was Theodorus Frelinghuysen (1723-1761).
Under his leadership the Coetus of Churchmen in America
declared itself to have all of the powers of a classis.[35] In the
minds of at least half of the Reformed Churchmen this act
settled the issue of the right to ordain. Others were not convinced and felt that the Coetus had violated Church order and
assaulted proper authority.

Even though this issue was to tear violently at the fabric of
the Dutch Church in America until 1771, efforts continued,
nevertheless, to establish an American school to train pastors in
the Dutch Reformed tradition. In 1755 Frelinghuysen was
asked by the Coetus to go to the Netherlands to raise funds for
such a school. His commission gives some idea of educational
concerns at that time. In part it read:

Inasmuch as it is expedient, for the glory of God, and conducive to the
salvation of men, to establish in these recently inhabited ends of the earth
seminaries of true philosophy as well as of sound doctrine, that men may
be imbued with the principles of human wisdom, virtue and unostentatious
piety: Therefore, we, pastors and elders of the Reformed Church of both
provinces, viz., of New York and New Jersey, in North America, being
assembled in a Coetus, and having established an alliance among ourselves,
do resolve in these present critical times to strive with all our energy, and
in the fear of God, to plant a university or seminary for young men

destined for study in the learned languages and in the liberal arts, and who are to be instructed in the philosophical sciences; also that it may be a school of the prophets in which young Levites and Nazarites of God may be prepared to enter upon the sacred ministerial office in the Church of God. Indeed, because our country is yet new, and not possessed of so great wealth as is required for the work prescribed, therefore, we earnestly beseech all the well disposed, and implore them to be willing to help us with the power of money. . . . [36]

Preoccupied with efforts to heal the sad breach in the Church, Frelinghuysen was prevented from leaving for the Netherlands until 1759. By then the Netherlands Church was so aware of the wretched struggle between its American clergymen that few persons cared to invest in what must have seemed a very partisan venture. In 1761 a disillusioned Frelinghuysen returned to America only to be washed overboard and drown less than one day from New York Harbor. [37]

It is one of the ironies of Reformed Church history that while the "Coetus" (that group which first saw the need for American training of American churchmen) was so totally unsuccessful, their antagonists in the "Conferentie," who had so argued against American ecclesiastical freedom and educational autonomy, had almost no trouble in securing a charter which provided for a Dutch professor of theology in Kings College (now Columbia University) when it was established in 1753. When Frelinghuysen's dream was finally realized in 1766 and a charter was obtained for Queens College (now Rutgers University) the ecclesiastical authorities in the Netherlands found themselves attempting to arbitrate and heal a deep schism in which each side was convinced that its school and its method of ministerial preparation was the only one that merited acceptance.

To further confuse the issue some American (and some Dutch) churchmen suggested that neither Kings nor Queens College was the best way and that a Dutch theological professor should be attached to the College of New Jersey (now Princeton University). Perhaps it was this last proposal which suggested to the Dutch Church a way out of the dilemma. In writing to the Coetus (January 8, 1771) the Classis of Amsterdam proposed:

As soon as the desired reconciliation of the now divided brethren shall be effected, a Professor (or rather two Professors) of Theology should be elected, as was proposed in the first plan, with a sufficient salary, and that such Professor, without standing in any relation to any existing academy, give lessons in theology etc., in his own dwelling, to such students only, as can show by certificates, that they have been two or three years, either at one of the Colleges, or at a High School, or Gymnasium, under able teachers in the languages, philosophy, etc., who may now be in your country, or who may come hereafter.[38]

In October, 1771 the "desired reconciliation" was consummated with what have come to be called the "Articles of Union." In Articles 28 and 29 the Reformed Churchmen in America agreed to the following:

Concerning the Professorate, we will act according to the advice of the Rev. Classis of Amsterdam. We will provisionally choose one or two professors to teach didactic, eleutic, exegetic, etc. theology, according to the received doctrines of our Low Dutch Reformed Church, to which office we, according to the judgment of the classis, will choose, on favorable terms, such divines from the Netherlands as are of acknowledged learning, piety, and orthodoxy, and immutably attached to the Netherlands formulas of union, said Classis having promised to recommend suitable characters.

The professor or professors above mentioned, as soon as the wished for reconciliation in this country is obtained and finally established, shall be chosen and called on a sufficient salary, though not without the approbation of the general assembly, with this provision, that such professors shall not stand in any connection with English academies, but shall give lectures in their own dwellings, to such students only who can produce testimony that they have studied two or three years at a college or academy under approved teachers, and improved themselves in preparatory studies, such as the languages, philosophy, etc. Such professor or professors shall also preach once every month or fortnight, in Dutch or English, as well as to assist the minister of the place where he or they reside as to afford the student a good model of preaching, in consequence of which the Rev. professor or professors shall be subject to the particular and general assemblies in the same manner as is already specified particularly of the minister.[39]

This action committed the Reformed Church to a new method of ministerial preparation—a method so common today that we take it for granted. Prior to this action a man studied theology in some university and was thereby qualified for pastoral office. If such university training were not possible, a candidate spent a period of months observing the daily activities of an outstanding clergyman and discussing theology with him.

By the actions of 1771 there was created for the first time the concept of a separate, professional school of theology, outside any university structure and quite distinct from parish life. The American Revolution may have delayed its actualization until 1784 and financial expediencies may have distorted some of its intended shape, but by 1771, in response to the politics of the Coetus-Conferentie fight, the theological seminary of the Reformed Church was conceived. This unexpected "middleway"—this pragmatic solution to an intensely emotional situation— became for America the accepted method of ministerial training. In 1794, the Associate Presbytery (in Western Pennsylvania); in 1805, the Associate Reformed Church; and in 1807, the Andover Congregationalists followed the Dutch Church's example and founded seminaries. So popular and accepted did this method of theological education become that between 1810 and 1840 more than forty seminaries were established by American denominations.

For the Reformed Church this development was once more a practical response to the denomination's theological commitment to education. There can be no doubt that Queens/Rutgers College suffered because of the development of the seminary we now call New Brunswick. As a matter of fact, during the period from 1810 to 1825 the college virtually gave up its existence so that the seminary could live. A quick check of the colleges attended by seminary students during this same period can perhaps help us understand why the Reformed Church seems to have been so willing to live with this kind of arrangement. Of the ninety men who entered the ministry of the Reformed Church as graduates of New Brunswick from 1810 to 1825 only nine were graduates of Queens College. Perhaps even more instructive are the figures for the years from 1784 to 1810 when only eight out of eighty-six were Queens graduates. [40] Perhaps it was such data that led the great John Henry Livingston so to analyse the situation that in 1813 he could observe (in a letter to his friend, the Rev. Dr. John B. Romeyn) that "as a literary institution, Queens College is not necessary; its funds are inadequate and will so continue, nor will nor can it ever prosper in the neighborhood of two powerful rivals [Princeton and Columbia]...."[41] This conclusion encouraged Dr. Livingston to suggest that the College be merged with the Seminary to form a "Theological College." This proposal was forwarded to the General Synod in June, 1815. The "Plan of a Theological

College, to be formed by a union between Queens College, and the Professorate" included the following:

1. Let this College, when formed, have, for its object, primarily, the education of young men for the Gospel ministry. For securing this object, the religion of the scriptures, as explained in the Belgic Confession of Faith and Heidelbergh Catechism, shall be the basis of all the instruction given in this institution.
2. As it is not probable that so many youth, designed for the ministry, will offer themselves for admission in this College, as to occupy the time and exercise the talents of the teachers; let a select number, designated for any other profession (say, 20,30,40,50) be admitted, *speciali gratia*, who shall be subject to all the rules and regulations of the College. The age at which students are to be admitted, to be not less than 14 years.
3. Let there be four professors who shall be appointed as follows:
   1. The professor of theology.
   2. The professor of Biblical Criticism.
   3. The professor of Ecclesiastical History.
   4. The professor of Mathematics, &c.
   5. Let the three Theological professors be thus appointed by General Synod, who shall specify their departments in theological studies; their other services to be regulated by the trustees.[42]

As such, the plan was approved by the Board of Trustees of the College, but a shortage of funds prevented its ever being fully implemented. In future years Rutgers was to survive but only by the means of greater and greater public funding, becoming a state university in 1917.

We must once more observe that an action that would give every appearance of indicating that the Reformed Church had little commitment to education, when carefully scrutinized, is indeed evidence that the Church had very clear educational ideals and dealt pragmatically with them. In the attempt to assure the Church a thoroughly trained clergy, neither established ways of doing things nor existing institutions were sacrosanct.

The history of the Church's "western" institutions ought also to be read in this light. In their history, however, the "recent immigrant" nature of their public added a significant new factor to the educational ideal. The Church's educational program and institutions had to serve as bridges between the Dutch colonists and the English-speaking American culture. Primary parochial institutions were called into existence in places such as Holland,

Michigan in order to make a laity, already literate in one culture, equally able to understand and share God's Word within another culture. The Minutes of the Classis of Holland indicate that at the first meeting of the Classis (April 23, 1848) school districts (for parochial primary schools) were discussed.[43] At the second meeting (September 27, 1848) an extended discussion of education concerned the Classis, on the basis of which the members concluded: "the schools must be promoted and cared for by the churches, as being an important part of the Christian calling of God's church on earth. All lukewarmness and coldness toward that cause *must* be rebuked."[44]

Accordingly, parochial primary schools were begun as early as 1848.[45] In 1851, with the help of the eastern church, an Academy was undertaken. Eleven years later college level classes were offered and in 1866 the first class graduated from Hope College. When seven of the eight members of that class petitioned the General Synod asking permission to undertake theological studies in the midwest, the "Western" Seminary of the Reformed Church in America had its birth.

The histories of these western institutions to a surprising extent duplicated the rise and fall of their eastern predecessors. As facility with the English language grew among the Dutch in the midwest and as public schools were better equipped, concern for parochial education within the Reformed Church slowly shifted to concern for quality in public education. Even academies such as those in German Valley, Illinois and Cedar Grove, Wisconsin (as well as at Holland, Michigan), while they continued well into the twentieth century, faded into non-existence as public high schools met the educational needs of the Church.[46] Hope College very well might have been allowed to become a secular institution, as had Rutgers, if the times and situations had remained the same. By the end of the nineteenth century Darwinian biology, proclaiming that humanity was really not all that unique, was receiving an open hearing in secular universities. Only slightly later Freudian psychology further suggested that persons were not really responsible for their actions. These views revolutionized the traditional way of looking at human existence and galvanized the Reformed Church into insisting that the college education of her sons and daughters, while leading to a thorough understanding of men like Darwin and Freud, should always emphasize the unique relationship between human persons and their God. Rutgers University could no longer be expected to respond to this desire of the Church. Therefore the Church's attention was focused on Hope College and later on Central (purchased from the Baptists in 1922) and Northwestern.[47]

So the Church today relies upon public education to supply her sons and daughters with the basic tools of learning. She sees her colleges as instruments to provide a Christian context for higher learning, while her seminaries are charged with the responsibility of preparing men and women to clearly proclaim God's Word and minister to his people. Such institutions as Catechism, Sunday School and the Board of Education have also contributed to the Church's activity in education. But in this brief survey nothing could be said of them or of the very fine work done by Annville Institute and the Southern Normal School as well as by mission schools in North America and abroad, each of which richly deserves to have its own history told.

This history has shown our forefathers to have been motivated by a view of education which sought to provide the church with a literate laity and a well trained clergy. In seeking to maintain that noble objective, the Reformed Church of the past has proven to be determined and yet flexible, idealistic and yet pragmatic. As times and situations change and alter the effectiveness of our educational programs and institutions, the Reformed Church could do worse than to imitate her leaders of the past.

The Role of Women
in the India Mission, 1819-1880

Barbara Fassler

Today the Reformed Church in America is questioning old assumptions about male and female roles. On October 14, 1973, Ms. Joyce Stedge was installed as pastor of the Rochester Reformed Church of Accord, New York,[1] though debate about the legality of her ordination continued.[2] Throughout the denomination, women are becoming elders, deacons, and denominational administrators. In 1974, the Christian Action Commission presented to General Synod a resolution entitled "Feminism and the Church," calling upon the church to "reaffirm the equality of all men and women in Christ," and outlining steps by which the church could "correct its discrimination against women."[3] In Reformed Church families, husbands and wives are dividing tasks in new ways, and an article in the *Church Herald* of February 8, 1974, challenges Reformed Church men to achieve a masculinity which is enhanced, not threatened, by feeding the baby and changing the diaper.[4] The "new feminism" of the 1970's has forced church people to re-assess the meaning of "masculine" and "feminine" within the Christian community.

The same kind of re-assessment was taking place one hundred years ago, in the 1870's, in the Reformed Church India mission. An examination of the role of women in that mission, from its inception in 1819 to the end of the 1870's, can be useful in present-day evaluations of the meaning of men's and women's roles in the church.

In 1819 the Reformed Church sent John Scudder, M.D., and his wife Harriet, who joined other early American missionaries going to Ceylon, and then India. A crucial difference between American and Indian society was that in the United States of 1819, women freely attended worship services led by men, and were examined by male physicians. Thus a male evangelist or physician could reach women as well as men. But in the Indian society of 1819, women, especially women of the upper castes, did not readily attend evangelical services led by men, and there was a very strong taboo against a woman being examined by a male physician. Instead, Indian women were attended by female midwives. In order to build a mission that reached Indian women in equal numbers with Indian men, the missionaries would have had to change radically their concepts of male and female roles; they would have had to train their women in medicine, and free them from private domestic obligations so that they could work with Indian women. However, American families did not do this; they established a mission run primarily by men, reaching far more men than women. A more detailed analysis will show how this came about.

An examination of the activities of early Protestant missionaries, including the Scudders and their compatriots, shows that the male missionaries established two basic guides to their mission effort. First, missionaries must go where the people are, not wait for the people to come to them; second, missionaries should offer some valued service as a means of gaining access to people and building the rapport needed for successful evangelizing. As the first medical missionary ever sent from the United States to any country,[5] John Scudder's contribution to the mission field was to recognize the importance of this second principle, to demonstrate that medical care was one of the most effective services missionaries could offer, and to stick to his beliefs despite criticism from those who accused him of secularizing his mission by spending more time healing the body than the soul. Pioneer that he was, however, and sound as his principles were, he and the other missionaries practiced them in such a way as to make them effective primarily for Indian men.

The first principle was, go where the people are. The early missionaries decided that the people were in the marketplaces. Therefore, especially during the first thirty years, the primary activity of the missionary men was to travel from village to village, offering medical care, preaching, and distributing Christian literature in the marketplaces. From this task, which the men regarded as their most important, women were largely excluded. Mrs. William Chamberlain says that "early missionary women accompanied their husbands on tours, gathering the women, teaching the Lord's Prayer, Commandments, Apostle's Creed, Catechism,"[6] and Julius Richter lists village evangelizing as one of the types of work for women in India.[7] Nevertheless, a careful examination of the Arcot annual reports and of the earlier letters from John Scudder and his companion Miron Winslow to the Board, shows that, before 1870, with the occasional exception of the redoubtable Harriet Scudder, Reformed Church missionary wives did not commonly accompany their husbands on evangelizing trips. This is borne out by a 1823 letter to the Board from Scudder and Winslow, in which they state that "domestic duties . . . prevent [our wives] from laboring, to any great extent, among the people."[8] By "laboring among the people," they mean evangelizing of adults. The letter goes on to describe how the women take almost all of the responsibility for schools for children.

This evangelizing effort, run primarily by men, reached mostly men. In 1820, during his first year on the field, John Scudder listed the numbers attending evangelistic services. Typically the audience was eighty to ninety percent men.[9] By 1871, a typical village congregation was two-thirds men.[10] The annual reports of the Arcot Mission from 1854 to 1880 contain dozens of accounts of conversions, only a very few of which involve women.[11] The mission *Manual* of 1877 was very male oriented. Women were undoubtedly being converted, but in this summation of the mission's work, there are fourteen stories of native conversions, not a single one of which is a woman.[12] This same *Manual* contains an encomium to "village Christians" which lists not hardships women would face, such as abuse from husband or in-laws, divorce, or reduction of household allowance, but hardships men might face upon becoming Christian: loss of employment, foreclosure of debts, false court suits, loss of credit, and inability to find land for rent. The encomium ends by praising these village Christians for having "*manfully* and uncompromisingly breasted the waves of surging persecution.[13]

Principle two was, offer a valued service. The two major services offered by the missionaries were medical care and education. Both, as we shall see, were male-oriented.

Although the medical mission was justified to critics back home by the argument that it reached women who would have been inaccessible to the (male) missionaries in any other way,[14] the medical mission still reached far more men than women. Annual reports of the dispensary and hospital throughout the first fifty years show that even as late as 1870 the Arcot hospital was still treating two or three times as many men as women. One night more than seventy years after John Scudder first began healing in India, three different Indian men came in the course of a single night to the Arcot doctor's home asking for advice about their wives in difficult childbirth. However, all three men refused to allow a male doctor to examine their wives. There were no women physicians at the clinic. By morning all three wives were dead.[15]

Though Indian culture contained medical women who ministered to their own sex, American culture did not. In 1819, indeed up until the 1860's, American medical schools would not admit women students, and women did not even enter formal nurse's training until the Civil War.[16] The missionaries followed the practice of their own culture. During the first fifty years, they trained Indian men in medicine, but not American or Indian women.

A few steps, however, prepared for the changes which began to occur in the 1870's. Back in the 1820's John Scudder, to meliorate Indian people's objections to a male doctor treating women, took his wife with him. While he did the treatment, she talked to the women about Christ.[17] She is even described in one source as "following up" the doctor's patients, though whether this has any medical implication is unclear.[18] Later, native women took over this evangelizing role, and in 1867 a native woman "Bible reader" was employed in the Arcot hospital, though her role was evangelical rather than medical.[19] That same year, however, saw the first Indian "female nurse," listed in the hospital report. She did not earn as much as the male nurses or orderlies; in fact, she earned less than the water carriers and scavengers.[20] Since there is no mention of the hospital beginning a training program for female nurses, and since she was paid so little, it can be assumed that her duties were sanitary and menial rather than medical, but it was at least a small start.

At this same time, the hospital was desperately short of doctors. In 1871, the Board wrote to Dr. W. W. Scudder that, in spite of great efforts, they had failed to find another "medical man" to send to India.[21] There is no indication that it occurred to them to try to find, or to train in India, a "medical woman."

But conditions were beginning to change. In the United States, women had used the Civil War to work themselves into medical service as nurses.[22] In addition, the Women's College of Medicine in Philadelphia was now graduating the first American women doctors.[23] In 1869, the methodists sent Clara Swain, M.D., to India. She was the first woman medical missionary sent to any field by any American society or board.[24] Twelve years later the Reformed Church had a chance to send a woman to China, another culture where women were largely inaccessible to male physicians. China mission personnel pled for her; the Women's Board of Foreign Missions promised to meet her expenses, but the all-male Board of Foreign Missions, which had veto power over decisions of the Women's Board of Foreign Missions, turned down the proposal as "contrary to good policy and inexpedient."[25]

However, even if the Reformed Church was not yet ready to accept a woman physician, it did, in the 1870's, fifty years after John Scudder's arrival in India, finally begin to train Indian women as nurses and midwives. Doctors at Arcot had for quite some time been training native men in medicine; in 1870 three young men so trained were graduated and sent out in sole charge of medical dispensaries, capable of handling all but the most serious cases.[26] That year it occurred to Dr. Silas Scudder to propose training Indian women as nurses and midwives. Such women, he predicted, would be eagerly sought out by women of both high and low caste, and could save the lives of "hundreds upon hundreds of women and children."[27] However, though the Arcot hospital had been supporting a training program for males for some time, Dr. Scudder wrote that the government would have to support training of women nurses and midwives, since the Arcot hospital had no funds. This delayed the project seven years. Finally it was begun under British government support, and women were on their way.

A woman physician arrived in 1900. Dr. Ida Scudder, granddaughter of Dr. John Scudder, grew up in the Arcot mission, and, as a teen ager, had been present on that night when three Indian women were allowed to die rather than be examined by a male physician. On that night Ida Scudder decided to go to the United States for training as a physician and return to India's women.

It is clear, in summary, that missionary women did not follow the two principles which formed the basis of male missionaries' work; missionary women were guided by another principle: the priority of their wifely duties. During the first fifty years, only wives were allowed to go to the mission field.[29] Rufus Anderson, president of the American Board of Commissioners for Foreign Missions, under which Reformed Church missionaries operated for the first years, had many good reasons for women to go to the mission field, and they went in nearly as large numbers as men, but when it came to sending single women, all these reasons collapsed, because they were all based upon a woman's service, not to the mission or to Indian women, but to the missionary who was her husband. Anderson's rationale for women on the mission field begins, "woman was made for man,"[30] and goes on from there. The concept is apparent in one of John Scudder's fellow missionaries, who wrote in 1822, praising his deceased wife,

she had made it one principal object of her life, to stand between me and those cares which did not immediately relate to giving instruction to the people.[31]

In the 1850's, when the missionaries were establishing rules for the newly formed Arcot mission, they were still following these same priorities for women. The rule states,

The companions whom God has graciously given us are expected, so far as health, *family duties* and other circumstances may allow, to labor among heathen women by visiting them in their houses and using other appropriate means to bring them to a knowledge of truth.[32]

Within these priorities. American women evolved a strong mission: the operation of boarding and day schools for boys and girls. This mission did not follow either of the two principles which were the basis of the men's work. It asked the Indian children to come to the missionary rather than the missionary going to them; thus it was a mission which the wife could carry on while her husband was out evangelizing in the villages or handling a medical emergency. Second, the women offered a service—education—which was culturally acceptable to them (teaching, unlike medicine, was then a common profession for women in the United States), but not to Indian women. Indian women were accustomed to being attended by female midwives, but only the temple prostitutes were taught to read, and Indian men and women looked upon female education with deep suspicion and fear. However, as missionary wives struggled to overcome Indian prohibitions against female education, they developed a strong and effective mission to women, which had a tremendous effect upon Indian society.[33]

Other historians have discussed the value of these schools to Indian women, and the enormous effort missionary women expended to build and support them. This study will concentrate on an analysis of male and female roles in the schools.

To begin with, schools were regarded by the men as "women's work," and thought to be less important than the work the men did. In a letter to the Board in 1823, John Scudder describes the success of the boarding schools, but then hastens to assure his readers that he is not spending his valuable time on such low-priority work, away from his evangelistic duties, but that the work of the schools is carried on almost entirely by missionary wives:

By some of the above remarks, you will understand that our boarding schools still continue to be a source of great encouragement. We have recently commended a school of this description at Manepy, so that we now have one at each station. Perhaps it may be thought by some, that we are forsaking the more appropriate work of a missionary, and confining our attention too much to the education of these children and youth. But it should be distinctly understood, that the care and instruction of these schools devolve, in a great degree, on the females of our mission, assisted by natives; and though domestic duties may prevent them from laboring, to any great extent, among the people, they may in this way be very useful to the cause.[34]

Although the women did a great deal of the every-day work, it was always men who were supervisors, who represented the work of the schools to those outside, and who wrote the annual reports back to the Board in America. Behind-the-scenes coaching in these reports is revealed by such statements as "Mrs. Scudder informs me ... " followed by the report. One of the signs of change in the 1870's was that Mrs. J. W. Scudder stopped informing and started writing the report herself.[35]

The wives who were the first teachers were gradually replaced by more and more native men, even in the all-girl schools. At first the instruction in the girls' boarding schools was given almost entirely by wives. But by 1861 "one of the catechists" (only men were trained as catechists then) was giving three hours of academic instruction per day in the girls' boarding school, after which the girls assembled on the veranda of the mission house to be "further examined and taught" by Mrs. Ezekial Scudder, who heard their lessons of the morning and taught them sewing.[36] In 1864 the Arcot report stated that the female seminary, under the immediate care of Mrs. Scudder,

was hampered by the lack of a competent teacher.[37] The next
year they hired a male teacher and later also a "headmaster,"
who was a graduate of Arcot Seminary (for boys).[38] Eventually
the girls at Chittoor Female Seminary were taught entirely by
males, under the supervision of a missionary wife, and with a
woman "matron." This trend, common to American mission
schools in general, was somewhat reversed when single women
began to come to the Protestant mission fields in the 1850's and
60's (Arcot received its first single women in 1870). Because
they had the freedom from family responsibilities and the
professional standing, single women often took teaching positions which otherwise might have been held by men.

The schools enrolled more boys than girls, and usually boys'
boarding schools were established before those for girls. This
was, of course, not surprising in view of the Indian cultural
resistance to female education. Typical of the early days is the
report from John Scudder in 1822 that at the Tillipally station
in Ceylon there were seven schools, enrolling a total of 315
boys and 14 girls.[39] Gradually the proportion of girls in these
schools increased. However, even into the 1860's there were
nowhere near as many girls in the schools as boys.[40] For
example, at Vellore in 1862 there were two boarding schools—
one enrolling 40 boys and another enrolling 17 girls.[41]

When the missions began to establish boarding schools, those
for boys were usually established first. Even in the 1850's, the
boys' school at Arcot was established first, and the Chittoor
Female Seminary two years later, in 1855. Missionary wives at
first gave their efforts to the boys' schools. Mrs. Jared Scudder
and Mrs. W. W. Scudder at first examined the boys in the new
Arcot Seminary and heard their recitations.[42] But gradually the
women became more involved in the girls' boarding schools, and
in primary schools, so that instruction in the boys' boarding
schools was done almost entirely by men.

The schools offered a different type of education to girls
than to boys. The purpose of the boys' schools was to train
helpers, Bible readers, schoolmasters, and later medical workers
for the mission. In addition, many graduates went on into
government service or into other professions outside the mission; so many, in fact, that in the 1850's the Arcot mission, as
well as other Protestant missions in India, curtailed their English
language instruction because too many young men were using

the mission schools as preparation, not for work that would help the mission, but for advancement into profitable careers.[43]

The girls' schools had a far different purpose. They were to change the role of women in Indian society, but only in the ways in which that role differed from American ideas of the proper role of women. The missionaries were appalled by the practices of child-marriage, compulsory widowhood for girl children whose intended husbands died, immolation of widows on the funeral pyre of their husbands, female infanticide, and temple prostitution.[44] These practices were opposed by the missionaries and by the British government, and were eventually outlawed.[45] Beyond these most shocking practices, missionaries were concerned about those kinds of oppression which it is more difficult to outlaw: woman's isolation in the home, callous and brutal treatment by their husbands who beat them or laid on them the most irksome manual labor, their total lack of education, and what the missionaries called their "superstition."[46]

Missionaries, through their schools, tried to encourage a different role for women—a role like that of women in American society. The missionaries were convinced that the role they envisioned was a much better role. They may have been right, though it is also clear that they to some extent exaggerated the oppression of Indian women, either because they never obtained an accurate picture of such things as the real power exercised by Indian women in the home,[47] or because it was to their advantage to exaggerate the oppression of women, so as to stir American women to greater zeal in the support of mission work aimed at Indian women.[48] One interesting circumstance is that in Ceylon, real estate was largely the property of women, handed down from mother to daughter, and not to be touched without their consent.[49] John and Harriet Scudder were in Ceylon from 1819 to 1837. The records from those years, in so far as they touch on the Scudders' view of native women, emphasize their oppression, and do not indicate whether, in a time when American women had almost no property rights whatsoever,[50] any of the American missionaries were struck by the power of women in Ceylon and the contrast with their own American laws.

Thus the missionaries, through their schools, tried to bring about what they considered a better role for women. We have said that the missionary wives were considered to owe first priority to their wifely function. The schools they ran taught the same role to Indian girls. The schools were primarily for the purpose of training suitable wives for Indian male Christians. Typical is this statement of purpose, written in 1860 for the Chittoor Female Seminary:

> The object of this school is to train up a class of girls who will be fitted to become the wives of our native helpers. While we strive to give them a good plain education, we do not neglect those things which the wife of a native should know. They learn to cook, to sew, and to do all kinds of house work. We do not wish to raise them above, but to fit them for the position they will be called upon to fill. [51]

Reports of the success of the Chittoor Seminary were frequently stated in terms of the number of graduates who married native Christian men, especially if those men were graduates of Arcot Seminary and/or readers and catechists in the mission. [52] These schools did not primarily train the women themselves for positions in mission work, except that, as the wife of a catechist, a woman might set up a small village school—again, following the pattern of the missionary wife.

The 1870's, however, saw the beginnings of change. In 1869 the first female was hired as a mission teacher, though there were still no female catechists or assistant catechists. [53] By the next year the report listed 12 Christian school mistresses (21 Christian schoolmasters), and, for the first time, a female Bible reader. However, she is not listed with the male Bible readers, but is placed at the bottom of the list, after the Colporteurs. [54] By 1877, in the mission *Manual* section written by Mrs. Jared Scudder, the first mentioned purpose of the seminary is to train not wives but native teachers, though their sphere is limited to the elementary schools, and their future role as wives is still important:

> The great object of the school is to train up a class of girls, who shall be fitted to teach in the primary schools of our Christian villages, and to become good and faithful wives to our native helpers." [55]

Indian girls were not being trained in the use of the privileges their culture gave them, such as offering medical care to other women. Rather, they were being trained to follow the role concepts of American women, and to enter teaching.

Given these concepts of the role of the girls' schools, it is not surprising to find considerable difference in the type and quality of academic education in boys' and girls' seminaries. From the beginning, the subject matter differed. Boys usually studied English and Tamil; girls studied Tamil only.[56] One has only to read the lists of subjects studied by the boys in Arcot Seminary, as they appear year after year in the Arcot reports, and compare them to the subjects studied by the girls at Chittoor Female Seminary, to see that the boys were receiving a much more rigorous academic education. When missionaries reported on the girls' school, they proudly pointed to the non-academic aspects of the girls' education: their skill at sewing, the proceeds from the sale of handmade articles, and the fact that the girls did all their own housework and cooking.[57] The parallel to this for the Arcot Seminary was that the boys were expected to raise part of their own food. However, when the missionaries wrote about this, their main concern was to assure their readers that this activity did not interfere with the academic excellence of the boys' program.[58] Even when studying the same subjects, the girls were not expected to achieve as well as boys: in 1823 as a statement of highest praise, the girls in the Oodooville school were said by John Scudder to "read and write Tamul nearly as well as the boys in the boarding school."[59]

In many ways, then, as we have seen, the schools in which missionary women were so heavily involved remained male oriented. However, their contribution can only be fully appreciated when one recognizes the difficulty of teaching girls anything at all in a society deeply opposed to the education of women, where only temple prostitutes learned to read. A letter to the Board from John Scudder's fellow missionary in 1826 outlines the opposition faced in the early years by missionaries trying to educate Indian girls:

Prejudice and interest combine against us. To raise females is, in the opinion of the other sex here, to raise a pestilence. It is to give them greater opportunities of doing wrong. Besides, it is to take away from the Brahmins and priests one principal source of support—the females, having a very considerable control of money matters, and being most devoutly superstitious . . . the parents think, that though the girls learn to sew, there is no benefit, as they have no clothes to be made; and in the present state of society, it is very much so. With regard to learning to read, write, etc., the effects, which they calculate upon, are not *good*, but *bad*. They only look for an increase of pride and obstinacy in the female, proportioned to her acquirements, and of course an increase of the difficulty, which the husband now has to manage his wife, so that more *whippings* will be necessary.[60]

Mr. Winslow continues that even Christian young men are often not inclined to accept the Oodooville seminary graduates as wives, because the school routine has rendered them unaccustomed to heavy and unpleasant manual labor. The girls themselves presented opposition, since they were aware that learning to read exposed them to reproach and shame in their society. They would much rather spend their time learning to sew.[61] Fifty years later this was evidently still a problem, since the British government inspector, examining the students in 1877, pronounced the girls strong in sewing but weak in math.[62]

In the face of such opposition, missionaries alone persisted. Even the British government did not make any attempt to educate girls until after 1850. By then, missionary schools all across India were already teaching thousands of girls. [63]

We have said that the 1870's were a decade of changes in the sex role concepts which guided the Arcot mission. It was the decade when Dr. Silas Scudder first proposed training Indian women in medicine; it was the decade when Ida Scudder was growing up in India; it was the decade when single women began arriving to serve as professional teachers and administrators in the girls' schools, thus slowing the shift to male teachers who had replaced the missionary wives; it was the decade when a woman first wrote a part of the mission annual report; it was the decade when the girls' boarding schools began to place more emphasis on preparing not just wives but teachers; it was the decade when the mission began to train and employ Bible women and female catechists.

Finally, it was the decade in which a mission to adult women in their own homes began to receive a stronger emphasis. This mission was called the Zenana mission, after the "zenana" or women's section of an Indian home. Before 1870, missionary women had attempted to evangelize adult Indian women both by a limited program of visiting them in their homes, and by assembling them in groups.

One of the early groups was the prayer meeting. It was a way of reaching women who did not come to the mixed-sex prayer or preaching services led by men and attended mostly by men.

Accounts of these prayer meetings abound in the Arcot reports, year after year. Even missionary wives who play an otherwise marginal role in mission activities appear as leaders of women's prayer groups. At these meetings, Scripture was read, and often elementary reading instruction was given, aimed at enabling women to read Christian literature on their own. Occasionally we read that lessons in hygiene, maternal care, or other aspects of household life were given to village women.[64] These began very early in the century, and they might have provided an early entry for women into the medical mission in a visiting-nurse role which would win them acceptance into Indian women's homes. However, this was never followed through.

Native women, mostly wives of catechists and/or graduates of Chittoor Seminary, were in due time trained to lead the women's prayer groups.[65] Even when women taught such groups, however, men often handled supervision and final examination.[66]

Evangelization of adult women had always been practiced in a limited way, but in the 1870's, the zenana mission gave it much more emphasis. Finally the first principle which had been used by male missionaries since 1819 was being applied to women's work—go where the people are. Married missionary women had always lacked the mobility to do very much of this, but now, with the influx of single women onto the mission field, and with the greater numbers of native women being graduated from the female seminaries, staff was available. The native "Bible women" were introduced into Protestant missions in the 1860's and 1870's, about fifty years after their male counterparts, the catechists and readers.[67] Mrs. Mayou of the Arcot Mission began to use Bible women in 1866.[68] A Bible woman would enter the zenana to read Scripture, give elementary reading instruction, conduct prayer, explain Christian principles, and offer comfort especially to poor, aged and blind women. There is no record of either missionary or native women offering nursing, hygenic or midwife services.

By 1868, the work of these Bible Women was being mentioned and praised in the Arcot Report. By 1873, a female Bible reader is listed as a member of the mission staff, though, as we might expect, she is not listed with the "Bible Readers" (all male) but in a separate category called "Female Bible Readers," at the bottom of the list, after "Colporteurs."[69]

Zenana work was an immediate success,[70] an indication,

perhaps, that the field was ready long before the missionaries were ready to commit the time and effort of their women to carry it on.

These changes in the 1870's were undoubtedly influenced by two important developments in America. First, a significant American feminist movement was forcing changes in property and marriage laws, gaining entry for women into schools of higher education, opening up formerly all-male careers, and gradually making it more acceptable for women to speak in public. The second development in America was that the support for missions was coming more and more from women. American women, stirred by stories of the degradation of heathens, especially heathen women, and fired by reports of the courage and steadfastness of missionaries, rallied in ever increasing numbers. They formed mission societies, contributed money, built nation-wide support networks, sent boxes of supplies, and kept the mission effort in the public eye.[71] At least some of these women undoubtedly began to insist that the mission reach out more effectively to Indian women. In 1869 the criticism of the male-centeredness of the evangelizing effort was strong enough for the missionaries to answer it in their annual report:

We not unfrequently see or hear the remark that the "preaching method," though well adapted to the lower classes, does not and cannot reach the high, and fails altogether in reaching the female population. From this we dissent. We do not deny, that in large cities the proud and wealthy may keep aloof from the preaching missionary, nor that the ladies of the Zenana are beyond the range of his efforts. But our experience does deny, that he fails to reach the higher classes whether male or female. Throughout this district, the Vellala, and the Reddi, the Chetty and the Mudaliar listen as readily as the Pariah and Chuckler. Even the secluded Brahmin is sought and preached to in his Agraharam. As for the women, they seldom fail to compose a part of our audiences. Standing in doorways and on the outskirts of the crowd, they listen as attentively as the men. In many Telegu villages, the weaker sex cluster about the preacher, while their less courageous husbands and brothers listen at a greater distance.[72]

The very existence of such a discussion, never before broached in such an important forum as the annual report, makes it clear that the 1870's, like the 1970's, was a period in which various forces were causing the church to examine ways in which their concepts of the proper role of women may have been effecting their mission.

Footnotes

Introduction

1. Rufus W. Clark, "The Relations of Religion to Civil Liberty," *Centennial Discourses* (New York: Board of Publication of the Reformed Church in America, 1877), p. 16.
2. *Ibid.*, p. 11.
3. Alexis de Tocqueville, *Democracy in America*, edited by J. P. Mayer and Max Lerner (New York: Harper & Row, 1966), pp. 268 and 271.
4. Students interested in Dutch Colonial history should consult John Romeyn Brodhead, *History of the State of New York: First Period, 1609-1644* (New York: Harper, 1853), Thomas J. Condon, *New York Beginnings: The Commercial Origins of New Netherland* (New York: New York University Press, 1968), Edward Tanjore Corwin, ed., *Ecclesiastical Records of the State of New York*, 7 vols. (Albany: J.B. Lyon, 1901-1916), Gerald F. De Jong, *The Dutch in America, 1609-1974* (Boston: Twayne Publishers, 1975), David Maldwyn Ellis, *et. al.*, *A Short History of New York State*, revised edition (Ithaca, New York: Cornell University Press, 1967), Paul Demund Evans, *The Holland Land Company* (Buffalo, New York: Buffalo Historical Society, 1924), Henry S. Lucas, *Dutch Immigrant Memoirs and Related Writings* (Assen, the Netherlands: Van Gorcum Press, 1955), John Pershing Luidens, "The Americanization of the Dutch Reformed Church," unpublished Ph. D. Dissertation, University of Oklahoma, 1969, George L. Smith, *Religion and Trade in New Netherland, Dutch Origins and American Development* (Ithaca: Cornell University Press, 1973), James Tanis, *Dutch Calvinistic Pietism in the Middle Colonies: A Study in the Life and Theology of Theodorus Jacobus Frelinghuysen* (The Hague: Martinus Nijhoff, 1967), Arnold J.F. Van Laer, ed., *Documents Relating to New Netherland, 1624-1626, in the Henry E. Huntington Library* (San Marino, Calif.: Henry E. Huntington Library and Art Gallery, 1924), M.G. Van Rensselaer, *History of the City of New York in the Seventeenth Century*, 2 vols. (New York: Macmillan Co., 1909).
5. In 1688-89 Jacob Leisler led an unsuccessful rebellion of craftsmen, shopkeepers, and small farmers against merchants, landowners and royal officials in New York City.
6. Jacob Arminius was a seventeenth century Professor of Theology at the University of Leyden who opposed the Calvinist doctrine of election.
7. For a good brief study of the role of these lay workers see Gerald F. De Jong, "The *Ziekentroosters* or Comforters of the Sick in New Netherland," *New York Historical Society Quarterly*, LIV (Oct., 1970), pp. 339-359.

8. In 1772 the American branch of the Dutch Reformed Church declared itself independent and became known as the Reformed Protestant Dutch Church in North America. In 1867 it changed its name to the Reformed Church in America, its present designation.
9. For more information on the life of Megapolensis see Gerald F. De Jong, "Dominie Johannes Megapolensis: Minister to New Netherland," *New York Historical Society Quarterly*, LII (Jan., 1968), pp.7-47.
10. N.P. Stokes, *Iconography of Manhatten Island* (New York: 1915-28), IV, p. 55.
11. Edward Tanjore Corwin, ed., *Ecclesiastical Records of the State of New York*, vol. I (Albany: J.B. Lyon, 1901), p. 318.
12. Franklin J. Jameson, ed., *Narratives of New Netherland, 1609-1664* (New York: Charles Scribner's Sons, 1909), pp. 259-260.
13. *Ecclesiastical Records*, I, p. 602.
14. *Ibid.*, IV, p. 2587.
15. Quoted in James Tanis, *Dutch Calvinistic Pietism in the Middle Colonies: A Study in the Life and Theology of Theodorus Jacobus Frelinghuysen* (The Hague: artinus Nijhoff, 1967), p. 82. For a less complimentary estimate of Frelinghuysen see Herman Harmelink III, "Another Look at Frelinghuysen and his Awakening," *Church History*, XXXVII (Dec., 1968), pp. 423-438.
16. *Ecclesiastical Records*, I, p. 525.
17. *Ibid.*, III, p. 1661; IV, p. 2591.
18. *Ibid.*, III, pp. 1719 and 1858.
19. *Ibid.*, IV, pp. 2706-2710.
20. *Ibid.*, V., p. 3645.
21. *Ibid.*, VI, p. 3992.
22. *Ibid.*, p. 3995.
23. See, for example, Nat Hentoff, ed., *The Essays of A.J. Muste* (Indianapolis: Bobbs- Merrill Co., 1967), Graham Taylor, *Pioneering on Social Frontiers* (Chicago: University of Chicago Press, 1930), Norman Vincent Peale, *The Power of Positive Thinking* (New Jersey: Prentice-Hall, 1952).

The American Revolution

1. See J.A. Todd in *Centennial Discourses* (New York: Board of Publication of the Reformed Church in America, 1877), pp. 107 ff.; Willard D. Brown: *History of the Reformed Church in America* (New York: Board of Publication and Bible School Work, 1928), Chapter V. These represent anniversary publications of past years. There is also an abundance of local church histories having the same tendency.
2. T.J. Wertenbacker: *The Founding of American Civilization:* The Middle Colonies (New York and London: Charles Scribner's Sons, 1938), p. 99, quoting A.C. Flick: *Loyalism in New York During the American Revolution* (New York: Columbia University Press, 1901), p. 66.

3. "All the *churches* and schools are closed" after 1776 (H.W. Dunshee: *History of the School of the Collegiate Reformed Dutch Church,* (New York: Aldine Press, "By authority of consistory," 1883), p. 58; "The *congregation* dispersed, and what had been the Reformed Protestant Dutch Church in New York City *disbanded* until after the war" (J.P. Waterbury: *A History of the Collegiate School, 1638-1963,* (New York: Clarkson N. Potter, 1965), p. 63 (italics added).

4. [The designation "Civil Religion" was made popular by Professor Robert N. Bellah and refers to that religious dimension in the life of every people through which it interprets its historical experience in the light of transcendent reality. See Robert N. Bellah, "Civil Religion in America," *Daedalus,* Vol. 96, No. 1 (Winter, 1967), pp. 1-21; Robert N. Bellah, *The Broken Covenant: American Civil Religion in Time of Trial* (New York: The Seabury Press, 1975).—ed.]

5. Rev. James Romeyn (1797-1859), quoted in Benjamin Taylor: *Annals of the Classis of Bergen,* p. 187.

6. A.C. Leiby: *The Revolutionary War in the Hackensack Valley* (New Brunswick: Rutgers University Press, 1962), p. 83.

7. *Centennial Discourses,* p. 524. Pastor Weyberg of Philadelphia, supported by the Classis of Amsterdam, is also sometimes reckoned among our ministers of the period. But he really belonged to the German Reformed Coetus of Pennsylvania.

8. Henry M. Cox: *History of the Reformed Church of Herkimer, N.Y.,* (Herkimer, 1886), p. 13.

9. Taylor, *Annals of the Classis of Bergen,* p. 203; Leiby: *Revolutionary War in the Hackensack Valley,* passim.

10. George Z. Collier: *Tercentenary Studies,* p. 367.

11. Thomas Jones d. 1792: *History of New York During the Revolution* (New York: N.Y. Historical Society, 1879), Vol. I, p. 45; Lorenzo Sabine: *Biographical Sketches of Loyalists of the American Revolution with an Historical Essay* (Boston: Little, Brown, and Co., 1864) Vol. II, p. 214.

12. *Two Hundredth Anniversary of the Old Dutch Church of Sleepy Hollow,* (Tarrytown, N.Y.: Consistory of the First Reformed Church, 1898) pp. 138 ff.

13. *A Glance at Three Hundred Years,* "substance of an address given before General Synod . . . 1927," Privately printed.

14. Leiby: *Revolutionary War in the Hackensack Valley,* p. 228, citing Henry Clinton papers in the Clements Library, Ann Arbor, Michigan.

15. [The term Arminian has roots in the seventeenth century conflict over the doctrine of election in the Netherlands. Jacob Arminius, a professor of Theology at the University of Leyden, headed the opposition against election. In eighteenth century American religion an "Arminian" was one who asserted the free-will of man in the salvation process. —Ed.]

16. [See introduction, pp. 11-13 for another discussion of the Coetus-Conferentie controversy. —Ed.]

17. [The "True Dutch Reformed Church" was organized in 1822 by a small number of Reformed churches which protested what they considered to be the denomination's "liberal" stance on the doctrine of election. It remained in existence as a separate body until 1865, when some of the churches merged with the newly formed Christian Reformed Church. See *True Reformed Dutch Church, Acts and Proceedings, Oct. 1822-June, 1865 (New York: John A. Gray, 1865); James Van Hoeven, "Salvation and Indian Removal: The Career Biography of the Reverend John F. Schermerhorn, Indian Commissioner," Unpublished Ph.D. Dissertation, Vanderbilt University, 1972,* pp. 64-67; Herman Harmelink III, *Ecumenism and the Reformed Church* (Grand Rapids: Eerdman's Publishing Co., 1968), pp. 29-32. —Ed.]

18. The conflict Among the Jersey Dutch during the Revolution," in *Papers presented at the First Annual New Jersey History Symposium,* December 6, 1969, (Trenton: New Jersey Historical Commission, 1970), p. 31.

19. Alice P. Kenney: "The Albany Dutch, Loyalists and Patriots," in *New York History,* XLII (October, 1961).

20. Edward A. Collier: *A History of Old Kinderhood* (New York: G.P. Putnam's Sons, 1914), pp. 165-195; F.N. Zabriskie: *History of the Reformed P.D. Church of Claverack* (Hudson, N.Y.: Stephen B. Miller, 1867) pp. 18-20,25.

21. The pastoral succession, and notes on the affiliation and activity of individual pastors, can be found in Charles Corwin: *Manual of the Reformed Church in America* (Fifth Edition, New York: Board of Publication and Bible School Work, 1922).

22. Leiby: *Revolutionary War in the Hackensack Valley,* p. 203.

23. Ibid., pp. 186-190.

24. [Erastianism is the term pertaining to the Swiss theologian Thomas Erastus (1524-83) who taught, in a loose sense, that the Church must be subservient to the State. —Ed.]

25. Richard P. McCormick: *New Jersey from Colony to State* (Princeton: D. Van Norstrand and Co., 1964,) p. 153.

26. William S. Myers: *The Story of New Jersey* (New York: Lewis Historical Publishing Company, 1945), Vol. I, p. 169.

27. Collier. *History of Old Kinderhood,* p. 180.

28. A.F. Flick: *History of the State of New York,* (Port Washington: Ira J. Friendman for the N.Y. Historical Society, 1962), Vol. III, pp. 347-358.

29. Arthur H. Bill: *New Jersey and the Revolutionary War* (Princeton: D. Van Nostrand and Co., 1964), p. 105; McCormick: *New Jersey From Colony to State, p. 174.*

30. *Cox:* Reformed Church of Herkimer, N.Y., p. 22.

31. See his "Second Memorial Sermon" (1842) entitled "The Revivals of Religion in the Church of Raritan" in *Forty Years at Raritan: Eight*

Memorial Sermons with Notes for a History of the Reformed Dutch Churches in Somerset County, N.J. (New York: A. Lloyd, 1873), pp. 20-39. This document seems to be the basis of the common interpretation of Theodorus J. Frelinghuysen's relation to the "Great Awakening," and to its place in later coetus-conferentie disputes. Evidence now available of which Messler was unaware has received scant critical attention except for Herman Harmelink's article "Another Look at Frelinghuysen and His Awakening," *Church History,* XXXVII (Dec., 1968), pp. 423-438.

The American Frontier

1. Stryker report, 1800 (unpublished), General Synod Archives, New Brunswick Theological Seminary, New Brunswick, New Jersey.
2. *Ibid.*
3. *Minutes,* General Synod, 1791, p. 217.
4. Jacob Jinnings to General Synod, April 15, 1791 (unpublished), General Synod Archives, New Brunswick Theological Seminary, New Brunswick, New Jersey.
5. *Ibid.*
6. *Minutes,* General Synod, 1797, p. 473.
7. *Ibid.*
8. Gerald F. De Jong, *The Dutch in America, 1609-1974* (Boston: Twayne Publishers, 1975), pp. 60-61.
9. *Minutes,* General Synod, 1806, p. 352.
10. *Ibid.*
11. *Ibid.,* p. 353.
12. Charles E. Corwin, *Manual of the Reformed Church in America* (Fifth Edition; New York: Board of Publications of the Reformed Church in America, 1922), p. 221.
13. *Minutes,* General Synod, 1786, p. 150.
14. *Reformed Church in America, Centennial Discourses* (New York: Board of Publications of the Reformed Church in America, 1877), p. 512.
15. *Minutes,* General Synod, 1821, p. 57.
16. *Ibid.,* p. 56.
17. *Ibid.,* 1822, p. 15.
18. *Ibid.,* p. 14.
19. Corwin, *Manual,* p. 222. See also David D. Damarest, *The Reformed Church in America: Its Origin, Development, and Characteristics* (New York: Board of Publications of the Reformed Church in America, 1889), p. 109.
20. *The Magazine of the Reformed Dutch Church,* July, 1828, p. 125.
21. *Ibid.,* p. 95.
22. *Minutes,* General Synod, 1827, p. 52.
23. Minutes of the Proceedings of the Board of Managers of the Mis-

sionary Society of the Reformed Dutch Church, November 20, 1828
(unpublished), General Synod Archives, New Brunswick Theological
Seminary, New Brunswick, New Jersey.
24. *Ibid.*, April 28, 1830.
25. "Circular: Office of the Board of Managers of the Missionary Society
of the Reformed Dutch Church," *Christian Intelligencer*, II (Sept. 24,
1831), p. 31.
26. "The Minutes of the General Synod of the Reformed Dutch Church,"
ibid., II (Sept. 17, 1831), p. 26.
27. *Ibid.*
28. "For the Christian Intelligencer," *The Christian Intelligencer*, II (Sept.
3, 1831), p. 17.
29. *Minutes*, Albany Synod, May, 1830, p. 17.
30. "For the Christian Intelligencer," *Christian Intelligencer*, II (Sept. 17,
1831), p. 25.
31. *Ibid.*, p. 27.
32. *Ibid.*
33. "Circular: Office of the Board of Managers of the Missionary Society
of the Reformed Dutch Church," *ibid.*, II (Sept. 24, 1831), p. 31.
34. "Minutes of the General Synod of the Reformed Dutch Church,"
ibid., II (Sept. 17, 1831), p. 16.
35. "For the Christian Intelligencer," *ibid.*, p. 27.
36. *Minutes*, General Synod, 1830, p. 297.
37. "For the Christian Intelligencer," *Christian Intelligencer*, II (Sept. 3,
1831), p. 18.
38. *Minutes*, General Synod, 1831, p. 378. For a complete study of this
issue see my "Salvation and Indian Removal: The Career Biography of
the Rev. John Freeman Schermerhorn, Indian Commissioner," Unpublished Ph.D. dissertation submitted to the faculty of the Graduate
School of Vanderbilt University, 1971, pp. 57-98.
39. Sydney E. Mead, *The Lively Experiment* (New York: Harper and
Row, Publishers, 1963), p. 91.
40. *Minutes*, General Synod, 1836, p. 470.
41. *Ibid.*, p. 521.
42. *Ibid.*, 1845, p. 499.
43. *Ibid.*
44. *Ibid.*
45. *Ibid.*, 1836, p. 521.
46. Report of the Board of Domestic Missions, 1871, p. 3.
47. *Minutes*, General Synod, 1843, p. 188.
48. *Ibid.*
49. *Ibid.*, 1849, p. 462.
50. See pp. 61-69, this volume.
51. *Minutes*, General Synod, 1848, p. 425.
52. *Ibid.*, p. 427.
53. *Centennial Discourses*, p. 518.

54. Report of the Board of Domestic Missions, 1870, p. 6.
55. *Ibid.*
56. *Ibid., 1871*, p. 7.
57. See pp. 60-61, this volume.
58. Report of the Board of Domestic Missions, 1860, p. 7.
59. *Ibid.*, 1871, p. 5.
60. *Ibid.*, p. 4.
61. *Ibid.*, p. 5.
62. *The Semi-Centennial Convention of the Board of Domestic Missions* (Newark: Board of Publications of the Reformed Church in America, 1883), pp. 16-18.
63. *Minutes*, General Synod, 1899, p. 445.
64. H. Shelton Smith, Robert Handy, Lefferts A. Loetscher, *American Christianity: An Historical Interpretation with Representative Documents, 1820-1960*, II (New York: Charles Scribner's Sons, 1963), p. 220.
65. *Minutes*, General Synod, 1900, p. 762.
66. See Roger D. Kemp, The Reformed Church in America and the Indian American," unpublished thesis presented to the faculty of New Brunswick Theological Seminary, May 1970, for a good historical study of this topic.
67. *Minutes*, General Synod, 1842, p. 503.
68. Report of Committee on the Southern Industrial School at Brewton, Alabama, Sept. 22, 1919 (unpublished), General Synod Archives, New Brunswick Theological Seminary, New Brunswick, New Jersey.
69. *Ibid.*
70. *Ibid.*
71. Annual Report, Southern Normal School, Brewton, Alabama, Aug., 1945 (unpublished), General Synod Archives, New Brunswick Theological Seminary, New Brunswick, New Jersey.
72. *Ibid.*
73. *Ibid.*
74. *Ibid.*
75. See Sharon T. Scholten, "The Rise and Decline of the Reformed Church in Oklahoma," unpublished thesis presented to the faculty of New Brunswick Theological Seminary, May, 1957, for a good study of the mission program of the Reformed Church in Oklahoma.
76. See pp. 71-72, this volume.
77. Corwin, *Manual*, p. 227.
78. See p. 72-73, this volume.
79. Report of the Board of Domestic Missions, 1938, p. 5.
80. *Ibid.*
81. Justice William O. Douglas, *Zorach v. Clauson*, 343 U.S. 306, 313 (1952).
82. Sydney Ahlstrom, *A Religious History of the American People.* (New Haven and London: Yale University Press, 1972), p. 952.

83. Church affiliation for the twentieth century is reported as follows:

Year	Percentage of Total Population
1910	43
1920	43
1930	47
1940	49
1950	55
1956	62
1960	69
1970	62.4

See Ahlstrom, Op. Cit., p. 952.
84. Report of the Board of Domestic Missions, 1950, p. 5.
85. *Ibid.*, p. 15.
86. *Minutes*, General Synod, 1955, p. 86.
87. Stryker Report, 1800 (unpublished), General Synod Archives, New Brunswick Theological Seminary, New Brunswick, New Jersey.

Immigration

1. Benjamin Munn Ziegler, ed., *Immigration, An American Dilemma*, (Boston: D.C. Heath & Co., 1953), p. 17. The immigration figures are as follows:

1821-1830 -	143,439	1891-1900 -	3,687,564
1831-1840 -	599,125	1901-1910 -	8,795,386
1841-1850 -	1,713,251	1911-1920 -	5,735,811
1851-1860 -	2,598,214	1921-1930 -	4,107,209
1861-1870 -	2,314,824	1931-1940 -	528,431
1871-1880 -	2,812,191	1941-1950 -	1,035,039
1881-1890 -	5,246,613		

The literature on immigration is voluminous. The following volumes are good surveys on the subject: Marcus Lee Hansen, *The Immigrant in American History* (Cambridge: Harvard University Press, 1940), and *The Atlantic Migration, 1607-1860, A History of the Continuing Settlement of the United States* (New York: Harper and Row, 1961); Maldwyn Allen Jones, *American Immigration* (Chicago: University of Chicago Press, 1960); Oscar Handlin, *The Uprooted, the Epic Story of the Great Migration that Made the American People* (Boston: Little, Brown & Co., 1951); George M. Stephenson, *A History of American Immigration, 1820-1924* (New York: Russell & Russell, Inc., 1964); and Carl Wittke, *We Who Built America, the Saga of the Immigrant* (New York: Prentice-Hall, 1945).
2. Richard C. Wolf, "The Middle Period, 1800-1870," *Religion in Life*, XXII (Winter, 1952-1953), pp. 72-84.
3. See this volume, pp. 34-42.
4. The basic resource for the Germans and other immigrant groups is the

annual reports of the Board of Domestic Missions of the Reformed Church in America, 1832-1964. There also is information in the *Acts and Proceedings* of the General Synod of the Reformed Church in America for the same years. A report of the work of the Board was made to the General Synod each year. An essay of particular value for the German immigrant situation is George Schnucker, "The German Element in the Reformed Church in America," *Tercentenary Studies, 1928, Reformed Church in America, A Record of Beginnings* (New York: Board of Publications, 1928).

5. Edward Tanjore Corwin, *A Manual of the Reformed Church in America, 1628-1902* (Fourth ed; New York: Board of Publications of the Reformed Church in America, 1902), p. 501. Corwin called Guldin "the Apostle of the Germans."

6. *Minutes*, General Synod, 1845, pp. 424-430. See also Herman Harmelink III, *Ecumenism and the Reformed Church* (Grand Rapids, Wm. B. Eerdmans Publishing Co., 1968), pp. 32-35.

7. See essay by Eugene Heideman, this volume, pp. 102-104. A summary of the relationship of the Reformed Church in America and the Reformed Church in the United States is found in Edward Tanjore Corwin, *A Digest of Constitutional and Synodical Legislation* of the Reformed Church in America (New York: The Board of Publication of the Reformed Church in America, 1906), pp. 584-586. The Reformed Church in America suspended correspondence with the German Reformed Church in 1853. The General Synod of the (Dutch) Reformed Church passed the following resolution at the same time:

Resolved, that this Synod do hereby express, in the most decided and unequivocal manner, their protest against all those sentiments of a Romanizing character and tendency which are technically known as the 'Mercersburg theology,' as being essential departure from the faith, as calculated to lead yet farther astray from the old landmarks of the truth and to undermine the great principles of the Reformation from Popery.

Minutes, General Synod, 1853, p. 319.

8. *Annual Report of the Board of the Domestic Missions*, 1857, pp. 38-87.

9. *Ibid.*, 1858, p. 31.

10. *Ibid.*

11. *Ibid.*

12. See Benjamin C. Taylor, *Annals, the Classis of Bergen, of the Reformed Dutch Church, and of the Churches Under its Care* (3rd ed; New York; Board of Publication of the Reformed Protestant Dutch Church, 1857), for a useful study of the Germans who joined the Reformed Church.

13. The Germania Classis was not formed until September, 1915. When this occurred, Pleasant Prairie Classis had twenty-two member

churches and the Germania Classis seventeen, for a total of thirty-nine. See *The Annual Report of the Board of Domestic Missions*, 1916, p. 11. This report notes that these German speaking churches "have been second to none in their loyal support of the Home and Foreign Missions of the Church."

14. After World War I the development of these German speaking churches was decidedly hindered when the state of Iowa enacted laws forbidding the speaking of any foreign language in public assemblies. Regarding this, the Board of Domestic Missions reported in 1919,

> Possibly none of the mission churches were more seriously affected by the war than were some of the Holland and East Frisian churches in Iowa and the northwest. In some communities, feeling against those Germans or those remotely associated with that country ran so high that churches using anything but the English language in their services were viewed with the utmost suspicion; a suspicion which followed their members to their homes and their vocations. One of our church buildings in the west was burned a few months ago, and there is strong suspicion that its destruction was the result of lawlessness directed by misguided patriotism. In the state of Iowa, where we have over thirty mission churches, many of them using other than English in some of their services, a proclamation of the governor forbade the use of other languages in public assemblies.

Annual Report of the Board of Domestic Missions, 1919, p. 7.

15. Gerald F. DeJong, *The Dutch in America, 1609-1974* (Boston: Twayne Publishers, 1975), p. 262. De Jong's excellent volume is the most recent study of Dutch immigration in America. See also the definitive study by Henry S. Lucas, *Netherlanders in America, Dutch Immigration to the United States and Canada, 1789-1950* (Ann Arbor: The University of Michigan Press, 1955). The companion volumes are also very useful: *Dutch Immigrant Memoirs and Related Writings*, 2 vols. (Assen, the Netherlands: Van Gorcum & Comp. N.V., 1953).

16. Arnold Mulder, *The Peoples of America: Americans From Holland* (Philadelphia and New York: J.B. Lippincott Co., 1947). p. 109.

17. De Jong, *The Dutch in America*, p. 130.

18. *Ibid.*, p. 131.

19. *Dutch Immigrant Memoirs*, I, p. 186. See also De Jong, *The Dutch in America*, p. 133.

20. Amry Vandenbosch, *The Dutch Communities of Chicago* (Chicago: the Knicerbocker Society, 1927), pp. 8-9.

21. De Jong, *The Dutch in America*, pp. 132-133.

22. *Minutes*, General Synod, 1847, p. 92.

23. *Ibid.*, 1848, p. 425.

24. *Classis Holland, Minutes, 1848-1858* (Grand Rapids, Wm. B. Eerdmans Publishing Co., p. 1950), pp. 36-37.

25. *Minutes*, General Synod, 1849, p. 84.
26. For information on the Dutch migration to Wisconsin, see De Jong, *The Dutch in America*, p. 143.
27. "Special Work of the Reformed Church among the Hollanders and Germans," p. 18. This is one of several addresses delivered at Newark, New Jersey in 1882. These addresses were published in *The Semi-Centennial Convention of the Board of Domestic Missions* held at Newark, New Jersey on Wednesday, November 8, 1882 (Newark: The Board of Publications of the Reformed Church, 1883).
28. [On the development of the educational Institutions in the Reformed Church see the essay by Norman Kansfield, this volume, pp. 130-148.—Ed.]
29. See Herman Harmelink III, *Ecumenism and the Reformed Church*, pp. 38-52.
30. *Minutes*, General Synod, 1967, pp. 302-303.
31. [For a discussion of the theological issues within the Reformed Church, see the essay by Eugene Heideman, this volume pp. 95-110.—Ed.]
32. *The Semi-Centennial Convention of the Board of Domestic Missions*, p. 18.
33. *Annual Report of the Board of Domestic Missions*, 1890, p. 12.
34. *Ibid.*, p. 13.
35. *Ibid.*, 1894, p. 6.
36. *Minutes*, General Synod, 1907, p. 790.
37. *Annual Report of the Board of Domestic Missions*, 1907, p. 26.
38. *Ibid.*, 1913, p. 10.
39. *Ibid.*, 1929, p. 16.
40. *Ibid.*, 1922, p. 35. For further information on Hungarians and their churches in America, see David Aaron Sounders, *The Magyars in America* (New York: George H. Doran Company, n.d.); Joseph S. Roucek, "Hungarian Americans," in Frances J. Brown and Joseph S. Roucek, eds., *One America—The History, Contributions, and Present Problems of Our Racial and National Minorities* (New York: Prentice-Hall, Inc., 1946); R.A. Schermerhorn, *These Our People: Minorities in American Culture* (Boston: D.C. Heath & Co., 1949), pp. 320-346; and "Hungarian Reformed Church in America," in Frank S. Mean, *Denominations in the United States* (5th ed.; Nashville: Abingdom Press, 1970) pp. 187-188.
41. Gerald De Jong, *The Dutch in America*, p. 173.
42. *Ibid.*, pp. 174-193.
43. *Minutes*, General Synod, 1949, p. 111.
44. *Ibid.*
45. *Ibid.*
46. See page 70, this volume.
47. *Acts of Synod of the Christian Reformed Church*, 1950, p. 203.
48. *Minutes*, General Synod, 1951, p. 99.
49. *Ibid.*, 1953, p. 93.

50. "Report of the Special Committee to Study the Theological Basis for the Existence of the Reformed Church in America in Canada," *Minutes*, General Synod, 1963, p. 271.

51. Included in this number are some congregations organized before World War II.

World Mission

1. George L. Smith, *Religion and Trade in New Netherland* (Ithaca: Cornell University Press, 1973), pp. 77-78.

2. [See Introduction, pp. 1-16.—Ed.]

3. The Address and Constitution of the New York Missionary Society (New York: T. &. J. Swords, 1796), p. 13.

4. John F. Schermerhorn, "Letters to the Editor," *Christian Intelligencer*, IX (Oct. 6, 1838), p. 29. See also Alexander Gunn, *Memoirs of the Rev. John H. Livingston* (New York: Rutgers Press, 1829). [The *Christian Intelligencer* published Livingston's sermon in a three part series: IX (Aug. 25, 1838), p. 17; IX (Sept. 1, 1838), p. 21; and IX (Sept. 8, 1838), p. 25. For an examination of the place of Livingston's theology in the Reformed Church, see the essay by Eugene Heideman, this volume, pp. 96-98.—Ed.]

5. "Sermon by John H. Livingston," *Christian Intelligencer*, IX (Aug. 25, 1838), p. 25.

6. Revelation 14:6-7.

7. Livingston's sermon, *Christian Intelligencer*, IX (Sept. 8, 1838), p. 25.

8. *Ibid.*

9. J.B. Waterbury, *Memoir of the Rev. John Scudder, M.D.* (New York: Harper and Brothers, 1870), pp. 22-25.

10. [See essay by James Van Hoeven, this volume, pp. 40-42.—Ed.]

11. [For a discussion of the contribution of Mills to the missionary impulse of the early nineteenth century see Thomas C. Richards, *Samuel J. Mills, Missionary Pathfinder, Pioneer, and Promoter* (Boston: The Pilgrim Press, 1906); Gardiner Spring, *Memoirs of the Rev. Samuel J. Mills, Late Missionary to the South Western Section of the United States, and Agent of the American Colonization Society Deputed to Explore the Coast of Africa* (New York: New York Evangelica Society, 1820); and John Freeman Schermerhorn and Samuel J. Mills, *A Correct View of that Part of the United States Which Lies West of the Allegheny Mountains, With Regard to Religion and Morals* (Hartford: Peter D. Gleason & Co., 1814). For a discussion of the "Brethren" see "Constitution of the Society of Brethren," *Constitution and Records of the Society of Brethren* (Williams College: n.p., 1808). Discussion of the appearance of the Brethren before the Congregational Association in Massachusetts is in James W. Van Hoeven, "Salvation and Indian Removal: The Career Biography of the Rev. John F. Schermerhorn, Indian Commissioner," Unpublished Ph.D. dissertation, Vanderbilt University, 1972.—Ed.]

12. *First Ten Annual Reports of the American Board of Commissioners for Foreign Missions, with Other Documents of the Board* (Boston: Crocker and Brewster, 1834), pp. 9-14.
13. *Minutes*, General Synod, 1818, p. 18.
14. *Ibid.*, 1820, p. 74.
15. Waterbury, *Memoir*, p. 25.
16. In 1826 the United Foreign Missionary Society merged with the American Board of Commissioners for Foreign Missions. See *Minutes*, General Synod, 1826, p. 61.
17. *Report of the American Board of Commissioners for Foreign Missions* (Boston: T.R. Marvin, 1857), pp. 22-23.
18. Charles E. Corwin, *Manual of the Reformed Church in America* (Fifth Edition; New York: Board of Publications of the Reformed Church in America, 1922), p. 188.
19. Letter of Doty to Rufus Anderson, in A.B.C.F.M. correspondence, Reel 1, General Synod Archives, New Brunswick Theological Seminary, New Brunswick, New Jersey.
20. See Corwin, *Manual*, pp. 190-191, and 197.
21. *Ibid.*, p. 197.
22. Letter of Doty to Rufus Anderson, in A.B.C.F.M. correspondence, Reel 1, General Synod Archives, New Brunswick Theological Seminary, New Brunswick, New Jersey.
23. *Minutes*, General Synod, 1856, p. 112.
24. See essay by James Van Hoeven, this volume, pp. 42-44. For a discussion of the ecumenical relationship between the Reformed Church in America and the German Reformed Church see my *Ecumenism and the Reformed Church* (Grand Rapids: Wm. B. Eerdman Publishing Co., 1968), pp. 32-35.
25. *Reformed Church in America, Centennial Discourses* (New York: Board of Publications of the Reformed Church in America, 1877), p. 417.
26. *Minutes*, General Synod, 1857, p. 235.
27. *Ibid.* See also Corwin, *Manual*, p. 193.
28. For a full review of this issue see *Minutes*, General Synod, 1863, pp. 333-340.
29. *Ibid.*, p. 335.
30. *Ibid.*, p. 337.
31. *Ibid.*, 1864, p. 490.
32. Corwin, *Manual*, pp. 207-215.
33. *Ibid.*, pp. 215-218. See also Alfred D. Mason and Frederick J. Barn, *History of the Arabian Mission* (New York: Board of Foreign Missions, R.C.A., 1926). Legend has it that Phelps put an asterisk behind his name when he signed the compact, noting below that he was "uncertain." He never went to Arabia.
34. *Centennial Discourses, pp. 418-424.*
35. See *Women's Board of Foreign Mission Reports* (New York: Board of

Publications of the Reformed Church in America), for the years 1875 to 1946.
36. John T. McNeill and James Hastings Nichols, *Ecumenical Testimony* (Philadelphia: Westminster Press, 1974), p. 204.
37. Norman Goodall, *Christian Ambassador* (Manhasset: Channel Press, 1963).
38. See pp. 82-84.
39. McNeill, *et. al.*, *Ecumenical Testimony*, p. 205. See also Ruth Rouse and Stephen C. Neill, *A History of the Ecumenical Movement* (Philadelphia: Westminster Press, 1968), pp. 462-463.
40. *Ibid.*
41. Wallace N. Jamison, *The United Presbyterian Story* (Pittsburgh: The Geneva Press, 1958), pp. 180-185.
42. William Ernest Hocking, *Rethinking Missions* (New York: Harper and Brothers, 1932). See also Elizabeth Gray Vining, *Friend of Life* (Philadelphia: J.B. Lippincott Co., 1958).
43. Barnerd M. Luben, personal letter.
44. *Church Herald*, May 30, 1975.
45. *Ibid.*, Nov. 5, 1971, pp. 4ff.
46. John Piet, *The Road Ahead: A Theology for the Church in Mission* (Grand Rapids: William B. Eerdmans, 1970).

Theology

1. Throughout its history, there have been persons who believed that the Reformed Church compromised too much as it tried to maintain both orientations. Among such persons, many of whom left the membership of the denomination, there have been individuals and groups who understood particular matters more clearly than has the denomination as a whole. Any complete account of the history would have to include those who vigorously dissented from the central position. In this brief essay, space permits only consideration of those who struggled with the problem of maintaining the tension.
2. For an exposition of this theme, see Rev. T.B. Romeyn, "The Adaptations of the Reformed Church to the American Character," in *Centennial Discourses, A series of sermons delivered in the year 1876.* (New York: Board of Publication of the Reformed Church in America, 1877), pp. 441-464. See also, James F. Zwemer, "Our National Vocation" (address given at Holland, Michigan on July 4, 1919, on file at The Netherlands Museum, Holland, Michigan).
3. See M. Eugene Osterhaven, "The Experiential Theology of Early Dutch Calvinism," *Reformed Review*, Spring, 1974, pp. 180-186. It is important to note that within the strand which stresses The Standards of Unity, the experiential theology which emphasizes the Catechism has lived in some tension with the emphasis on predestination as stated in the Canons of Dort.

4. *Articles of Dort, 1619*, Art. XXVIII, in E.T. Corwin, *A Digest of Constitutional and Synodical Legislation of the Reformed Church in America, 1906* p. xxxii.

5. Charles E. Corwin, *A Manual of the Reformed Church in America, 1628-1922*, (New York: Board of Publication and Bible School Work of the Reformed Church in America, 1922, fifth ed. revised) pp. 6-21.

6. There are many accounts of the Conferentie-Coetus controversy. See *Ibid.* pp. 61-74. [See also pp. 11-13 and 28-30 this volume.—Ed.]

7. The best study of Frelinghuysen is James R. Tanis, *Dutch Calvinistic Pietism in the Middle Colonies* (The Hague: Martinus Nijhoff, 1967). See also Eugene Oosterhave, *Op. Cit.*, pp. 186-188, and Abraham Messler, *Forty Years at Raritan: Eight Memorial Sermons with Notes for a History of the Reformed Dutch Churches in Somerset County, New Jersey* (New York: A. Lloyd, 1873), pp. 34-47, 61-71. [For a decidedly different interpretation of Frelinghuysen see Herman Harmelink III, "Another Look at Frelinghuysen and His Awakening," *Church History*, XXXVII (Dec., 1968, pp. 423-438.—Ed.]

8. John De Witt, *A Funeral Discourse Pronounced in the Reformed Dutch Church of New Brunswick Occasioned by the Decease of the Rev. John H. Livingston D.D. S.T.P.*, (New Brunswick: William Myer, 1825) pp. 18-24, 34-35.

9. *The Christian Intelligencer*, August 25, 1838, p. 17. In emphasizing the milleniam, Livingston accepted a theme which is to be found in American preachers at least from the time of the Mathers. See Robert Middlekauff, *The Mathers, Three Generations of Puritan Intellectuals, 1596-1728*, (New York: Oxford University Press, 1971), pp. 179-87.

10. In the twentieth century, pre-millennialism became linked with dispensationalism and a low estimation of the church. As a result, it has been generally rejected by Reformed Church ministers, although many members in the churches continue to promote the doctrine. See Albertus Pieters, *The Seed of Abraham* (1950) and *Studies in the Revelation of St. John* (1943) both published by Wm. B. Eerdmans, Grand Rapids, Mich. [See also pp. 78-79 this volume.—Ed.]

11. See "Preface to the Entire Constitution, Embracing Doctrines, Liturgy, and Government, 1792" in E.T. Corwin, *Op. Cit.*, pp. v-vii.

12. E.T. Corwin, *Op. Cit.*, p.v. See W. Hudson *The Great Tradition of the American Churches* (New York: Harper & Row, 1963) pp. 42-55, for a discussion of the Puritan background.

13. [See pp. 114ff, this volume.—Ed.]

14. The literature on "Hopkinsianism" is immense. For a brief statement of the doctrines and issues involved, see George M. Marsden, *The Evangelical Mind and the New School Presbyterian Experience* (New Haven and London: Yale University Press, 1970) pp.34-46. Marsden's book is also important in providing a full discussion of the Old School split in the Presbyterian Church. The Reformed Church watched the development of the controversy with intense interest, with full reports

appearing in *The Christian Intelligencer* during the period 1830-1869. While adopting a position of neutrality, *The Christian Intelligencer's* sympathy tilted toward the Old School. In doing so, it favored Dort over the American orientation.

15. *Minutes of the General Synod,* October, 1820. pp. 24-31.

16. See James W. Van Hoeven, "Salvation and Indian Removal: The Career Biography of the Rev. John Freeman Shermerhorn; Indian Commissioner," Unpublished dissertation submitted to the faculty of the Graduate School of Vanderbilt University, Nashville, Tennessee, 1971), pp. 65ff. This dissertation contains much excellent material on the history and theology of the Albany-New York area of the Reformed Church during the first half of the nineteenth century.

17. See, for example, *The Christian Intelligencer,* March 31 and April 7, 1832.

18. Van Hoeven, *Op. Cit.* p. 68.

19. This stance was later to prove puzzling to the Dutch settlers in the midwest, many of whom came to America to escape the "oppression" of the Synod of the Hervormde Kerk in The Netherlands. In 1868, they overtured the Synod to refuse to permit Freemasons to become members of The Reformed Church. The Synod refused on the ground that while it advised against membership in secret societies, "The right and power to receive members into the Church belongs solely to the consistory." Some of the settlers thereafter defected to the Christian Reformed Church. This attitude of the Synod remains one of the basic differences from the Christian Reformed Stance to this day. See *Minutes of General Synod,* 1868, p. 461, and 1870, pp. 96-7. See also B. Grotenhius, "Ons kerkelijk standpoint in de geschiedenis" *De Hope* 14 August 1889.

20. C.G. Finney, (arr. by E.E. Shelhamer), *Finney on Revival* (London: Marshall, Morgan & Scott, Ltd., no date) pp. 58-60.

21. W. Hudson, *American Protestantism, (Chicago: The University of Chicago Press, 1972, 7th impression)* p. 79.

22. Dominie Boel in 1723 had questioned the orthodoxy of Frelinghuysen's doctrine of regeneration and of judgment for the unregenerate; see G.J. Van Heest, "The Life of Theodorus Jacobus Frelinghuysen", *The Western Seminary Bulletin,* Dec. 1952, p. 8.

23. "And let the enemies of vital experimental piety, who are ever prepared to stigmatize such exercises as constituted the very life of our revered friend's soul as enthusiasm in its worst sense, be put to silence by facts now detailed. . . . Does enthusiasm pursue a uniform, persevering course in holy living; . . . Does enthusiasm know the meaning of the words—habit—order—piety? No, brethren, views and exercises of heart, producing such results, is such an enthusiasm, as we may well desire and pray to possess *our hearts, to influence our actions, and to close our eyes.* " John De Witt, *Op. Cit.* pp. 27-8.

24. "Revivals of Religion", *The Christian Intelligencer,* May 5, 1932, p. 158.

25. [In September, 1858, Jeremiah C. Lanphier organized a neighborhood nood-day prayer meeting at the Old Dutch Church on Fulton Street, New York. The program attacted great attention and by mid-winter, 1859, the crowds had overflowed into the John Street Methodist Church, around the corner. Subsequently, the noon-day prayer meetings spread to other major cities, and sparked a revival mood within American protestantism. See Timothy Smith, *Revivalism and Social Reform: American Protestantism on the Eve of the Civil War* (New York: Harper & Row, Publishers, 1957), pp. 63 ff.—Ed.]

26. This attitude prevails to the present; see the issue of the *Reformed Review*, Autumn, 1970, on "evangelism." In footnote 3 above, the distinction between the experiential tradition of the Catechism and the Predestination of Dort was noted. In the Ten Eyck case and in revivalism, it was possible for Reformed revivalists to emphasize the experiential tradition. In the ecclesiastical assemblies as well as in published materials, they, rather than the defenders of predestination, were compelled to prove their loyalty to the Standards.

27. "The Westminster Confession of Faith," Chapter III, III, in John H. Leith (ed) *Creeds of the Churches* (Richmond, Va.: John Knox Press, rev. ed., 1973) p. 199.

28. *Belgic Confession*, Art. 16; *Heid. Cat* Q & A. 54. For a careful consideration of the doctrine in the Canons of Dort, see J.G. Woelderink, *De Uitverkiezing*, (Delft: Van Keulen, 1951) pp. 19-23.

29. See the excellent discussion in John W. Beardslee III, *Reformed Dogmatics* (New York: Oxford University Press, 1965) pp. 16-22, as well as E. Dowey, *The Knowledge of God in Calvin's Theology* (New York: Columbia University Press, 1952) pp. 212-220.

30. Dowey points out that for Calvin, God is never merely sovereign. He is sovereignly good, sovereignly just, sovereignly merciful and righteous." *Op. Cit.* p. 210. This is more apparent in the confessions of Dort than of Westminster.

31. Marsden, *Op. Cit.* p. 177.

32. William Carlough, "German Idealism and the Theology of John W. Nevin," *Reformed Review*, March 1962, pp. 37-45.

33. Reformed Church ministers could call upon the Heidelberg Catechism, Question and Answer 80 and the Belgic Confession, Art. 36, for divine approval in keeping the "idolatry" of the Mass out of the land. Rev. W.C. Brownlee, a Dutch Reformed Minister, led the New York clergy in their opposition to the Roman Catholics.

34. *The Christian Intelligencer*, August 7, 1845, p. 14 and August 28, 1845, p. 26. Edward Pusey was the English Anglican leader of the Oxford movement, whose views led John H. Newman to become a Roman Catholic.

35. The most direct theological influence against Nevin entered the Reformed Church in the person of Joseph F. Berg, who left the German church in protest against Nevin in 1852 and was professor at New Brunswick, 1861-71; see his *A Vindication of the Farewell Words of*

the German Reformed Church (Philadelphia: William S. Young, Printer, 1852).

36. Throughout its history, the Reformed Church in America has experienced difficulty in maintaining the doctrine of infant Baptism. Readers are referred to *Minutes of General Synod*, 1804, pp. 332-3; W.R. Gordon, *The Church and Her Sacraments* (New York: Board of Publications of the Reformed Church in America, 1870); J.R. Mulder, "A Calvinistic Conception," *The Leader*, March 7, 1934, pp. 8-9; M.E. Osterhaven, *Meaning of Baptism* (Grand Rapids: Society for Reformed Publication, 1955, and "The Report of the Theological Commission," *Minutes of the General Synod*, 1967, pp. 189-199.

37. James Hastings Nichols, *Romanticism in American Theology* (Chicago: The University of Chicago Press, 1961) pp. 114, 108. Samuel Woodbridge, dean of New Brunswick Seminary, called the study of the doctrine of providence "the *appropriation* of theology by history;" "Historical Theology", *Centennial of the Theological Seminary of the Reformed Church in America, 1784-1884.* (New York: Board of Publication of the Reformed Church in America, 1885) p. 31.

38. *Ibid.* p. 90.

39. *Ibid.* p. 115.

40. *Ibid.* pp. 95-98.

41. *Centennial of The Theological Seminary* pp. 23, 43-4.

42. See pp. 61-66, in this volume.

43. Rev. P. Moerdyke, *The Immigrant Fathers* (an unpublished address given at the meeting of the Classis of Michigan, 1911, on file at The Netherlands Museum, Holland, Michigan) p. 3.

44. Yet the defenders of orthodoxy in the mid-west were more under the influence of their environment than they realized. For example, at the moment when they were defending orthodoxy against Freemasonry, the Rev. J.H. Karsten translated Josiah Strong's *Our Country* into Dutch. It was recommended by seven mid-western ministers as the best American Christian statement of the reason for missionary activity. In actuality, Strong's book is rooted in Social Darwinism and elitist racial theory.

45. See Herman Harmelink, *Ecumenism and the Reformed Church* (Grand Rapids, Mich., Wm. B. Eerdmans Publishing Co., 1968) pp. 38-53.

46. *Thirty-Ninth Annual Report of the Board of Domestic Missions of the Reformed Church in America, 1871*, pp. 3-4. See also Frederick Zimmerman, "The Outreach of Missions," *The Leader*, Feb. 28, 1934, p. 12.

47. Milton J. Hoffman, "The Reformed Church in America, 1928-1953", *The Western Seminary Bulletin*, Dec., 1952, p. 3.

48. Elton M. Eenigenberg, "The Christian Hope," *The Western Seminary Bulletin*, March 1953, p. 4.

49. See above, footnote 44.

50. E. Worchester, *The Parish Minister and His Theology.* (phamphlet inaugural address in archives of New Brunswick Theological Seminary, 1923) p. 44. In 1925, W.A. Weber, in his inaugural address, *How Shall the Church Speak to the New Age out of Eternity?*, made a similar statement; see pp. 59-60 of his address.

51. Charles Hodge, *What is Darwinism?*, quoted in E.S. Gaustad (ed), *Religious Issues in American History.* (New York: Harper & Row, 1968) pp. 182-185.

52. E.J. Blekink, unpublished lectures on systematic theology in Western Theological Seminary Archives, Holland, Mich., Lectures IV-IX. Frederick Schenck of New Brunswick Seminary had previously dealt with the problem of evolution. See his *The Sociology of the Bible.* (New York: Board of Publications of The Reformed Church in America, 1909) pp. 25-26, 153, and *Christian Ethics and Evidences* (New York: Young Men's Christian Association Press, 1910) pp. 23, 26-69.

53. J.E. Kuizenga, *The Leader,* August 23 and 30, Sept. 6 and 13, 1922, pp. 8-9 in each issue. The followers of Van Raalte have often been understood to be almost sectarian and reactionary in their attitudes. Actually, the leaders in the Holland, Michigan, area were remarkably open to cooperation and intensely interested in becoming "American". See Henry E. Dosker, *Levenschets van A.C. Van Raalte, D.D.* (Nijkerk: C.C. Callenbach 1893) and the long series on general and special revelation by Kuizenga in *The Leader,* 1922. The leadership became wary of cooperation when the "modernists" began to make inroads in organizations such as the YMCA and the Federal Council of Churches.

54. A. Pieters, *Notes on Genesis* (Grand Rapids, MIch.; William B. Eerdmans Pub. Co., 1943) pp. 11-101. Taylor Lewis, a Reformed Church teacher at Union College in Schenectady, had already published a similar statement in 1857! See Marsden, *Op. Cit.*, pp. 144-5.

55. For a statement of the theological significance of the Sabbath in Protestant America, see Herbert W. Richardson, *Toward an American Theology* (New York: Harper & Row, 1967) pp. 112-126.

56. The last full-scale reference to this dream in Domestic Missions reports in 1937. See footnote 43 above.

57. Classis of Holland, *Memorial to the General Synod of the Reformed Church of America with reference to the treatise of Rev. John De Witt, D.D., L.L. D. on Inspiration* (Holland, Mich.; Ottawa County Printing Office, 1894); see also John De Witt, *What is Inspiration?* (New York: Anson D.F. Randolph, 1893) and E. Winter, *What is Inspiration?* (phamphlet printed at Grand Rapids, 1894, on file at Western Theological Seminary archives.

58. L. Kuyper, "The Righteouness of God in the Old Testament" (Inaugural address on file in Western Seminary archives, 1943); see Heid. Cat. Q. & A. 11, Belgic Confession, Art. 16.

59. L. Kuyper, "The Suffering and Repentance of God," *Scottish Journal of Theology*, 1967, pp. 257-277.
60. L. Kuyper, "Interpretation of Genesis Two-Three", *Reformed Review*, Dec. 1959, pp. 4-14.
61. John Piet, *The Road Ahead* (Grand Rapids, Mich.: Eerdmans Publishing Co., 1970), pp. 20-47, 54-55.
62. "The Report of the Committee on Overtures", *Minutes of General Synod*, 1931, p. 945.
63. *Ibid.*, 1937, pp. 102-3, 1938, p. 432. Dr. Weber of New Brunswick Seminary was a key figure in attempts to develop new approaches to religious education; see footnote 42 above.
64. George Hankamp, "Trends toward Modernism in the Reformed Church in America," *The Intelligencer Leader*, Sept. 10, 1937, pp. 7-8.
65. "Report of the Committee on Revision of the Constitution", *Minutes of General Synod*, 1957, pp. 118-123; see the background though supplied by a member of the committee, Loring Andrews, "Unity in Program and Action" *The Church Herald*, April 11, 1958, pp. 4, 22; April 18, 1958, pp. 12-13, 23.
66. During that period, the Holland, Michigan leadership had maintained contact with the more conservative church related to Abraham Kuyper, the Gereformeerde Kerk, and the Vrije Universiteit.
67. Although the ecumenical question lies outside the scope of this essay, it is important to recognize that the question of church merger and cooperation was a central issue to the men in The Netherlands as well as in the Reformed Church in America. See for example, E. Heideman, *Reformed Bishops and Catholic Elders* (Wm. B. Eerdmans Publ. Co., 1970.) I.C. Rottenberg played a key role in helping the American church become familiar with trends in The Netherlands. For an example of his thought, see, "Perspectives on Christian Ministry" *The Reformed Review*, Dec. 1965 pp. 20-26.
68. G.T. VanderLugt, (ed), *The Liturgy of the Reformed Church in America together with The Psalter.* (New York: The Board of Education, 1968); see also Howard Hagemen, *Pulpit and Table* (Richmond, V.: John Knox Press, 1962), especially pp. 84-108 where he takes a favorable view toward's Nevin liturgical reform.
69. Donald J. Bruggink and Cral H. Droppers, *Christ and Architecture* (Grand Rapids, Mich.: Wm. B. Eerdmans Pub. Co., 1965).
70. See, for example, Henry Bast, *The Lord's Prayer* and *The Authority of the Bible;* Gordon Girod, *The Deeper Faith* (1958); George Douma, *Meaning of the Lord's Supper* (1951). The editor of *The Church Herald*, Dr. Louis Benes, was closely related to this group in emphasizing the continuing relevance of the predestination tradition (modified by contemporary evangelicalism) to American life.
71. See, for example, John W. Beardslee III, *op. cit.*; Eugene Oosterhaven, *Our Confession of Faith: A Study Manual of the Belgic Confession* (Grand Rapids: Baker Book House, 1964) and *The Spirit of the*

Reformed Tradition: The Reformed Church Must Always be Reforming (Grand Rapids: Wm. B. Eerdmans Publishing Co., 1971).
72. Justin Vander Kolk, "A Re-examination of Calvin's Doctrine of Scripture Based on Reading in his Commentary," Unpublished Ph.D. Dissertation presented to the faculty of the Divinity School at the University of Chicago, 1951. I. John Hesselink, Jr. has published many articles on Calvin; see, for example, "The Catholic Character of Calvin's Institutes," *Reformed Review*, Dec., 1965, pp. 13-19. Hesselink and Hageman became presidents of Western and New Brunswick Seminary respectively in 1973. The exchatological approach in accord with the phrase, "Catholic, Evangelical, and Reformed" can be expected to continue at both seminaries.
73. "The Report of the Theological Commission", *Minutes of General Synod* 1967, p. 188, and subsequent years. Others in the Reformed Church prefer to recognize the continuing role of "status" as well. See E. Heideman, *Op. Cit.*, p. 211ff.
74. *The Book of Church Order of the Reformed Church in America* (1973) Part II, Art. 9, p. 23, and Appendix, pp. 71-2.
75. E. Heideman, *Our Song of Hope.* (Wm. B. Eerdmans Publishing Co., 1975) pp. 11, 79-80.

Social Concern

1. Anson Dubois, "America for Christ," *The Christian Intelligencer*, Vol. 32 (February 14, 1861), p. 2.
2. *Minutes*, General Synod, 1876, pp. 456-457. For a comprehensive study of the idea of a Christian America see Robert T. Handy, *A Christian America: Protestant Hopes and Historical Realities* (New York: Oxford University Press, 1971).
3. The Report is found in *Acts and Proceedings of the General Synod*, 1872, p.4.
4. C. H. Edgar, "Thoroughly Furnished," in *Centennial Discourses of the Reformed (Dutch) Church in America* (2nd ed., New York: Board of Publications of the Reformed Church in America, 1877), p. 395.
5. (New York: Abingdon Press, 1957).
6. *Christ and Culture* (Torchlight ed., New York: Harper, 1956), pp. 190-229.
7. Winthrop S. Hudson, *American Protestantism* (Chicago: University of Chicago Press, 1961), pp. 62-78.
8. "The Descendants of Van Raalte," *Reformed Review*, Vol 12 (March, 1959), pp. 33-42.
9. On ethnic isolationism see Isaac C. Rottenberg, "Tendencies and Trends in a Century of Theological Education at Western Seminary," *Reformed Review*, Vol. 20 (December, 1966), pp. 22-24, 41-49; Henry S. Lucas, *Netherlanders in America* (Ann Arbor: University of Michigan Press, 1955), pp. 541-562.
10. Hudson, *American Protestantism*, p. 83.

11. *Minutes*, General Synod, 1894, p. 160.
12. "Constitutional Basis of Our Sunday Laws," *Christian Intelligencer*, Vol. 32 (June 20, 1861), p.2.
13. Lucas, *Netherlanders*, pp. 543-544.
14. *Minutes*, General Synod, 1914, pp. 154, 181-182.
15. *Minutes*, General Synod, 1925, p. 957.
16. *Slaveholding Not Sinful* (New York: John A. Gray, 1855).
17. Lucas, *Netherlanders*, pp. 549-550. [H.P. Scholte believed that the abolitionists posed a threat to the preservation of the Union, which was his primary concern. See his *American Slavery in Reference to the Present Agitation of the United States* (Pella, Iowa: Gazette Book and Job Office, 1856), which was the first book on the slavery issue published west of the Mississippi River.—Ed.]
18. *Christian Intelligencer*, Vol. 31 (October 25, 1860), p. 70; (December 27, 1860), p. 106; (January 17, 1861), p. 118.
19. "Paul on Slavery," *Christian Intelligencer*, Vol. 31 (January 3, 1861), p. 10.
20. *Minutes*, General Synod, 1862, pp. 210-211; *Christian Intelligencer*, Vol. 32 (August 22, 1861), p. 1.
21. *Slaveholding Not Sinful*, p. 31.
22. *Minutes*, General Synod, 1863, p. 279.
23. "The Adaptation of the Reformed Church to the American Character," *Centennial Discourses*, p. 459.
24. *Christ and Culture*, p. 84.
25. There are files on both Muste and Taylor in the Reformed Church Archives, New Brunswick, New Jersey.
26. *Christian Intelligencer*, Vol. 67 (September 2, 1896), p. 581.
27. "Paternalism," *Christian Intelligencer*, Vol. 73 (October 29, 1902), pp. 697-698.
28. These articles appeared under the title, "Special Grace and General Culture," in the *Leader* (1922).
29. "The Kingdom of God," an address delivered November 19, 1931.
30. *Minutes*, General Synod, 1921, pp. 571-572.
31. "The Church and the Social Question," *Leader* (June-August, 1934).
32. The events leading to the formation of the Committee on Social Welfare may be traced in the *Minutes* of General Synod, 1931, pp. 986, 1124-1125; 1932, pp. 148-161.
33. *Minutes*, General Synod, 1922, p. 839.
34. *Minutes*, General Synod, 1931, p. 973.
35. *The Christian Attitude toward War* (Grand Rapids: Eerdmans, 1932).
36. "The Church in Time of War," *Intelligencer Leader*, Vol. 8 (November 28, 1941), pp. 3-4; B. D. Dykstra, "From Christ to Constantine," *Intelligencer Leader*, Vol. 8 (July 25, 1941), pp. 3-4; *Minutes*, General Synod, 1942, p. 538.
37. "Our Faith and a Durable Peace," *Intelligencer Leader*, Vol. 10 (January 29, 1943- February 19, 1943).

38. "The Christian and World Order," *Church Herald,* Vol. 4 (October 31, 1947), pp. 6-7; "God and the Security Council," *Church Herald,* Vol. 5 (April 23, 1948), p. 6.
39. Letter from Norman Vincent Peale, *Church Herald,* Vol. 8 (March 9, 1951), p. 10; Louis Benes, "The Gospel and Communism," *Church Herald,* Vol. 8 (January 19, 1951), pp. 6-7.
40. *Minutes,* General Synod, 1939, pp. 146-147; 1940, pp. 545-546; 1946, p. 148; 1967, pp. 207-208, 214. The disposition of a specific case, that of Glenn Pontier, is described in *Minutes,* General Synod, 1971, pp. 228-230.
41. [In 1900 the Reformed Church began a mission among "the colored people" of Orangeburgh, Magnolia, Shiloh and Timmonsville, South Carolina. This work was transferred to the Southern Presbyterian Church in the 1920's because the "type of worship in the Reformed Church was not attractive to the rank and file of the Negroes, who preferred the more emotional service offered by other churches. The better educated only were reached by our churches." Corwin, *Manual,* p. 226.—Ed.]
42. *Minutes,* General Synod, 1905, p. 146.
43. *Minutes,* General Synod, 1957, p. 181; 1961, pp. 209-210; 1964, pp. 99 and 231.
44. *Minutes,* General Synod, 1969, p. 98. [In 1969 James Foreman and the Black Economic Conference issued a Black Manifesto which demanded $500,000,000 in reparations from the churches and synagogues of America.—Ed.]
45. Robert A. Geddes, "Shall the Reformed Church Serve Negro Communities?" *Church Herald,* Vol. 6 (February 25, 1949), pp. 10-11; Don De Young, "Evangelical Dynamic for Social Change," *Church Herald,* Vol. 22 (June 4, 1965). pp. 18,30; Howard Hageman, "Inner City Turbulence and the Church," *Church Herald,* Vol. 26 (September 19, 1969), pp. 4-7, 28-30.
46. "The Church at the West," *Reformed Review,* Vol. 20 (December, 1966), p. 15.
47. Louis Benes, "The Business of the Church," *Church Herald,* Vol. 15 (July 25, 1958), pp. 6-7. See the issue of August 29 for spirited responses to this editorial and a further effort by Benes to state his position.
48. For an excellent analysis of this see Handy, *A Christian America,* pp. 184-225.
49. *The Spirit of the Reformed Tradition* (Grand Rapids: Eerdman's, 1971), pp. 144-158.
50. *Faith and Politics* (New York: G. Barziller, 1968), p. 137.

Education

1. E. B. O'Callaghan, ed., *Documents Relative to the Colonial History of*

the State of New York (Albany: Weed, Parson and Company, printers, 1856), vol. I, p.123.

2. William Heard Kilpatrick, *The Dutch Schools of New Netherlands and Colonial New York* (New York: Arno Press and the New York Times, 1969) p. 39.

3. *Ibid.*, p. 83.

4. Composite translation of the Latin and German text as published in H.E. Vinke, *Libri Symbolici Ecclesiae Reformatae Nederlandicae*, Utrecht: J.G. van Terveen, 1846) pp. 376-379.

5. Zacharias Ursinus, *Summe of Christian Religion* (London: Arthur Johnson, 1617), pp. 998-999.

6. Kilpatrick, *The Dutch Schools*, p. 19.

7. *Ibid.*, p. 20. Note that here even the language of the synodical order reflects the Catechism.

8. *Harmonie, dat is overeenstemminge der Nederlandtsche Synoden, ofte Regulen* . . . Tot Leyden voor David Jantz, van Ilpendam . . . 1618, p. 12.

9. *Kerken-ordeninge Gestelt in den Nationale Synode der Gereformeerde Kerken* . . . *1618-1619* (Rotterdam: Nicholaas Topyn, 1733), p. 12.

10. *Ibid.*, p. 22.

11. *Ibid.*, p. 27.

12. *Ibid.*, p. 7, (Italics mine).

13. *Ibid.*, p. 11.

14. *Ibid.*, p. 12.

15. *Ibid.*

16. *Ecclesiastica Records of the State of New York* (Albany: Office of the State Historian, 1905), p. 122. (Hereinafter cited as *Ecclesiastical Records.*)

17. Kilpatrick, *The Dutch Schools*, pp. 67-68.

18. See *Ibid.*, pp. 216-217. Fortunately one of these early schoolhouses, the Voorlezer's House, has survived. It is situated at 59 Arthur Kill Road, Richmondtown, Staten Island, New York. Built before 1696, this building is probably the oldest schoolhouse in the northern United States. The building is now part of the Richmondtown Historic District and is open to the public, April through October only, Saturdays and Sundays from 2:00 to 5:00 p.m.

19. A copy of the *Historie van David* in Beardslee Library, Western Theologican Seminary, Holland, Michigan, comprises only the biblical text of I Samuel 16—II Samuel 24, interspersed with rather primitive woodcuts.

20. Kilpatrick, *The Dutch Schools*, pp. 223-225.

21. Some measure of the Dutch Church's political power can be guessed at in an event in 1717. Although Trinity Church (Episcopal) had been seeking an organ since about 1703, the first organ in New York was given to the Dutch Church in Garden Street by Governor Burnet, in

1717. Since Governor Burnet was himself a member of Trinity parish this gift, apart from political effect, is most difficult to understand. See *Ecclesiastical Records*, p. 1520, and *Christian Intelligencer* (April 11, 1878), p. 3.

22. Kilpatrick, *The Dutch Schools*, p. 152.
23. *Ibid.*, p. 150.
24. *Minutes*, General Synod, 1859, p. 14.
25. *Ibid.*, p. 257.
26. Edward Tanjore Corwin, *Digest of Constitutional and Synodical Legislation of the Reformed Church in America*(New York: Board of Publication, 1906), pp. LXIII-LXIV.
27. *Minutes*, General Synod, p. 398.
28. *Ibid.*
29. See Newton Edwards and Herman G. Richey, *The School in the American Social Order* (2nd. ed. Boston: Houghton Mifflin, 1963), p. 238.
30. For Example, *Minutes*, General Synod, 1840, p. 421, recommendation that music be introduced into district schools; 1846, pp. 73-74, concern over school books "teaching doctrines contrary to Holy Scripture."
31. Corwin, *Digest*, p. 482. See pp. 482-483 for full discussion.
32. *Minutes*, General Synod, 1892, p. 661.
33. University of Utrecht, 1656, and University of Leyden, 1661.
34. See "Chronological List of the Ministers," in Edward Tanjore Corwin, *A Manual of the RCA* (New York: Board of Publications, 1902), pp. 1045-1071.
35. Minutes of Coetus, 1754, in *Minutes*, General Synod, I, sci-scii.
36. *Centennial of the Theological Seminary of the Reformed Church in America, 1784-1884* (New York: Board of Publication, 1885), p. 331.
37. Corwin, *Manual*, p. 269.
38. *Ecclesiastical Records*, p. 4196.
39. *Ibid.*, pp. 4215-4216.
40. Corwin, *Manual*, pp. 1048-1051. It would appear that during this era most candidates were graduates of Union College, Schenectady, New York.
41. Alexander Gunn, *Memoirs of the Rev. John H. Livingston* (New York: Rutgers Press, 1829), p. 419.
42. *Minutes*, General Synod, June, 1815, pp. 44-45. Cf. *Minutes*, General Synod, October, 1815, pp. 5-7.
43. *Classis of Holland, Minutes: 1848-1858* (Grand Rapids: Wm. B. Eerdmans, 1950), p. 24.
44. *Ibid.*, p. 26.
45. Aleida J. Pieters, *A Dutch Settlement in Michigan* (Grand Rapids: Reformed Press, 1923), p. 131.
46. Northwestern Academy, Orange City, Iowa slowly changed its func-

tion from Academy to Junior College to college in an alternate
response to such changing needs.
47. Central College is in Pella, Iowa, and Northwestern College is in
Orange City, Iowa. Along with Hope College, both are presently
strong Liberal Arts Colleges.

The Role of Women in the India Mission, 1819-1880

1. "Ordination," *Church Herald*, XXX, no. 36 (Oct. 26, 1973), p. 20.
2. See, for example, "Overtures to the General Synod, 1974," *Church Herald*, XXXI, no. 9 (May 3, 1974), p. 18.
3. *Christian Action Resolutions and Background Papers. General Synod, 1974*. (Reformed Church in America, n.p., n.d.), p. 8.
4. Korshak, Miriam Frazier, "Will the Real Man Please Stand Up," *Church Herald*, (Feb. 8, 1974), pp. 14-15.
5. Scudder, Dorothy Jealous, *A Thousand Years in Thy Sight: The Story of the Scudders in India*. unpub. Ms. (New Brunswick, N. J.: New Brunswick Theological Seminary, 1970), p. 2.
6. Chamberlain, Mrs. William Isaac, *Fifty Years in Foreign Fields: China, Japan, India, Arabia* (N. Y.: Women's Board of Foreign Missions of the Reformed church in America, 1925), p. 28.
7. Richter, Julius, *A History of Missions in India*, trans. Sydney Moore (Edinburgh & London: Oliphant Anderson and Ferrier, 1908), p. 199.
8. "Ceylon Mission; Joint Letter of the Missionaries," *Missionary Herald*, XIX (January, 1823), p. 6.
9. "John Scudder's Journal, Aug. 27, 1820," *Missionary Herald*, XVIII (1822), p. 47. Also "John Scudder's Journal, Sept. 24, 1820, *Ibid.*, p. 49.
10. "Abstract of the 19th Annual Report, 1871," *Annual Reports of the Arcot Missions, 1854-1880* (Madras: American Mission Press, 1854-1880), p. 1.
11. *Annual Reports*, passim.
12. Women's Board of Foreign Missions, *A Manual of Missions of the Reformed (Dutch) Church in America*, ed. Mrs. Margaret E. Sangster (N. Y.: Board of Publications of the Reformed Church in America, 1877), pp. 5-55.
13. Women's Board, *Manual*, pp. 40-1. Italics mine. See also Kenneth Ingham, *Reformers in India, 1793-1833* (Cambridge: Cambridge University Press, 1956), p. 29.
14. "John Scudder's Journal, Aug. 12, 1820," *Missionary Herald*, XVIII (1922), p. 47. Jared Scudder, "Historical Sketch," in *Arcot Assembly and Arcot Mission of the Reformed Church in America, Jubilee Commemmoration, 1853-1928* (Madras: Methodist Publishing House, 1931), p. 32.
15. Scudder, Dorothy, *op. cit.*, ch. 3.

16. Flexner, Eleanor, *Century of Struggle* (N. Y.: Atheneum, 1973), pp. 106-7.
17. "Letter from John Scudder, March 29, 1849," *Missionary Herald*, XLIV (1849), p. 263.
18. Scudder, Dorothy, *op. cit.*, p. 40.
19. *Annual Medical Report of the Dispensary and Hospital in Connection with the American Arcot Mission, 1867*, p. 10. Bound in *Annual Reports*, 1854-80.
20. *Ibid.*, p. 19.
21. Letter to E. C. Scudder, July 14, 1871, in *Letters from the Board to Missionaries on the Fields* (microfilm available from New Brunswick Theological Seminary, New Brunswick, N. J.), vol. II.
22. Flexner, *op. cit.*, p. 106.
23. Beaver, Robert Pierce, *All Loves Excelling: American Protestant Women in World Mission* (Grand Rapids, Mich.: Eerdmans, 1968), p. 131.
24. *Ibid.*
25. Mrs. Chamberlain, *op. cit.*, pp. 23-4.
26. *Annual Medical Report of the Dispensary and Hospital in Connection with the American Arcot Mission, 1870*, p. 7. Bound in *Annual Reports*, 1854-80.
27. *Ibid.*, pp. 11-12.
28. Beaver, *op. cit.*, p. 172.
29. There were a few exceptions: single women relatives of missionaries; family servants (the John Scudders took an unmarried black woman) and missionaries' widows, who sometimes stayed on the field.
30. Anderson, Rufus, *To Advance the Gospel: Selections from the Writings of Rufus Anderson*, ed. Robert Pierce Beaver (Grand Rapids, Mich.: Eerdmans, 1967), p. 210.
31. "Some Account of the Last Sickness and Death of Mrs. Susan Poor, who died at Tillipally May 7th, 1821. Communicated by the Husband of the Deceased," *Missionary Herald*, XVIII (1822), p. 126.
32. "Rules of the Arcot Mission." *Annual Reports*, p. 8. Italics mine.
33. Ingham, *op. cit.*, pp. 86-7.
34. "Ceylon Mission; Joint Letter of the Missionaries," *Missionary Herald*, XIX (January, 1823), p. 6.
35. *Annual Reports*, 1870, p. 32. But even at the very end of our period women were not very much involved in writing reports or correspondence with the Board. In 1881 Mrs. Chamberlain was caring for, supervising, and instructing girls at the Madanapalle girls school in Arcot, yet when it was necessary to write to the Women's Board of Foreign Missions to plead for funds for a proper building, her husband wrote the letter (Mrs. Chamberlain, pp. 27-8).
36. *Annual Reports*, 1861, p. 15.
37. *Annual Reports*, 1864, p. 29.
38. Women's Board, *Manual*, pp. 7-8. *Annual Reports*, 1865, pp. 15-17.

39. *Missionary Herald* XVIII (1822), p. 369.
40. See Warneck, Gustav, *Outline of a History of Protestant Missions from the Reformation to the Present Time*, authorized trans. from the 7th German edition, ed. George Robson (Edinburgh and London: Oliphant, Anderson and Ferrier, 1901), p. 257. See also William Chamberlain, *Education in India* (N. Y.: Macmillan, 1899), pp. 40-1.
41. *Annual Reports*, 1862, p. 35.
42. *Annual Reports*, 1864, p. 39 and 1867, p. 14.
43. Anderson, Rufus, *Memorial Volume of the First Fifty Years of the American Board of Commissioners for Foreign Missions*, 5th ed. (Boston: American Board of Commissioners for Foreign Missions, 1862), p. 313.
44. Phillips, Clifton Jackson, *Protestant America and the Pagan World: The First Half Century of the American Board of Commissioners for Foreign Missions, 1810-1860* (Cambridge, Mass.: Harvard University Press, 1969), p. 273. See "John Scudder's Journal, July 5, 1820," *Missionary Herald*, XVIII (1822), p. 46. See also *Missionary Herald*, XV (1819), p. 136.
45. Pathak, Sushil Madhava, *American Missionaries and Hinduism: A Study of their Contacts from 1813 to 1910* (Delhi: Munshiram Manoharlal, 1967), p. 66. But for continuance of infanticide and widow-burning, see *Missionary Herald*, L (1854), p. 241.
46. "Hindu Womanhood," in Women's Board, *Manual*.
47. Pathak, *op. cit.*, pp. 80-1. Ingham, *op. cit.*, p. 84.
48. Pathak, *op. cit.*, pp. 80-4.
49. Strong, William E., *The Story of the American Board* (Boston: Pilgrim Press, 1910), p. 181. See also S. Arasaratnam, *Ceylon* (Englewood Cliffs, N. J.: Prentice-Hall, 1964), pp. 108-9.
50. Flexner, *op. cit.*, pp. 62-4.
51. *Annual Reports*, 1860, p. 11, and 1867, pp. 25-6. A similar statement for Oodooville occurs in Anderson, *Memorial Volume, op. cit.*, p. 313.
52. For example, see *Annual Reports*, 1864.
53. *Annual Reports*, 1869, pp. 10-13.
54. *Annual Reports*, 1870, pp. 8-12.
55. Women's Board, *Manual* p. 102. See also p. 78: "Primary schools are taught by graduates of seminaries, both male and female."
56. "Madras—General Letter from the Mission," *Missionary Herald*, XXXIV (1838), p. 158.
57. *Annual Reports*, 1867, pp. 44-6.
58. *Annual Reports*, 1869, p. 57.
59. "Ceylon Mission—Account of the Boarding School at Tillipally," *Missionary Herald*, XIX (1823), p. 310.
60. "Mr. Winslow's Journal," *Missionary Herald*, XXII (1826), p. 181.
61. "Ceylon Mission—Account of Daniel Smead," *Missionary Herald*, XXI (1823), p. 35. See Scudder, J. W., "Historical Sketch of the Arcot Mission," (1879), p. 22. Bound in Arcot Reports, 1854-1880.

62. Women's Board, *Manual*, pp. 70-1.
63. Chamberlain, William, *op. cit.*, pp. 40-1. Richter, *op. cit.*, p. 343. Pathak, *op. cit.*, p. 63.
64. *Missionary Herald*, XLV (1849), p. 257.
65. For example, see *Annual Reports*, 1870, p. 67.
66. *Annual Reports*, 1856, p. 9.
67. Strong, *op. cit.*, p. 181.
68. *Annual Reports*, 1866, pp. 20 and 27.
69. *Annual Reports*, 1873, p. 90.
70. *Annual Reports*, 1866, p. 20.
71. Beaver, *op. cit.*, p. 86.
72. *Annual Reports*, 1869, p. 5.